'This book is essential reading for anyone who wants to understand the methods deployed in the growing 'datafication' of education at ever younger ages and the consequences of this national and international trend, with the authors combining vivid examples and incisive critique of a powerful human technology.'

Emeritus Professor Peter Moss, *UCL Institute of Education, UK*

'No sector of society appears to be escaping the rapid proliferation of data-based technologies of control and surveillance. In this insightful book, Bradbury and Roberts-Holmes comprehensively demonstrate that Early Years and Primary education is no exception. This book recognizes the need to initiate critical conversations about the current (mis)uses of data throughout schools and education systems. It also offers some perceptive ideas about what might be done differently … a must-read for anyone concerned with the future of schools and schooling.'

Neil Selwyn, *Professor in the Faculty of Education, Monash University, Australia*

THE DATAFICATION OF PRIMARY AND EARLY YEARS EDUCATION

The Datafication of Primary and Early Years Education explores and critically analyses the growing dominance of data in schools and early childhood education settings. Recognising the shift in practice and priorities towards the production and analysis of attainment data that are compared locally, nationally and internationally, this important book explores the role and impact of digital data in the 'data-obsessed' school. Through insightful case studies the book critiques policy priorities which facilitate and demand the use of attainment data, within a neoliberal education system which is already heavily focused on assessment and accountability. Using an approach influenced by policy sociology and post-foundational frameworks, the book considers how data are productive of data-driven teacher and child subjectivities. The text explores how data have become an important part of making teachers' work visible within systems which are both disciplinary and controlling, while often reducing the complexity of children's learning to single numbers.

Key ideas covered include:

- The impact of data on the individual teacher and their pedagogical practice, particularly in play-based early years classrooms
- The problems of collecting data through assessment of young children
- How schools respond to increased pressure to produce the 'right' data – or how they 'play with numbers'
- How data affect children and teachers' identities
- International governance and data comparison, including international comparison of young children's attainment
- Private sector involvement in data processing and analysis

The Datafication of Primary and Early Years Education offers a unique insight into the links between data, policy and practice and is a crucial read for all interested in the ways in which data are affecting teachers, practitioners and children.

Alice Bradbury is Senior Lecturer (Associate Professor) in the Department of Education, Practice and Society at the UCL Institute of Education, UK.

Guy Roberts-Holmes is Senior Lecturer (Associate Professor) in the Department of Learning and Leadership at the UCL Institute of Education, UK.

Foundations and Futures of Education

Peter Aggleton, *UNSW Australia*
Sally Power, *Cardiff University, UK*
Michael Reiss, *UCL Institute of Education, UK*

Foundations and Futures of Education focuses on key emerging issues in education as well as continuing debates within the field. The series is interdisciplinary and includes historical, philosophical, sociological, psychological and comparative perspectives on three major themes: the purposes and nature of education; increasing interdisciplinarity within the subject; and the theory-practice divide.

A full list of titles in this series is available at:
www.routledge.com/Foundations-and-Futuresof-Education/book-series/FFE.

THE DATAFICATION OF PRIMARY AND EARLY YEARS EDUCATION

Playing with Numbers

Alice Bradbury and Guy Roberts-Holmes

Routledge
Taylor & Francis Group

LONDON AND NEW YORK

First published 2018
by Routledge
2 Park Square, Milton Park, Abingdon, Oxon OX14 4RN

and by Routledge
711 Third Avenue, New York, NY 10017

Routledge is an imprint of the Taylor & Francis Group, an informa business

British Library Cataloguing in Publication Data
A catalogue record for this book is available from the British Library

Library of Congress Cataloging in Publication Data
Names: Bradbury, Alice, author. | Roberts-Holmes, Guy, author.
Title: The datafication of primary and early years education : playing with numbers / Alice Bradbury and Guy Roberts-Holmes.
Description: Abingdon, Oxon ; New York, NY : Routledge, 2018. | Series: Foundations and futures of education | Includes bibliographical references.
Identifiers: LCCN 2017021008 | ISBN 9781138242159 (hardback) | ISBN 9781138242173 (pbk.) | ISBN 9781315279053 (ebook)
Subjects: LCSH: Early childhood education–Evaluation. | Education, Primary–Evaluation. | Education–Data processing. | Educational tests and measurement. | Educational indicators. | Educational evaluation.
Classification: LCC LB1139.23 .B72 2018 | DDC 372.21–dc23
LC record available at https://lccn.loc.gov/2017021008

ISBN: 978-1-138-24215-9 (hbk)
ISBN: 978-1-138-24217-3 (pbk)
ISBN: 978-1-315-27905-3 (ebk)

Typeset in Bembo
by Wearset Ltd, Boldon, Tyne and Wear

MIX
Paper from
responsible sources
FSC
www.fsc.org FSC™ C013985

Printed in the United Kingdom
by Henry Ling Limited

AB: For Jenny, Susan and Andrew
GRH: For Pamela and Simon

CONTENTS

ILLUSTRATIONS

Figures

Table

PREFACE

My hope and dream is that primary schools can once again be places where creativity, imagination and joy are valued more than numbers on a spreadsheet. Year two and six teachers are a dying breed. We are dropping like flies after struggling to cope with constant regulations, changes and unrealistic expectations placed on us and the children we teach. I swore I would never teach to the test but the current system is forcing me to do so. I spend my days cramming facts and knowledge into young growing brains then assessing in the hope that something sticks. I teach bright sparky children who the assessments will record as failures and I despair. My classroom is a happy place and my school is an incredibly supportive one and I am still struggling to do this again for a second year.

(Year 2 teacher, More Than a Score Campaign)

In Reception there are still a lot of children who find it difficult to settle in. So my daughter wanted somebody to cuddle when she first comes in when I say goodbye, so I am thinking that the teachers have a pile of papers on their desk waiting and they have to think 'Will I be there for the children or will I be there for the paperwork?' So I can see that they get taken away from actually being there with the children when I just want them to play with the children and keep them safe and cuddle them.

(Parent, Research Project 2)

It has been a long day of writing about data and education. I arrive at my daughters' nursery to pick them up. Through the window of the 'baby room' where my younger daughter spends her time, I see a nursery practitioner with an iPad, tapping in information. Another sits cuddling a child, talking about a teddy bear she holds. Another is wiping food off the floor. Next door, in the room for three- and four-year-olds, I go to pick up my older daughter; in there, another member of staff sits leafing through a folder of brightly colour-coded sheets, at a table with three children playing with construction toys. She occasionally stops to reprimand someone or pick up pieces from the floor. When I come for parents' evening, I won't be shown these colour-coded plans, but I will be shown pictures and notes about what my daughters can do. In the meantime, I can log on to my online personal account and see the 'data' that have been collected about them and their learning: videos, notes and photographs, all linked with particular curriculum areas.

(Reflection on writing process, Alice Bradbury)

These quotes and reflection reveal the reality of a data-obsessed education system: those who work with children, some just babies, collect data constantly, attempting to prove that their judgements about where to place children against set criteria are correct; in turn this produces more data, as children are graded, levelled and compared against standards. Teachers are forced to narrow the curriculum or 'teach to the test' due to the pressures to produce the right assessment data. Parents are concerned that 'the paperwork' will distract teachers from the emotional support young children need as they start school.

The education system in England is engaged in a huge project of data production, sometimes with beneficial consequences, and sometimes not. But at the same time as collecting data, the staff cuddle children, manage behaviour and clean up; these things do not show in 'their data', but are nonetheless essential. The teacher above identifies children as 'sparky' and longs to prioritise 'creativity, imagination and joy', but what matters is what can be recorded, tracked and predicted. That changes people's roles and the values of a school or early years setting, as well as how we think about ourselves and about children. This 'datafication' is prominent in compulsory education, where the 'early years' section of primary schools (Nursery and Reception classes) is involved in accountability systems which judge the entire school. This trend is not restricted to England, but occurring around the world in different ways and at different rates. In this book, we explore this phenomenon and how it affects teachers, school leaders and children.

ACKNOWLEDGEMENTS

First, we wish to thank our research participants: this work would not have been possible without the involvement of a number of teachers and school leaders, who gave up their time to be interviewed or complete a survey. The commitment of teachers to research which aims to inform policy, despite their heavy workloads, is always impressive and essential to our work.

We would like to thank the series editors for their support with this project, particularly Michael Reiss for his useful comments, and the help of our editors at Routledge.

We are grateful to the two funders for the Baseline project, the Association of Teachers and Lecturers and the National Union of Teachers, for their vital support of timely research and commitment to research-based policy-making. We have benefitted hugely in the formation of our ideas from discussions with Anne Heavey at ATL and Ken Jones at NUT, and continue to do so. We would also like to thank our colleagues at the IoE and elsewhere who have discussed this work with us and provided useful advice, notably Stephen Ball, Annette Braun, Merryn Hutchings, Gemma Moss, Terry Wrigley, Carol Vincent, Dominic Wyse and our colleagues at More Than a Score. In particular we want to thank Professor Peter Moss for his wise early education critique and passion for justice, which has inspired us both. Finally, we are also indebted to our research assistant, Emma Jones, for her accurate and detailed work on the quantitative data and insightful analysis.

Alice:
On a personal note, I am deeply grateful for the unwavering support of my husband, Alistair; he has always respected my work and delighted in my achievements. I also want to thank my sister Katy for her insights into how policy works in her school, and my father for his advice on writing. This project has always been linked in my mind with my own children: the Baseline project described here was conducted

while I was heavily pregnant with my second daughter, and completed three days before she was born. I would therefore like to thank my extended family for their support, particularly my daughters' grandparents. My mum and my parents-in-law have provided a great deal of support during my girls' early years. I would not be able to function as an academic and mother without them, and this book is dedicated to them.

Guy:
To Pamela for your love, encouragement and belief in me! Also to our teenage children, Justin, Pia and Isabelle, who during the writing of this book were studying for A levels, GCSEs and Sats and variously described themselves as 'robots', 'test machines' and 'numbers'. I am very grateful for wonderful family dinner discussions which taught me your experiences of datafication as you conscientiously 'passed the tests for teachers'. Thank you to my brother Simon, who as a nursery headteacher first showed me the professional realities of datafication as I sat in his office watching him opening dozens of comparative spreadsheet emails! This book is dedicated to you.

ABBREVIATIONS

BA	Baseline Assessment
CEM	Centre for Evaluation and Monitoring, a DfE-approved Reception Baseline Assessment provider
Development Matters	Non-statutory guidance to support the implementation of the Statutory Framework for the Early Years Foundation Stage
EAL	English as an Additional Language
Early Excellence	A DfE-approved Reception Baseline Assessment provider
EExBA	Early Excellence Baseline Assessment
EYFS	Early Years Foundation Stage (children aged 3–5)
EYFS Profile	Early Years Foundation Stage Profile, the statutory assessment at the end of Reception
FSM	Free school meals
KS1	Key Stage 1: includes Year 1 and 2 (children aged 5–7)
KS2	Key Stage 2: includes Year 3 to 6 (children aged 7–11)
LAs (or LEAs)	Local Authorities (previously Local Education Authorities)
Leuven Statements/Scale	A 5-point scale to assess 'well-being' and 'involvement' in the early years
NFER	National Foundation for Educational Research, a DfE-approved Reception Baseline Assessment provider
Nursery	Class for children aged 3–4, may be based in a primary school
OFSTED	Office for Standards in Education
Reception	Class for children aged 4–5; first compulsory year of school

Sats	Standard Assessment Tests at end of each Key Stage
SEN/SEND	Special Educational Needs/Special Educational Needs and Disabilities
SIMS	School Information Management System
Summer-born	Children born between 1 April and 31 August
Target Tracker	Assessment package to support the monitoring of pupil progress

1

INTRODUCTION

The state, data and primary education

Introduction: why research the use of data in schools?

This book begins with two simple questions: how important are data in primary schools and early years settings? And what is the impact of data on these educational sites? The two research studies we discuss here explored assessment policy and practices in early years settings, and one specific policy – Baseline Assessment – which was an assessment for children aged four and five. Through both of these projects, we identified the increasing importance of data in the every-day lives of those working in primary schools and early years settings – a phenomenon we (and others) call 'datafication' (Roberts-Holmes 2015; Williamson 2016b; Lingard, Martino and Rezai-Rashti 2013). By this we mean a change both in the classroom, where data collection drives pedagogy and dominates workloads, and in school management, where inspection is organised around a school's data. In this latter vein, the basis for Baseline Assessment itself is a reliance on numerical data as a method of judging schools. We also use 'datafication' to describe the changes in subjectivity wrought by the current obsession with data, particularly the changing role and status of teachers in the data-driven school and the way in which children come to be 'made up' through data.[1] Thus we explore, in all senses, what Ball has called 'the tyranny of numbers' (2015). Our subtitle 'playing with numbers' serves as a reminder that we discuss largely play-based contexts where numerical data are collected, and that numbers are something that can be manipulated.

This work is driven by the research data we collected in England, but also reflects a wider concern with the use of data in education from academics and practitioners internationally (Selwyn 2016b; Lawn 2013; Ozga *et al.* 2011).[2] Increasingly, issues relating to data have a huge impact on education practices, yet this remains an under-researched area. Thus, we respond here to Selwyn's call to 'make visible the flow and circulation of data and begin to understand the ways in which data are then integrated back into everyday education practices' (2015, 76). This interest in data in education in turn reflects a wider interest in the impact of 'big data' in society and culture more broadly (Bowker and Star 1999; Kitchin 2014; Eynon 2013). Much of this work claims that digital technology is central to the functioning and values of society: as Beer comments, 'Questions of data, metrics, analytics and number in the cultural sphere are not marginal, rather they are central to contemporary cultural formations' (2013, 11). This change is based on the technological innovation of the advent of computing power; data are now cheaply produced, collected and analysed in contexts where in the past they were expensive, leading to claims of an 'industrial revolution in data' (Hellerstein cited in Manovich 2012). This has resulted in overwhelming volumes of digital data: 'the production of data is increasingly becoming a deluge; a wide, deep torrent of timely, varied, resolute and relational data that are relatively low in cost and, outside of business, increasingly open and accessible' (Kitchin 2014, xv). This volume of data is largely due to increased computing power, which has meant 'we no longer have to choose between data size and depth' (Manovich 2012, 3); thus the age of either in-depth studies or mass surveys is over. These developments have resulted in new fields of academic study focused on the impact of data as a productive force:

> This wave of interest in the constitutive power of data, software and code is increasing as it becomes clear that data are, in a number of ways, central to the make-up of contemporary social formations of different types. Despite this excellent emergent body of literature, we are still only at the foothills in our critical analysis of the role of data in culture and society.
>
> *(Beer 2015, 3)*

As in many fields, the educational research world has only recently begun to consider the impact of data, and in many cases this has been limited to consideration of governance, known as 'governing through data' (Ozga *et al.* 2011). In this text, we aim to redress this imbalance by adding a significant contribution to the limited research focused on school and classroom practices (Finn 2016; Pratt 2016).

The context for this study is the primary education system (age 4–11) and early years settings (age 2–4) in England; education in other areas of the United Kingdom is governed by devolved policies. This is pertinent as England is an extreme example which demonstrates many concerns voiced in the international literature; the education system is described as 'the most "advanced" in Europe in terms of data production and use' (Ozga 2009, 149; see also Silliman 2015). Since this was written, the reliance on data has only increased with policy changes, so that the issue has attracted media attention with headlines such as 'Teachers "worn out by demand for data"' (Metro 2017). An article by a school inspector in the *Times Educational Supplement* commented that the guidance for Ofsted inspectors on analysing data for primary schools was 50 pages long.

> Think about it: how have we reached a situation where the data associated with primary assessment need 50 pages of explanation to professionals

involved in inspection? What does this say about our current data-obsessed assessment system? It says that it's far too complicated; far too dependent on numerical data which have a spurious air of precision, reliability and validity; far too impenetrable; far too far from the judgments that teachers need to make about real children's progress towards greater, genuine understanding. The guidance gives a glimpse into a parallel universe far too removed from classroom reality.

(Richards 2016)

Thus, our work provides a case study – or cautionary tale – of what happens when an education system becomes data-obsessed, and loses sight of the complexities of the identities and learning taking place in an early years or school setting. This data obsession is an essential part of the current functioning of a neoliberal education system driven by values of competition and comparison (Ball 2012a; Ball 2013a), so, for us, studying data is an important part of studying the operation of policy and how these values are both accepted and contested. As Selwyn comments, 'the discourses, practices and objects of digital data offer a direct "way in" to many of the struggles and conflicts that now characterise contemporary education' (2015, 79). These struggles include social justice concerns: who is defined as what by data, and how can datafication work to solidify, reveal or challenge disparities between different groups of children?

In this introductory chapter, we consider the politics of data, how data and datafication are defined, and then attempt to map out the existing research on data and education internationally. We end the chapter with a description of the relevant policy context in England, and an outline of the structure of the book. This sets the scene for our overall argument, which has these main strands:

- datafication is **productive** – of particular data-driven subjectivities, including new roles and hierarchies, and reproductive of some inequalities;
- datafication is **reductive** – reducing complexity of learning to single numbers and defining quality through proportions;
- datafication results in **increased visibility of performance** and has thus become an important part of performativity;
- the attraction and danger of datafication both reside in the **permanence of beliefs about accuracy** and therefore the usefulness of tracking and prediction.

The politics of data

Data are[3] political; they reinforce arguments, 'prove' effectiveness and demonstrate the success or failure of policy. At a local level, data determine the course of children's educational trajectories and teachers' careers, and, in England, a school's rating by the Office for Standards in Education (Ofsted). Data are fundamental to the relationships between the state and schools (Ozga *et al.* 2011; Ozga 2016). The use of data must be seen within the political context of an international education system which is driven by neoliberal values of managerialism and accountability (Ball 2015; Lingard, Martino and Rezai-Rashti 2013; Apple 2006). The collection of data facilitates accountability at greater levels of precision and fosters increasingly reliance on numerical comparisons as the basis of assessments of quality; an 'audit society' (Power 2013). This makes it very attractive to those who wish to engender market-driven values of competition into the education system: data are the 'ideal means of bringing market values and free market mechanisms into otherwise closed public education settings' (Selwyn 2016a, 92). Nowhere is the competition dimension of data in education more prominent than the PISA tests (Programme for International Student Assessment), the Organisation for Economic Cooperation and Development's international comparison of attainment at secondary school. The PISA results rank countries by attainment in the international tests, driving national policies, encouraging 'policy borrowing' from successful systems and, in the case of lower-ranking countries, generating 'PISA shocks' (Grek 2009; Sellar and Lingard 2013), which provoke public debate. In 2017 a new international comparative assessment from the OECD began to be piloted for younger children – the International Early Learning Study for four- and five-year-old pupils – which has been described as a 'pre-school PISA' (Moss, Dahlberg, Grieshaber *et al.* 2016). We return to this recent development in later chapters. On a national level, statutory assessment systems such as the 'Sats' tests in England, NAPLAN[4] in Australia, state-wide standardised tests after the No Child Left Behind Act in the United States and the SIMCE[5] in Chile provide examples of the use of data to provide parents with information to choose schools, within a marketised system. In these cases, data become powerful indicators of the 'quality' of schools and teachers, with performance made visible.

Data in education are integral to a particular political understanding of what matters in education, based on neoliberal values of competition. Related to this is the great attraction of the apparent *precision of data*, a positivist discourse, within the world of education which is seen by many as 'messy', ad hoc or unregulated – what Biesta calls the 'pseudo-security of numbers' (2017, 317). This is part of a 'broader deference to statistical reasoning which permeates our understanding of social practices' (Hardy and Boyle 2011, 214). As we discuss in later chapters, the allure of reduction can be seen as relating to the uncertainties of what has been described as the 'late neoliberal' era (McGimpsey 2017).

At an institutional level, data use in schools also has to be seen in the context of discourses of 'digital revolution' and the concordant disruption to established educational practice. From the 1990s on, the promise of technology to transform education became an established trope, but 'it should be clear to all but the most zealous technophile that the much heralded technological transformation of schools and schooling has yet to take place' (Selwyn 2010, 5). This tale of 'high tech hope and digital disappointment' (ibid.) has not prevented new waves of hype about the power of technology to improve education, most recently through online learning, and the continued interest of private companies in the educational market. When considering the use of data in schools, we need to acknowledge the complex interests involved in reproducing this discourse about the power of data and other digital technology to change education; as Selwyn argues, 'we need to recognize the corporate, commercial and economically-driven nature of much of the prevailing talk about disruption and deinstitutionalization' (2016a, 21). The scale of money described through this discourse is vast: he quotes a 2013 McKinsey Global Institute report which argued that efficient use of data could add 1 trillion dollars to the value of education each year through improved effectiveness (Selwyn 2016a, 92). Education data are big business; as we discuss in more detail in later chapters,[6] the private businesses tasked with providing Baseline Assessment received a share of between £3.5 and £4.5 million (Heavey 2016).

Defining 'data'

In a world where discourses of 'big data' and the 'data revolution' regularly circulate, the term 'data' has become one which is commonly used without much thought to its exact definition. As Pratt notes, in schools the term 'data' has been reduced to mean only *numbers*: 'the very meaning of the term has been commandeered to ensure only that which is enumerated counts; as if data could only be numbers and not more qualitative descriptions of the children's world' (2016, 897). We include in our definition non-numerical forms of data (written observations, photographs, colour coding), though the majority of the data discussed do take numerical form. In the study of data beyond education, they are described as: 'the raw material produced by abstracting the world into categories, measures and other representational forms – numbers, characters, symbols, images, sounds, electromagnetic waves, bits – that constitute the building blocks from which information and knowledge are created' (Kitchin 2014, 1). Kitchin argues that data are: 'epistemological units, made to have a representational form that enables epistemological work' (2014, 19); the knowledge gained from data is contingent on how and why the data were collected in the first place. The simple scientific framing of data as benign, technical and neutral is mistaken; there are always influences in how data are collected, stored, analysed and used. As Gitelman and Jackson put it, data are always 'cooked'; there is no such thing as 'raw data', untouched by human influence (2013, 5 cited in Kitchin 2014, 20; see also Bowker 2005). This is obviously true in education, where the most common form of data collected, assessment data, are inevitably affected by the mode of assessment, as well as many other factors. There is also no neutral method of analysing data: however neutral the processes of code and algorithms may appear, they are always imbued with some underlying values about what matters in education:

> The work of policymakers, education leaders and educators, the choices of parents, and the behaviour and progress of learners alike are all being sculpted or governed by technologies that are instructed by the code and algorithms written by technical experts according to particular discourses about what education is or should be.
>
> *(Williamson 2016b, 4)*

This view of the technology as part of the social context – a 'sociotechnical system' – is drawn from a range of fields including science and technology studies, software studies, geography, philosophy and sociology (Williamson 2016b). This perspective draws attention to the original context in which the technologies were produced, and then 'fold back to re-shape the contexts in which they originated' (Williamson 2016b, 6). In this book we conceptualise data in this broader sense as a record of something which *also does work itself*; data are not a purely technical form of information, but a socially created set of information or knowledge which also have influence on practices and subjectivities.

Defining 'datafication'

The use of data in education is not a new phenomenon: schools have always kept records of attendance, attainment and other practices such as punishments (Selwyn 2016a; Goldstein and Moss 2014). However, the advent of digital technology and societal expectations around the promise of this new technology to improve education have led to data having an increased prominence in schools and other educational settings – on an 'an unprecedented scale' (Selwyn 2016a, 81). Ozga *et al.* describe 'the incessant production of data to monitor performance in education' (2011, 1).

We use the term datafication to describe this broad phenomenon of increased prominence, as it offers a shorthand for a complex process. In earlier work we have defined datafication in terms of increased significance, visibility and constant governance through dataveillance, and as being what happens when people or systems are 'subjected to the demands of data production' (Roberts-Holmes and Bradbury 2016). Ozga describes the use of data as a policy instrument as growing in 'strength, speed and scope' (2009, 150). Others have described the increased use of data in education using the 'three Vs' (Laney 2001 cited in Selwyn 2016a, 81): *volume*, describing increased amounts of data produced; *variety*, in terms of types of data and their sources; and *velocity*, of both the production and processing of data. This is a useful categorisation which helps us to move forward from descriptions of 'more data'. It is helpful to think about how data are produced from multiple sources and have multiple forms in classrooms, how they are transferred from one site to another and with whose permission, who has the power to alter them, and of course who controls how they are processed and delivered back to serve some purpose. For us, changes in volume, variety and velocity are all component parts of datafication. We are interested in the different forms and purposes of data, such as the distinctions between 'compliance data' produced to fulfil a commitment (usually policy-based) and 'useful data' which aid learning (Selwyn, Henderson and Chao 2015). Thus this work builds on Bradbury's previous explorations of assessment processes in early years and their complex relationships with concepts of 'teacher knowledge' (Bradbury 2013c). We also develop our discussions on the changing status of data within schools (Bradbury and Roberts-Holmes 2016a) and the related 'artefacts' of its collection (Souto-Otero and Beneito-Montagut 2016).

However, in this book we also use the term datafication to examine the *impact* of data, particularly on subjectivities, and so the process described is not simply a change to what is done and how, but also a change to *who people are*, or who they are expected to be. As Gitelman and Jackson note, data 'need to be understood as framed *and framing*' (2013, 5 cited in Kitchin 2014, 21, emphasis added). Datafication is something that happens to people, values and cultures as well as practices; data are 'productive measures' (Beer 2015). In this way we are broadening out others' use of the term to consider the impact on *subjectivities*, as well as practices and values. We examine datafication as a shift in what can be thought, or regimes of truth, in Foucault's terms, about what matters in education. Lingard and Sellar refer to 'the naturalisation of data as the most sensible medium for thinking about teaching and learning' (2013, 652); similarly Sellar refers to 'new modes of data-driven rationality' in education (2015, 138).

We include in this broader definition exploration of the processes of creating new actors and new spaces and flows of power (Piattoeva 2015; Lynch 2015; Manovich 2012, 2013): the data analysts, private companies that systematise data and the architects of software. We consider the role of private companies who were tasked with providing Baseline Assessment to schools and the (im)balances of power this created, within a context of increasingly private involvement in state education (Ball 2012a). A final aspect of datafication is the impact on *visibility* within processes of disciplinary power and surveillance (Foucault 1980, 1977); in the following chapter we explore how various theoretical perspectives can help to understand the role of data as disciplinary and as a key element of 'societies of control' (Deleuze 1995b).

Research on data and education

Having set out our area of interest, we use this section to map out the existing literature on data and education, concentrating on issues of data and governance and the limited specific research on primary and early years education. We then consider the problems and potential of datafication as set out in existing work, as context for our study.

Data and governance

The majority of work in the international field of data and education has explored the increasing role of data in processes of governance (Grek 2009; Ozga *et al.* 2011; Williamson 2015a; Selwyn 2015), while there has been limited empirical work on the impact on classrooms (Finn 2016). In the 2000s a major European-wide study considered the role of performance data in the governing and control of education. Data were collected from England, Denmark, Finland, Scotland and Sweden. The resulting literature focuses on quality assurance and the 'fabrication of quality' (Ozga *et al.* 2011) and the resultant new forms of governing. They argue that, in Europe, 'data are a powerful resource that link new forms of governance preoccupied with the measurement and improvement of performance to the constitution of society as a governable domain' (Ozga *et al.* 2011, 7). The 'governance turn' is 'intimately connected with the growth of data, and the increase in possibilities for monitoring, targeting and shifting cultures and behaviour that data apparently produce' (Ozga, Segerholm and Simola 2011, 85).

Considering the context in England, Ozga argues that the growth of data has 'unbalanced the relations of governing and created highly centralised system steering' (2009, 149). Her work, which focuses on the role of data in the relationships between the state and schools (rather than within schools, which is more our concern here), provides the context for our study. Since the 1980s, data have been used as a policy instrument within the shift from government to governance; from a system based on partnership to one based on neoliberal market-driven practices of accountability (Ozga 2009). In practice, this took the form of an increasing reliance on assessment data from national tests as the main form of accountability for schools. Currently, schools' assessment data are publicly available through 'data dashboards' and inspection regimes rely heavily on the data in a school's 'RAISEonline' profile (Ozga 2016). Ozga argues that the 'dispersed, distributed and disaggregated form' of governance is made possible by the use of data (2009, 150); thus it is essential to the functioning of this transformed system.

A major finding of Ozga *et al.*'s European-wide project was the description of a 'data turn' and new 'calculative rationality' in education (2011). Across Europe, they found that education systems were 'governed by numbers', heavily reliant on data as a method of control and surveillance, and as justification for policy. Similarly, in their research on state-wide responses to the publication of data from national tests in Australia, Lingard and Sellar (2013) argue these 'catalyst data' pressure politicians and policy-makers into action – for example, provoking state-wide reviews and new audit systems. Data become the driver for decisions, even though at times this results in 'perverse effects' to protect reputations. The reliance on data arises from the dominance of testing as an accountability measure:

> Around the globe, and particularly in Anglo-American and Asian nations, testing of various kinds, including high-stakes national census testing, has become a metapolicy, steering educational systems in particular directions with great effects in schools and on teacher practices, on curricula, as well as upon student learning and experiences of school.
>
> *(Lingard, Martino and Rezai-Rashti 2013, 540)*

In the United States, a shift towards standardised testing followed the No Child Left Behind Act of 2001, which mandated that each state have a standard test which could demonstrate 'adequate yearly progress'; this process of annual testing continues under the 2015 Every Student Succeeds Act, despite extensive criticism (Au 2011; Leonardo 2007; Apple 2009; Gilliom, 2010; Hursh 2013; Lipman 2013). This move towards the production of standard assessment data for comparison is not limited to the 'west'; in Chile, for example, for decades all children have sat the national SIMCE test, which provides data for parents to choose schools (Meckes and Carrasco 2010); but also, as in many neoliberal systems, contributes to social segregation (Valenzuela, Bellei and Ríos 2014). In South Africa, 'measurement … dominate[s] the educative process' (Davids 2017, 432).

Around the world, countries that have embraced neoliberal market values in education have produced assessments for accountability, creating a system where attainment data are an integral part of governance. As Rutledge, Anagnostopoulos and Jacobsen argue, 'policy makers direct student, teacher, and school performance from afar by controlling the collection, processing, and dissemination of data and attaching sanctions to them' (2013, 215 cited in Lingard, Martino and Rezai-Rashti 2013, 541). Within this turn towards governance through data, and particularly discussions of 'big data', data may appear distanced from the every-day operation of schools and teachers; however, we agree with Beer (2015) that large datasets should not be seen as separate from the social world but instead as *generative* in that they have an epistemological impact by defining what is known (and in turn what is valued). This is our focus here.

Research on data in schools

Research specifically on the use of data in primary and early years settings is limited, other than our own previous work (Bradbury 2013; Roberts-Holmes 2015; Bradbury 2016a; Roberts-Holmes and Bradbury 2016, 2017). The issue does arise in some studies of marketisation in general, such as Pratt's (2016), which includes small-scale study of internal competition in primary schools in England includes some discussion of the importance of data to teachers, and their sense of ownership over 'their data'. The teachers in this study comment on the importance of termly meetings with the headteacher to discuss attainment data for their class; Pratt argues that these data now represent 'individual capital acquired by teachers themselves', or as one teacher says, 'a sort of non-arguable level of proof' (2016, 898). However, the teachers also note the wider importance of producing the right data; one teacher is quoted as saying 'as a school [you] need that data to justify what you are doing' (Pratt 2016, 897). Pratt notes that the reliance on data is part of a 'changing emphasis from practice that is effective to practice that has *the hallmark* of effectiveness' (2016, 896, emphasis in original); building on work which has focused on the performative nature of teachers' work in a neoliberal era (Perryman 2009).

Hardy's work investigating the enactment of the NAPLAN national testing system in Queensland, Australia, using Bourdieu, found 'a habitus influenced by comparison of data at the national, state and local levels' (2014, 9). There was a 'data wall' in one staff room, which the principal described as part of his strategy of 'embedding data in the mindset of teachers'. Principals in primary schools under pressure to improve their results spoke of how 'powerful' it was to share their data with other schools and experts, and how it provided 'focus'. However, Hardy argues that the data were not simply used for political purposes of accountability, but there was a 'logic of appropriation' which meant teachers used the data to improve learning.

Finn's (2016) research in England provides a rare example of an exploration of data which focuses on the impact on students and involves research data from young people. His work, based on an ethnographic study of a secondary school, argues that data have an affective dimension, bringing positive 'atmospheres of progress' into classrooms; these make some students feel optimistic and motivated, while others are left feeling isolated. Similarly, Sellar (2015) argues for the affective dimension of data, although his work concentrates on data at the national level, rather than in the classroom.

Further empirical work includes Selwyn's study of two secondary schools in Australia, which focused on the 'diverse but often mundane ways that [the schools] had become orientated towards the everyday use of digital data as a means of accountability' (Selwyn 2016b, 61). Selwyn found three distinct forms of data-based governance: the use of data for 'system-wide' accountability, for 'within school' accountability, and for 'within class' accountability (2016b, 56). The 'within class' forms included teachers' own methods of collecting information on how confident students felt about a particular topic, which in their methods reflected the school-wide systems of colour-coded spreadsheets. Thus the teachers in this study employed practices with student data which mirrored how they were held accountable themselves. Selwyn comments on the visibility of data around the school in the form of graphs and summaries on display, and their prominence in staff meetings. This trend towards visualisation of data was also noted by Hardy in his study of Australian primary schools (2015). In Selwyn's study, teachers saw data as strategic, in that they gave them early warning of 'upcoming situations', so they could predict 'bumps in the road' (2016b, 61); this is in keeping with 'risk management' approaches. However, there were limitations to the use of data: teachers saw printouts of figures as 'a crude distillation of what were initially more nuanced measures' (Selwyn 2016b, 62). Moreover, data use was often simple, ad hoc and unsophisticated; Selwyn argues it was a 'trickle' rather than a 'data deluge' (2016b, 63). Importantly, however, Selwyn, Henderson and Chao note that schools engaged in data practices beyond those officially mandated, such as 'real time reporting' of student attainment; thus 'prevailing external conditions of accountability, auditing and performativity had extruded into schools' internal practices and processes' (2015, 778–779). Data use had become a culture, a symbol of good educational practice.

Further research on teacher attitudes to data includes Kelly, Downey and Rietdijk's (2010) survey-based study of secondary teachers' use of and attitudes towards pupil performance data. They found that data use increased with seniority in the school, and younger and newer teachers used data least, but there was no variation in terms of gender or subject, counter to the stereotype that it is male, mathematically minded teachers who undertake data analysis. The majority of teachers in their survey felt confident about using data, and there was a strong commitment to their use to set targets and identify students in need of 'intervention'. However, teachers continued to produce their 'own data' in various forms, as they found it more useful than 'official data' and saw it as more trustworthy (Kelly, Downey and Rietdijk 2010; Kelly and Downey 2011). These findings mirror those of ethnographic and interview-based studies in emphasising the importance of data to schools' every-day operation, and the contingent nature of the enactment of policy. Teachers' utilise their own agency to find 'get arounds' (Selwyn, Henderson and Chao 2015) in response to the demands of data, and 'play games' with data (Kelly, Downey and Rietdijk 2010). We look in more detail at these responses to data in the next section.

The problems and potential of datafication

We use this section to set out briefly the range of arguments present in the literature regarding the positive and negative effects of datafication. We begin from a position which subscribes to neither a utopian nor a dystopian vision of data use in education, and argue that this dichotomy, present in debates about the use of data, does little to critically examine the phenomenon, or help educators to navigate it.

The use of data in education is part of, and cannot be separated from, the wider use of digital technology in schools over the last few decades. Discourses surrounding the increasing use of data sit within this broader discourse of 'digital revolution' in education, with its promises of the transformation of teaching and learning through technology. Selwyn argues that the scale of the promise of technology varies from 'modest improvement' through support and scaffolding of learning, through 'transformation', such as changing modes of learning through online provision, to 'revolution', which involves challenging institutions, curricula and qualification systems (2016a, 5–6). Data are part of each discourse, essential to the promise to 'fix' a broken system to varying degrees. As such, data use forms part of the current answer to the 'discourse of derision' (Ball 1990) over the school system. The overall story of schools' use of technology is described by Selwyn as one of 'high tech hope and digital disappointment' (2010, 1). Perhaps data use forms a new front in the drive to 'improve' education through technology. Parties outside of the traditional education establishment – private companies particularly – have an interest in reproducing this discourse of digital revolution as solution, and, as we see in the studies described in this book, are reaping the rewards through government policies which rely on private providers.

There are clearly some benefits to the use of data in education – or it would not be so prevalent. Data reveal problems and allow for improvement; they can be a 'useful vehicle for developmental purposes' (Hardy and Boyle 2011, 214). As Biesta comments, 'measurement culture' has 'allowed for discussions to be based on factual data rather than just assumptions or opinions about what might be the case' (2009, 35). However, as he continues, the facts about *what is* are combined with values about *what should be* in decisions about educational strategy; thus, the use of data in making decisions is not straightforward. The problems associated with the use of data in education can be broadly grouped into two categories: those related to effectiveness and those related to identities. The former group includes concerns about the applicability of measurement and assessment practices to educational settings, accuracy, manipulation and the change in practices that result. The latter includes concerns about what data 'do' to us, who they make us become, and the emotional or human cost of data-driven practices. We discuss both of these in later chapters, but sketch out here the main issues arising from existing research.

Effectiveness

As discussed, data promise certainty and precision within an uncertain world; in education they offer control and monitoring of learning at an unprecedented scale (Kelly and Downey 2011). But a major concern involved in the use of data is the disjuncture between this idea of precision and accuracy and the realities of classroom life. Moss describes this as the argument that 'complexity and messiness, diversity and context, the social and cultural must and can be controlled, reduced and tamed, spurred on by the belief that there must be one right answer for every question' (2014, 66). A result of this disjuncture is that data become limited to particular things; as Selwyn notes, 'The danger exists of educational data systems only measuring what can easily be measured, rather than what cannot be easily measured but is nevertheless important' (2016a, 98). This has an impact on concepts of validity:

> More than just the question of the technical validity of our measurements – i.e. whether we are measuring what we intend to measure – the problem here lies with what I suggest to call the *normative validity* of our measurements. This is the question whether we are indeed measuring what we value, or whether we are just measuring what we can easily measure and thus end up valuing what we (can) measure. The rise of a culture of performativity in education – a culture in which means become ends in themselves so that targets and indicators of quality become mistaken for quality itself – has been one of the main 'drivers' of an approach to measurement in which normative validity is being replaced by technical validity.
>
> *(Biesta 2009, 35)*

In early years in particular, there is the simple problem of accuracy in a subjective world; the incompatibility of a score or a decision on a criterion, and the reality of a young child who may behave differently one day to the next. Furthermore, one casualty of the rush to measure what we can easily measure is that the social context of education can be overlooked. As Kitchin argues, the analysis of data can 'unmoor' educational problems from the social, cultural and political realities of what the data are intended to record (2014, 22). This is particularly a problem when data are presented as neutral facts, separate from their origins in the complex world of a classroom or exam hall. Data 'have a kind of kudos that needs to be treated with care, as the values that are designed in to the analysis process are not always properly considered or made explicit' (Eynon 2013, 238). This can lead to problems where 'decontextualised student data ... may subvert concerns for social equity and justice' (Perrotta 2013, 119).

A further related problem is that, despite the promise of ever more effective practice driven by data, the use of data may actually produce less effective education systems, particularly where it is used inappropriately (Silliman 2015). Practices encouraged by the dominance of data collection – sometimes referred to as making education 'machine-readable' (Williamson, 2014 cited in Finn 2016, 31) – may in fact harm learning, through disruption to teaching time, distraction or, as we see in our research studies, alteration to pedagogy which is known to work. A huge amount of time is also spent by teachers on collecting and processing data, which may reduce their ability to spend time on planning or their time with children (Bradbury 2013c). Furthermore, problems can arise in the analysis of data due to lack of expertise and confidence; Selwyn refers to 'relatively unsophisticated' data processing in schools (2016b) which can affect how policy is enacted. Simplistic or incorrect analysis of data can lead to ineffective allocation of resources or unhelpful 'interventions'.

Another aspect of datafication that may produce a negative impact is the problem of 'gaming' or manipulation of results, as they are made more visible or 'high stakes':

> Productive measures [are] responsible for producing as well as tracking the social. They shape behaviours. As people are subject to these forms of measurement they will produce different responses and outcomes, knowing, as they often will, what is coming and the way that their performance will become visible.
>
> *(Beer 2015, 10)*

Assessments linked to school-level accountability are of immense importance for schools, and there is a risk that in a world where the analysis of data forms an essential part of school inspection, school leaders will be encouraged to manipulate their results in some way to produce the right narrative. As we described in our 2016 paper, there is a need for schools in England to produce an 'Ofsted story' of continual improvement, which involves a low level of attainment in the early years (Bradbury and Roberts-Holmes 2016a). Thus, as found in our previous work, it is attractive for teachers to keep assessment results in the early years as low as possible (Bradbury 2013c). We describe this production of data for the purposes of data analysis rather than real understanding of children's progress as 'fabrication', after Ball's specific use of the term (2003), and Ozga *et al.*'s discussion of 'fabricating quality' (2011). Although we are reluctant to engage in a discourse of 'effectiveness', with all its neoliberal overtones, any analysis of data in education must engage with the literature on the impact on practice.

Identities

Datafication changes how we think about individuals – their worth, role and achievements – and feelings. As Finn writes, 'data doesn't only change or enable particular modes of thought but also modes of individual or collective feeling' (2016, 30). Data and data analysis establish particular ways of thinking about what matters and what should be compared, often driven by competing visions of the purpose of education. Bradbury's previous research on the impact of the EYFS Profile found that the content of this assessment and the practices it engendered produced an ideal learner identity which was neoliberal in character (2013a): flexible, industrious, entrepreneurial, self-regulating. The statements which were used to judge children's 'development' shaped how teachers constructed the idea of 'good learner' and removed other possibilities from view. In analysing the numerical data produced by counting the number of statements children had met, teachers were forced to subscribe to a particular vision of the curriculum and learning, while solidifying children's identities as more or less 'developed'. This was uncomfortable for some teachers and at times frustrating, but overall they coalesced within the neoliberal paradigm of accountability through assessment. The idea that children, however young, should be assessed regularly and their attainments noted in numerical form has become what Foucault called a 'regime of truth' in education (Foucault 1980). Children are reduced to the data that represent them – as ones, twos and threes, or failing, meeting or exceeding in Roberts-Holmes' research data on the EYFS Profile (Roberts-Holmes 2013). This is not only found in research in the UK: Piattoeva's (2016) study of Russian public examinations found they have become a site for data production, with learners reduced to 'docile data producers'. In the US, Koyama and Menken (2013) discuss the framing of bilingual students as 'numerical calculations', 'defined by their lower scores'; while in Australia, Hardy (2015) examines the reductive effects of the 'enumerative nominalisation' of students. Similarly, Davids examines how South African education policy is 'trapped in a particular understanding of teaching and learning that can be understood only in terms of measurement' (2017, 422).

Children's worth rests on the impact they will have on the overall data for the class, particularly whether they will increase the proportion 'passing' the assessment. Thus, research on the use of data in schools builds on the existing field which examines the importance of assessment policy in building children's identities as learners. Gillborn and Youdell's (2000) research established the concept of 'educational triage', where some children are identified as 'hopeless cases', others as 'safe' and others 'suitable for treatment', based on the likelihood of them gaining a C grade in exams at age 16. This last group has more worth as they could potentially influence the school's performance figures, which were at the time based on the proportion of students gaining five A–C grades. Similarly, research studies have identified 'bubble kids' who are the target for intervention in US schools (Booher-Jennings 2005), and processes of educational triage in Australian primary schools (Lewis and Hardy 2015), and in Reception classes in England (Roberts-Holmes 2015). The identification of 'cusp children' who may gain a 'Good Level of Development' in the EYFS Profile, as shown in Vince's (2016) study of Reception classes in England, is based on analysis of data. Thus, there is a range of research which has established how children are constituted in terms of worth through discourses linked to data; what we do in this text is develop further our thinking about how this operates in the current data-obsessed climate. In particular, we are interested in the way that the use of data focused on progress has shifted the focus from the borderline children, to all children, who must be 'moving forward'.

We also examine how processes of datafication render students differently as subjects; less as individuals, and more as units of data production. Thompson and Cook comment that, 'Metaphorically, the teacher is being asked to turn away from the student to gaze at the virtual representations of the data' (2014, 139); we discuss how the individual child becomes less important in the data–obsessed classroom, but also how, conversely, some 'borderline' children become key within a target-driven culture (Hardy 2015; Roberts-Holmes 2013; Booher-Jennings 2005). Students are the producers of data, the 'raw materials' to be 'mined' (Manovich 2012). This shifting subjectivity, which builds on previous work on learner identities (Bradbury 2013a; Youdell 2006b), may be irrelevant to the young children in early years settings and primary schools, but it affects how their educational lives are organised and determined.

Our focus here is not only on the students themselves, but also on the role of data in the subjectification of teachers. There is an impact on their professional status, both within the school and in terms of salary, as progression up pay scales is dependent on satisfactory performance, usually framed by assessment data (Pratt 2016). As Beer puts it, 'certainty in measurement creates uncertainty in those being measured' (2015, 10). Survey research has indicated that teachers associate data use with a lack of trust in them as professionals (Kelly, Downey and Rietdijk 2010). This is pertinent in early years particularly, where teachers have traditionally had a complex relationship with issues of professionalism and gaining comparable status with other teachers (Bradbury 2012). We examine how this has been affected by their new role as collectors of vital data under Baseline policy, and their deployment of agency in response. We use Souto-Otero and Beneito-Montagut's (2016) discussion of the strategies employed in reaction to an increased volume of data to examine these responses. Souto-Otero and Beneito-Montagut aim to move beyond discussion 'compliance, surveillance, control and acceptance' to focus on resistance (2016, 15). They argue that alongside acquiescent practices of 'alignment' there are a variety of practices of resistance, including:

- Gaming: where 'the social actor plays within the proposed field but not under the set rules' (Souto-Otero and Beneito-Montagut 2016, 27), much like Ball's discussion of 'fabrication'. This is particularly relevant given our previous research on manipulation of results in primary schools (Bradbury 2011b) and the literature on institutional responses to high-stakes testing (Gillborn and Youdell 2000; Stobart 2008; Lingard and Sellar 2013).
- Bordering: where 'the use and credibility attached to commensuration is strategically deployed' (Souto-Otero and Beneito-Montagut 2016, 27). Data are used tactically; for example, universities' use of data from the Research Excellence Framework (REF) in promoting themselves.
- Folding: or 'opt[ing] out of the data deluge'. This may be passive, such as non-participation, or active, where activities take place but the data are not collected. There are costs to this strategy.

• Rebellion: which involves critiquing the system, refusing to accept its premises, and redefining key concepts.

This discussion of teachers' responses is informed by the literature on neoliberal subjectivities, particularly Ball's discussion of the 'terrors of performativity' (2003) and Ball and Olmedo's examination of 'care of the self' under neoliberal governmentalities (2013). The latter examines how teachers' informal responses form a 'struggle against mundane, quotidian neoliberalisations' (2013, 85). As we discuss in more detail in the following chapter, they argue: 'Neoliberalism requires and enacts a "new type of individual", that is a "new type of teacher and head teacher" formed within the logic of competition. The apparatuses of neoliberalism are seductive, enthralling and overbearingly necessary' (Ball and Olmedo 2013, 88). The nature of this new individual and the role of data in producing them are the focus for later chapters.

We also consider the status of teachers, in relation to each other and to the new actors required by datafication. As Manovich argues, the use of data introduces new hierarchies based on who has control over data and who has the skills to process or analyse them (2012, 2013; see also Selwyn, Henderson and Chao 2015). New divisions are created between the three categories of people, or 'data-classes', that emerge: those who create data, those who collect them and those who are able to analyse them (Manovich 2012). The final group is the smallest in number, but have great power. These distinctions, we argue, are important in schools, where increasingly data are analysed by consultants or an employed 'data manager', who remains at a distance from the classroom (Roberts-Holmes and Bradbury 2016). The 'rise of technical actors and data intermediaries producing and facilitating educational data' (Williamson 2016b, 3) introduces new roles and careers, and concomitantly new flows of power, and capital, into the education system. Jobs monitoring and managing the data appear at all levels from schools to governments, as the skills of the 'data guru' become essential (Lingard and Sellar 2013). Headteachers retain an important role, not least because they still conduct data analysis (Selwyn 2016b) and interpretation (Hardy 2014), but they too find themselves reliant on outside expertise, in the new 'expertocracy' (Grek 2013). While some schools become a 'data democracy', where all are enabled and trained to use data for overall improvements, others become 'data dictatorships' with data access controlled by one or two 'expert' members of staff (Kelly, Downey and Rietdijk 2010). Younger, newer teachers may have limited rights to access or change data within these new hierarchies, or they may be seen as the teachers who 'do technology' in contrast with others (Selwyn, Nemorin and Johnson 2016, 8). This discussion of new positions and hierarchies sits alongside research on the roles involved in policy enactment – for example, as 'translators', 'critics' and 'receivers' (Ball *et al.* 2011a) – which is also relevant here.

Beyond the individuals themselves who are involved in datafication, there are also important developments documented in the literature relating to the software underlying the collection and analysis of data, which is described as the 'hidden manager' by Lawn (2013). Lynch (2015) examines the 'hidden role of software', while Manovich (2012) discusses the importance of the 'software layer' of techniques of control and surveillance. The software is determined by the values and imperatives of those designing it, and those with the expertise to design it are vital, and powerful, within a data-reliant system: 'Software and data companies and agencies are becoming dominant sites for the instrumentation of education' (Williamson 2016b, 11). 'Educational data scientists are becoming new kinds of scientific experts of learning with increasing legitimate authority to produce systems of knowledge about children and to define them as subjects and objects of intervention' (Williamson 2016a, 401). Private companies and their role in the management of datafication, and thus a new educational knowledge infrastructure (Williamson 2016c), are our concern in Chapter 6. We also consider how these shifts of power – when teachers 'increasingly lose control of their stories to the database' (Thompson and Cook 2014, 137) – reconstitute teachers as subjects, in Chapter 3.

The policy context: the reification of progress

In this section we examine the current policy context of primary and early years education in England, with the aim of providing the background for the research data we discuss in later chapters. In particular, we explore the specific policy of Baseline Assessment in Reception classes (children aged 4–5 years old), which was the catalyst for our second research project (Bradbury and Roberts-Holmes 2016b). Throughout, as in previous work, we argue that a shift towards 'progress' as a key measure of schools' success has both been enabled by and in turn driven the increased significance of assessment data (Bradbury and Roberts-Holmes 2016a). This has also altered the dynamics within the early years and primary sectors, as key moments in the production of data have emerged giving some age groups more status. Baseline Assessment marked the epitome of this trend.

Primary schools in England are required to conduct statutory assessments at key points in children's educational journeys: the Early Years Foundation Stage Profile in Reception (age 4/5)[7]; a Phonics Screening Check in Year 1 (age 5/6); and statutory assessments in Year 2 (age 6/7) and Year 6 (age 10/11), known informally as Key Stage 1 and 2 'Sats'. The volume of data collected in each school simply for statutory purposes is therefore vast; in Ozga's research, the scale and scope of England's 'data machinery' was described by a senior analyst in Brussels as 'monstrous' (Ozga 2016, 73). Although in primary education this system has appeared relatively stable over the last decade, there have in fact been several key changes, including the introduction of a spelling and grammar paper in Year 6 and the introduction of the Phonics Screening Check (Bradbury and Roberts-Holmes 2016a), which have altered priorities and pedagogy in primary schools. The 'slimmed down' assessment regime proposed by the Conservative–Liberal Democrat coalition government of 2010–15 has not materialised (Bradbury 2013b); instead their commitment to providing more information to parents has dominated policy decisions. This complex array of assessments provides data on individual children's attainment, but is also used to assess the quality of the school by Ofsted, the inspection service (Ozga

2016). Each school's data dashboard (SDD) is available to Ofsted inspectors and poor attainment scores in terms of absolute attainment or progress measures (such as achievement between the Year 2 and Year 6 Sats) can provoke an inspection. The SDD compares the school's data with that of other schools with similar levels of attainment, indicating the importance of comparison and competition in this data-dominated system.[8] The SDD data also form an important part of the inspection process itself; before the inspection the team study the data to form their initial judgement and select their areas of interest, a key moment in the process (Ozga 2016). The final judgement rests not only on what inspectors observe during their visit, but on the attainment data, particularly in terms of progress; a school cannot be given an 'Outstanding' grade unless they show that 'Pupils make substantial and sustained progress throughout year groups across many subjects' (Ofsted 2014, 71).

In early years settings, the non-compulsory sector of education for under-fives made up of private and voluntary nurseries, Nursery classes in primary schools, nursery schools and children's centres, there is no statutory assessment system. There is, however, guidance on assessment – Development Matters – and curriculum guidance (the EYFS framework). As we discuss in later chapters, assessment nonetheless forms a key part of early years staff's work, and data are also vital to the operation and sometimes the continued existence of early years settings. This sector has come under increased scrutiny in recent years as investment has grown (Moss 2015); all three-year-old children and some disadvantaged two-year-old children are currently provided with 15 hours a week of free early education in a setting of their choice (for 38 weeks of the year). Thus there has been increased interest in concepts of quality and related issues such as educators' qualifications and child-to-staff ratios in early years, from the 1997–2010 Labour governments, the 2010–15 coalition government and the current (2015–) Conservative government (Bourne and Shackleton 2017). Moss argues:

> The basic structure of regulation and control has been fine-tuned, ensuring all children (and their educators) are governed by technologies of normalisation, which define their experience of early childhood education and initiate them into 'perpetual training', in which each stage of education 'readies' children and young people for the next and, ultimately, for a flexible labour market.
>
> *(2015, 230)*

As Moss argues, the rationale for increased investment and scrutiny is the long-term benefits of early years education within a neoliberal system. This has led, we argue in later chapters, to the need for early years settings to produce data which prove effectiveness, usually in the form of *measures of progress* between developmental criteria.

As we have argued elsewhere (Bradbury and Roberts-Holmes 2016a), the reification of progress has been a key development in primary education; Finn argues similarly that there has been a 'turn to progress' in secondary education (2016). The use of progress measures has a complex history in education in England: 'value added' measures have been included in league tables since 2002, using a calculation of proportions of children making expected progress between Sats at Key Stage 1 and Key Stage 2. A more complex 'contextual value added' measure was introduced in 2007; this measure compared progress between two given points with data from similar children for previous years. Controversially, it aimed to take into account the 'context' of the school, in terms of a number of characteristics of pupils, including gender, free school meals (FSM) status and ethnic group (Bradbury 2011a). This 'contextual' element was removed under the coalition government in 2011 on the basis that 'It is morally wrong to have an attainment measure which entrenches low aspirations for children because of their background' (DfE 2010, 68). There were also concerns over tactical game-playing (such as deliberately reducing earlier scores to ensure more progress – a topic we return to later in this book) and secondary school teachers' accusations of inaccuracy of assessments conducted at primary school (Kelly, Downey and Rietdijk 2010).

Thus the idea of using simple progress measures is established in the education system, but more complex calculations have been used with more caution. The introduction of Baseline Assessment in 2015, we argue, marked the epitome of a trend towards using what we call 'simple progress' as a key judgement on a school's quality. 'Simple progress' is a measure between two points without any contextual factors. When it was introduced in 2015, Baseline Assessment provided a single digit for each child, based on assessment in the first six weeks of Reception; the plan was to use this as the 'baseline' to judge each child's progress when they reached Year 6 seven years later. These scores would be aggregated and then used to judge the value added by the school. But in 2016 the government reduced the status of Baseline from statutory to voluntary as a result of research questioning the validity of the data produced (STA 2016) and a concerted campaign by educational groups against the policy (BWB 2015). However, in March 2017 a consultation was announced on a new Baseline Assessment in Reception, with the continued aim of measuring progress during a child's primary school years by comparing a starting point assessment with Key Stage 2 tests at age 10/11 (DfE 2017c). The consultation commented that the system of using Key Stage 1 assessments at age 6/7 as a starting point was ineffective and failed to take into account the progress made in Reception and Key Stage 1, so an assessment in Reception was the best option for a baseline.

> Any progress measure needs a reliable baseline, a starting point from which progress will be calculated. Ideally, that baseline should be established as early as possible to cover the maximum amount of a pupil's time in a particular school and therefore ensure that a school receives full credit for the value that it adds. It is also important that this baseline is robust and trusted.
>
> *(DfE 2017c)*

Thus the possibility of a 'robust' assessment of children at age four or five, as a baseline to measure progress, continues to dominate primary assessment policy in England.

Baseline Assessment

Baseline Assessment was introduced on a voluntary basis in the autumn of 2015, with the intention that it would be statutory in 2016 (with the existing assessment, the EYFS Profile, made optional) (DfE 2015a). Initially, Baseline was to provide key information for the main measure of judging primary schools; the guidance explained that from 2016 Baseline Assessment will be 'the only measure used to assess the progress of children from entry (at age 4–5) to the end of key stage 2 (age 10–11), alongside an attainment floor standard of 85 per cent' (DfE 2015b). This was a major shift in approaches to accountability in primary education which involves the early years phase more than ever before (Bradbury and Roberts-Holmes 2016b). There were also implications for the allocation of funding, as the Baseline Assessment data were intended to replace the EYFS Profile data as the basis for the allocation of low prior attainment funding to primary and infant schools from 2016. The DfE stated that this funding 'helps schools support pupils whose attainment was below the expected level before reception year' (DfE 2015a). It should be noted that there were antecedents to Baseline Assessment, as previous similarly timed assessments have been used in the past (1997–2002) and many Reception classes were already carrying out their own form of informal 'baseline' using teacher observations and comparisons with the EYFS early learning goals. However, the introduction of Baseline Assessment was unprecedented in that it was the first use of a baseline assessment for accountability purposes.

The origins of Baseline Assessment as a policy can be traced to comments from Ofsted's then chief inspector, who said in 2013 that the EYFS Profile was 'too broad an assessment' that did not link effectively to subsequent Key Stage assessments, and was 'a weak basis for accountability' (as reported in Gaunt 2013). One month later these comments were included in a DfE press release, paving the way for a consultation on reforming primary school assessment and accountability. This consultation included the proposal for a Reception baseline, alongside other alternatives, based on the principle that 'measures of progress should be given at least as much weight as attainment' (DfE 2013c, 4), and the government received over 1000 responses. The reaction to the idea of a baseline was largely negative, with 51 per cent of respondents answering 'No' to the question 'Should we introduce a baseline check at the start of reception?' (34 per cent 'Yes', 16 per cent 'Not sure'), on the basis of concerns that it was too young to test children, there would be a negative impact on the start of school and it would undermine the existing EYFS Profile (DfE 2014c, 16). When asked 'Should we allow schools to choose from a range of commercially available assessments?', 73 per cent of respondents said 'No'.

The coalition government's response to the consultation was the 'Reforming Assessment and Accountability for Primary Schools' document (DfE 2014c), which clearly stated that the primary purpose of the Baseline was accountability and not assessment:

> The purpose of the reception baseline is for an accountability measure of the *relative* progress of a cohort of children through primary school.
>
> *(DfE 2014c, 1)*

> We will use a reception baseline as the starting point from which to measure a school's progress.
>
> *(DfE 2014c, 7)*

This document also made clear that the result of the Baseline must be a single score, and stated the content to be included:

> The purpose of the reception baseline is to support the accountability framework and help assess school effectiveness by providing a score for each child at the start of reception which reflects their attainment against a pre-determined content domain.
> The clear majority of the content domain must … demonstrate a clear progression towards the key stage 1 national curriculum in English and mathematics.
>
> *(DfE 2014c, 1)*

This contrasts with the existing EYFS Profile, which covers all areas of the curriculum and particular 'learning dispositions'. The justification for Baseline Assessment, in common with other uses of progress measures such as 'value added', was 'to make sure we take account of: schools with challenging intakes [and] The important work in reception and key stage 1' (DfE 2015a). Thus, Baseline Assessment is presented as sympathetic to schools with lower attainment on entry, and a recognition of the value of early years education.

A further aspect of Baseline as a policy that was unprecedented in primary education in England was the use of private providers to produce the actual assessments. Contracts to provide a Baseline Assessment were put out to tender by the DfE in 2014. Six companies were selected and formed the 'approved list', from which schools were required to select an assessment. In 2015 schools paid these providers directly and were reimbursed by the DfE. After schools had selected their Baseline providers, the least popular providers were removed from the list, leaving only the following:

- Centre for Evaluation and Monitoring, Durham University (CEM);
- Early Excellence;
- National Foundation for Educational Research (NFER).

Schools that had selected other Baseline providers either had to change or were not reimbursed for the costs. The use of private providers is unusual in that other primary school assessments, such as Key Stage 2 Sats tests and the Phonics Screening Check, are provided by the Standards and Testing Authority (STA), a government agency. As we discuss in more detail in Chapter 2, this policy aligns with the trend towards greater private sector involvement in education (Ball 2012a; West and Bailey 2013). In 2015 a high proportion of schools selected the Early Excellence Baseline (known as EExBA), which is based on observations, like the existing EYFS Profile. This assessment was produced by a small consultancy, unlike the larger organisations, NFER and CEM. This choice was reported in the press as a rejection of the 'testing' of four-year-old children (Ward 2015c; Adams 2015). The choice of providers also means that data cannot be directly compared between schools using different assessments; this was given as a reason why the policy was made voluntary in 2016 (DfE 2016b; Ward 2016).

The introduction of Baseline was highly controversial in the education sector, with a well-organised 'Better without Baseline' campaign involving teaching unions, educational organisations and associations, and prominent campaigners (BWB 2015). This campaign discouraged schools from signing up to any of the Baseline options during the non-compulsory phase in 2015, as even the more 'early years friendly' observation-based options were driven by the government's criteria (Wrigley and Wormwell 2016). Concerns about the policy were widespread before its implementation: Ofsted argued it would discourage schools from working with nurseries and pre-schools to close attainment gaps, as that would affect their Baseline scores (Ward 2015a). Research conducted for the DfE by the National Federation for Education Research (NFER) in July 2015, which was intended to 'inform the approach to implementation of the reception baseline and to identify effective ways of communicating the results to parents' (DfE 2015b, 3), raised several issues. Through a small-scale survey, interviews with teachers and focus groups with parents, the NFER report found:

- lack of understanding of the assessment;
- existing on-entry assessments were used widely, often through observation;
- 'some evidence' of gaming results, in order to maximise progress measures;
- a desire to report results to parents orally.

(DfE 2015b)

Extensive research on the use of assessments for accountability has shown the potential impact on pedagogy and curriculum, classroom organisation, teachers' workloads and feelings of professionalism and, most significantly, on the issue of manipulation of results. Previous work on the EYFS Profile found that there was pressure to deflate results in order to maximise later progress measures (Bradbury 2013c), even though providing a baseline to measure progress was not a formal function of the assessment. The use of a 'high-stakes' assessment at age four/five also contrasts with considerable socio-cultural research which has demonstrated that children learn through sets of social relationships (Broadhead and Burt 2012; Fleer 2010). This body of work argues that authentic, holistic and developmentally appropriate assessment, based upon teachers' observations over time in a range of contexts, makes visible what young children are capable of learning in supportive and collaborative relationships. It is argued that a particularly useful time to engage in such observations and listening to children is when they are participating in rich and meaningful play activities (Fleer and Richardson 2009) and can be used to build up a 'learning journey' (Carr and Lee 2012). Such formative and summative assessment practices aim to make children's learning ever more stimulating, rich and successful. A child's well-being and the characteristics of effective learning, such as resilience, perseverance and self-regulation, learnt in the context of meaningful play, are seen to be more reliable predictors of later academic achievement rather than 'short-term academic results' which may not last (Bodrova and Leong 2007; Siraj, Kingston and Melhuish 2015; Whitebread and Bingham 2012). The prominence of this research and related view of holistic learning among early years practitioners is likely to be the reason why such a high number of schools (12,000, over 70 per cent) signed up to Early Excellence as their Baseline provider of choice (Ward 2015c; Wrigley and Wormwell 2016). Early Excellence has promoted itself to early years educators as retaining holistic teacher observations, including characteristics of effective learning, whilst dissociating itself with 'testing children' (Roberts-Holmes and Bradbury 2017). However, Early Excellence has to work within the government's guidelines for Baseline, so any maths, literacy or characteristics of effective learning are measured with a simple 'yes' or 'no', resulting in a number of points. As argued by the campaign group against Baseline, reducing a range of curriculum areas and the complexity of learning characteristics and dispositions to such a scoring system, and ultimately generating a single score for all the assessments, remains problematic in terms of the current dominant views of learning and child development (BWB 2015).

Following the move to make Baseline optional in 2016, numbers of schools signing up to do the assessment were reported to have 'plummeted' (Camden 2016), although thousands of schools still opted to do Baseline. As mentioned, at the time of writing, the government is consulting on a replacement for Baseline in Reception as they remain committed to some form of progress measure (DfE 2017c).

Structure of the book

The remainder of the book is divided into six chapters. The following chapter explains the theoretical framework utilised in this book, with a focus on the work of Foucault and Deleuze. We discuss how shifting patterns of data use and the related forms of surveillance can be theorised as *disciplinary power* in Foucault's terms, and also as part of a *society of control*, in Deleuze's formation. We consider how data operate as part of a neoliberal assemblage of policy tools in education, which involves notions of performance, accountability and the measurement of effectiveness and value. We consider the relationship between data and student and teacher subjectivities, and how data use can contribute towards inequalities in education, before detailing the methods used in our research and providing information about the multiple research sites.

In Chapter 3, we focus on the ways in which data are *productive*, beginning our analysis with a discussion of the prominence of data in early years settings and primary schools, and the impact on practices, pedagogy and relationships. We consider the ideological tensions for teachers, between engaging in pedagogy associated with assessment for accountability and their commitment to practices of care and child-centred learning. We then turn to our argument regarding the production of data-driven child and teacher subjectivities and the complex shifts in power and hierarchies associated with the involvement of new actors such as data analysts.

Following on from this discussion of subjectivities, Chapter 4 considers the *reductive* aspects of datafication. We explore issues of accuracy and judgement in relation to attainment data, and then consider how factors such as age, month of birth, language competency and emotional maturity can all affect the production of data with younger children. The research data presented here lead us to argue that processes of datafication are potentially dangerous in setting low expectations.

Chapter 5 considers how schools respond to policies which demand more data, and the resulting increase in visibility. We discuss the different potential reactions to this new transparency, including the temptation to manipulate results to improve performance. Using our research findings on how schools chose their Baseline providers, we argue that a reaction of 'limiting the damage' is logical in times of rapid policy change.

Our final analysis chapter, Chapter 6, takes a step back from the policy context of England to explore the wider context of datafication operating at an international level. We discuss the planned international comparison test for five-year-olds, known as the International Early Learning Study (IELS) or 'mini-PISA', and the relationship between the use of data at this national level and the micro level of the classroom. We also use this chapter to make links between the use of private companies in early years and primary schools in England and the wider privatisation of education, and discuss the role of intermediate agents in delivering difficult policy such as Baseline.

We end the book with a discussion of our arguments in relation to datafication and the overall conclusions we can draw from our case study of England. Chapter 7 concludes with a discussion of alternative uses of data in education.

Notes

1 For a full discussion of how teachers and children are 'datafied' see Bradbury and Roberts-Holmes (2016b) and Roberts-Holmes and Bradbury (2016).
2 We note the fact that we also deal here with 'data' in the form of research data, though this differs in that it is largely qualitative rather than quantitative. Furthermore, while our focus here is specifically on the use and production of data by schools, we acknowledge that, in writing this, we are ourselves entwined within the world of metrics and publication ratings, which we cannot escape.

3 In keeping with grammatical accuracy, we use 'data' as a plural in this text. However, when quoting research participants or other literature where it is used as a singular, we do not correct this.

4 National Assessment Program Literacy and Numeracy.

5 Sistema de Medición de la Calidad de la Educación, or Education Quality Measurement System.

6 For a full discussion of the role of edu-businesses in Baseline Assessment, see Roberts-Holmes and Bradbury (2017).

7 This was introduced in 2003 as the Foundation Stage Profile and has been revised and renamed since.

8 For a fuller discussion see Roberts-Holmes and Bradbury (2016).

2

THEORISING AND RESEARCHING DATA IN EDUCATION

Introduction

Our focus in this chapter is on making clear the *logics* of data in the current neoliberal educational context; we discuss why reducing education to numbers is attractive, useful and ever more possible. This in turn leads us onto how we can conceptualise the individual as 'made up' by numbers, or how subjectivities are shaped by the process we call datafication. We begin with two perspectives from Foucault and Deleuze which help conceptualise the role of data, before we explore key concepts such as performativity and surveillance within a neoliberal education system and the role of numbers and data within these. We argue that central to an understanding of datafication is neoliberalism's collapse of education into an economic activity rather than a social, cultural and political activity. Within this, schools become analogous to businesses as they commodify, compete, choose and calculate as they are driven to ever more rivalrous competition. We then consider the role of data in reproducing inequalities. We finish the chapter with a description of our research strategies and sites and a reflection on researching data in education.

Theorising data in education

Much of the theoretical discussion around data and education, and data in society more generally, uses concepts drawn from the work of Foucault, particularly *disciplinary power*, and Deleuze, particularly his description of *societies of control*. Much of this discussion focuses on the use of data as representing a shift from Foucauldian forms of discipline to Deleuze's more fluid forms of surveillance and control (Lyon 2014). We begin our theoretical discussion with these two perspectives, and how we interpret this shift.

Disciplinary power to societies of control

Foucault argues that power can only be understood through the *techniques* that are used in its exercise. One of these techniques is *disciplinary power*, which Foucault describes as an invention of bourgeois society, intended to ensure cohesion (McHoul and Grace 1998). Disciplinary power is exercised through 'conscious and permanent visibility' (Foucault 1977, 201), the idea of the panopticon providing the metaphor for this all-seeing position. Foucault describes how those who are subject to surveillance internalise those expectations and can be relied upon to police themselves. In his study of the prison, Foucault describes punishment as focused on the mind, rather than the body as in previous times. This operates within particular sites or enclosures, such as the school, prison or hospital, where activities are controlled.

Disciplinary power 'imposes on those whom it subjects a principle of compulsory visibility' (Foucault 1980); this concept has been used extensively within education to discuss how teachers are made visible and expected to 'self-govern' in response to demands (Ball 2003). Stephen Ball, most notably, describes how ideas drawn from Foucault's work can help us to examine the technologies of the neoliberal education system. 'Measurement, comparison and examination, numbers of many sorts, are embedded in and serve the techniques to produce domination and responsibilization and construct "calculating selves" and "centres of calculation"' (Ball 2013b, 59). The phenomenon of disciplinary power through calculation, numbers and statistics in the governance of education has been present since the advent of primary education, as Rose argues: 'The inculcation of calculating mentalities has been key to the practices of schooling since the nineteenth century' (Rose 1999, 214). As discussed, the 'data deluge' (Kitchin 2014, xv) enabled by ubiquitous computing technology has meant 'a whole variety of new calculable spaces are brought into existence' (Rose 1999, 213) but which nonetheless find their antecedents in the calculable spaces of the nineteenth-century schoolroom. Ball argues that in the current context numbers define the 'pertinent space within which and regarding which educators must act' (Foucault 2009, 75 cited in Ball 2013b, 104). This is a process we see in later chapters in relation to identification of particular groups as targets for intervention.

Deleuze describes his theory of societies of control (or 'control societies', depending on the translation) as the 'progressive and dispersed installation of a new system of domination' (1995a) which can be seen as replacing Foucault's disciplinary society. He argues that since the Second World War, discipline has been replaced by control, 'the new monster'. Instead of power operating within enclosed spaces, there are 'ultrarapid forms of free floating control'. Institutions remain, with a 'deceptive solidity', but power operates beyond and between the institutions: 'Enclosures are *molds*, distinct castings, but controls are a *modulation*, like a self-deforming cast that will continuously change from one moment to the other, or like a sieve whose mesh will transmute from point to point' (Deleuze 1995a). Numbers are vital within these modulations: 'the different control mechanisms are inseparable variations, forming a system of variable geometry the language of which is numerical' (Deleuze 1995a). In studies of data and surveillance, this shift 'from targeted scrutiny of "populations" and individuals to mass monitoring' reflects Deleuze's concepts of control, as opposed to Foucault's disciplinary power.

> Classically, studies of surveillance suggest that a shift in emphasis from *discipline* to *control* [...] has been a key trend associated with the increasing use of networked electronic technologies that permit surveillance of mobile populations rather than only those confined to relatively circumscribed spaces, and depend on aggregating increasingly fragmented data.
>
> *(Lyon 2014, 2, emphasis in original)*

This distinction is popular in discussions of surveillance and society, and relevant to education. Fendler provides a summary of the differences between these two analyses:

> first, both discipline and control societies are characterized by the self-monitoring gaze; but in a control society the monitoring is more frequent and continuous than in a disciplinary society. Second, standards in a disciplinary society tend to be fairly centralized and long-lasting; however, standards in a control society are more heterogeneous and quickly changing. Finally, a disciplinary society afforded the promise of closure or completion of a project; however, a control society offers no possibility of closure or completion.
>
> *(2001, 135)*

In education it is argued that the latest form of high-stakes testing 'with its emphasis on data-points, data-sets and databases, *disconnects* the disciplinary space of the classroom' (Thompson and Cook 2014, 132, our emphasis). Self-governing through visibility operates not only in the classroom, but in all aspects of working lives:

> There is not so much, or not only, a *structure* of surveillance, as a *flow* of performativities both continuous and eventful – that is *spectacular*. It is not the possible certainty of always being seen that is the issue, as in the panopticon, it is the uncertainty and instability of being judged in different ways, by different means, through different agents; the 'bringing-off' of performances – the flow of changing demands, expectations and indicators that make us continually accountable and constantly recorded.
>
> *(Ball 2000, 2)*

Similarly, Thompson and Cook argue that assumptions of 'fairly static organisation of power and power relations that are corporeal (aimed at the body) and enclosed within specific spatialised sites and enclosures' (2014, 130–131), based on Foucauldian disciplinary power, are now insufficient in education. Instead, they argue that analysis should focus on how Deleuze's 'ultrarapid forms of free floating control' overlie these assemblages of power (2014, 131). This follows Simon's argument that modern surveillance 'decouple[s] the imagined relationship between seeing and being seen; there is no longer (nor was there ever) a direct line of sight in the production of panoptic space' (2005, 15). But, this theoretical shift is not necessarily a refutation of Foucault, Simon argues: 'While discipline stabilizes and objectifies bodies, control modulates them. One way to understand this difference is that control does not act on the body so much as the environment through which the body moves' (2005, 15). This shift to control can be seen as a form of 'super-panopticism', according to Poster (1992, cited in Simon 2005); which 'does not operate via external force or internalized norms but rather in terms of discourse and the linguistic properties of digital computation' (Simon 2005, 16). Thus Deleuze's concept of societies of control is used to delineate the more recent computerised forms of surveillance from the physical surveillance of the panopticon.

Nonetheless, following Lyon, we argue here that concepts *both* of discipline and of control continue to have relevance in the study of data and education. A Deleuzian emphasis on the fluid and disparate forms of surveillance of teachers and children involved in datafication is important: for example, we consider in later chapters how different forms of personal parental data are collected by children's centres, and related to the children in attendance. The ongoing assessment of children through observation in early years settings and Reception classes fits with the argument that 'A control society is characterized by "continuous monitoring"' (Fendler 2001, 135). The changing demands of complex assessment systems similarly resonate with Deleuze's discussion of uncertainty, as opposed to heterogeneity in standards as discussed by Foucault, while the shift towards continuous progress as a measure of success chimes with Deleuze's warning of the impossibility of closure or completion. However, as Lyon argues: 'A Deleuzian approach is misleading if one imagines that the world of top-down government-based surveillance is a thing of the past. Such practices now appropriate data from the "rhizonomic" forms of surveillance described by Deleuze' (Lyon 2014, 7). Information drawn from multiple disparate sources is still used by central, disciplining forces, which control funding and determine centre closures. In education we can see how freer flowing forms of surveillance – or 'liquid surveillance' (Bauman and Lyon 2013) – through data collection are combined with long-established forms of discipline through high-stakes tests and inspection. These standardised measures, forming end-point assessments of educational 'success', continue to be disciplinary in nature, defining who proceeds and who is deemed as 'failing', or which school 'requires improving'. They still force us to act, alongside the freer forms of control. In their discussion of temporality in education, Thompson and Cook comment that teachers 'face timelines of accounting, associated with both discipline and control', subject to both regular observation and assessment 'with its attendant orientation to disciplinary data' and the 'production and flow of data through the network' (2017, 34). Thus, we would argue that the combination of both forms, discipline and control, makes education an interesting example of the power of data in shaping practices and subjectivities, and we use both concepts through our analysis.

Biopolitics and biopower

Furthering our discussion of the use of Foucault to consider aspects of data and surveillance, we are cognizant of Monahan and Torres' (2010) criticism that his theories of biopower are frequently neglected in favour of discussion of discipline and the panopticon. Biopower is defined by Rabinow and Rose thus:

> At its most general, then, the concept of 'biopower' serves to bring into view a field comprised of more or less rationalized attempts to intervene upon the vital characteristics of human existence [and] the living characteristics of collectivities or populations comprised of such living beings.
>
> *(2006, 196–197)*

Of the elements listed by Rabinow and Rose, which they argue form Foucault's 'somewhat imprecise' notion of biopower, the most relevant here is 'modes of subjectification, through which individuals are brought to work on themselves' (2006, 197). This subjectification relates to truth discourses and occurs under certain forms of authority, such as teachers who are encouraged to improve 'their data', as they are subject to truth discourses relating to the 'good teacher' and 'success'.

Biopower is relevant here in thinking about how data relate to the body, particularly how it works to produce 'docile bodies' (Foucault 1977; see also Simmons 2010). Educational data science is a 'significant, albeit emerging and disparate' field of biopolitical intervention (Williamson 2016a, 413). Given that some of the data collected on young children relate directly to their bodies, such as their ability to grip a pencil correctly, to go to the toilet on their own and to dress themselves, the notion of biopower as an 'attempt to intervene upon the vital characteristics' of individuals has a particular material resonance. We can see these forms of assessment as part of 'how educational data science constitutes a new politics relating to the measurement and pedagogic management of the corporeal, emotional and embrained lives of children' (Williamson 2016a, 402).

Haggerty and Ericson (2000), using Deleuze, comment that an emerging 'surveillant assemblage': 'operates by abstracting human bodies from their territorial settings and separating them into a series of discrete flows. These flows are then reassembled into distinct "data doubles" which can be scrutinized and targeted for intervention' (2000, 606). Thus, data have a function in reducing or abstracting the body, and designating some bodies as targets for intervention, as found in school practices. Furthermore, the concept of biopower 'mobilised through numbers as *inscription devices* in both constituting and targeting specific populations' in order to identify 'policy concerns' helps us to analyse how data on young children can be used to categorise, define 'policy problems' and prioritise funds – for example, in the 'early intervention' agenda which we discuss below (Allen 2011). We discuss the idea of a decorporeal-ised 'data double', as mentioned above, in more detail in the following section.

In our analysis we use both Foucault's concept of biopower alongside discipline; they are distinguished thus: 'Where discipline is the technology deployed to make individuals behave, to be efficient and productive workers, biopolitics is deployed to manage populations' (Kelly 2004, 59 cited in Lingard, Martino and Rezai-Rashti 2013, 546). Nonetheless, we follow Hope's comment that 'one should be wary of treating disciplinary and biopolitical power as isolated categories' (2016, 888) as schools are a site of intervention on the body and on the population. In both discipline and biopower, the norm has an important function: Foucault argues, 'The norm is something that can be applied both to a body one wishes to discipline and a population one wishes to regularize' (Foucault 2004, 253 cited in Hope 2016, 888). This is the case in schools, and in particular in the early years, where children are constantly compared to 'norms' based on developmental psychology (Fendler 2001), which define their subjectivity.

Performativity and subjectivity

> Performativity is a technology, a culture and a mode of regulation, or a system of 'terror' in Lyotard's words, that employs judgements, comparisons and displays as means of control, attrition and change. The performances (of individual subjects or organisations) serve as measures of productivity or output, or displays of 'quality', or 'moments' of promotion (there is a felicitous ambiguity around this word) or inspection. They stand for, encapsulate or represent the worth, quality or value of an individual or organisation within a field of judgement.
>
> *(Ball 2000, 1)*

As Ball explains, performativity is key to understanding subjectivities in the education system; through inspection, league tables, performance management meetings, teachers are regulated through the judgements made about them. They need to 'perform', whether this be producing the right data or an 'outstanding' lesson for Ofsted. These performances must be continuous: there is a never-ending pressure as 'success' is never permanent. The next year's results must be good, or the next set of data must show progress (Bradbury and Roberts-Holmes 2016a). We argue that data have a vital role in processes of performativity in the current education system, in terms of both practice and the identity of educators; like Ball, we are interested in:

> the ways in which lists, forms, grids and rankings work to change the meaning of educational practice – what it means to teach and learn – and our sense of who we are in terms of these practices – what it means to be an educator, and to be educated.
>
> *(Ball 2013b, 6)*

This focus on subjectivities is based on the idea that the subject is constituted through discourse, which defines possibilities of being and intelligibility in a particular space and time. As Butler argues, recognisability as a subject is dependent on norms in a particular context:

> Subjects are constituted through norms which, in their reiteration, produce and shift the terms through which subjects are recognized. These normative conditions for the production of the subject produce an historically contingent ontology, such that our very capacity to discern and name the 'being' of the subject is dependent on norms that facilitate that recognition.
>
> *(Butler 2010, 4)*

For teachers, in this case, their subjectivity is defined by norms which prescribe the 'good teacher' as one who is familiar with their data and responsive to it. To be recognised as successful, they must engage with these conditions for the production of the subject; thus they are also subject to these norms. Teachers are required to engage with this specifically neoliberal subjectivity, which prioritises productivity over care: 'The subject under the regime of performativity is made calculable rather than memorable, malleable rather than committed, flexible rather than principled, productive rather than ethical. Experience is nothing, productivity is everything [...] Social relations are replaced by informational structures' (Ball 2017, 43). We argue here that a system where data 'flow increasingly freely' (Lyon 2014, 9) produces data-driven subjectivities, both for the teacher and for the child, who is defined as a learner-subject through their engagement with neoliberal expectations (Bradbury 2013a). Foucault comments that students are productive subjects, or 'abilities-machines', whose output must be visible and monitored (cited in Ball 2013b, 107). However, many discussions of modern surveillance use Deleuze's concept of the *dividual* within societies of control: 'We no longer find ourselves dealing with the mass/individual pair. Individuals have become *"dividuals,"* and masses, samples, data, markets, or *"banks."'* (Deleuze 1995a, emphasis in original). This is useful in describing how (in this case) children are constituted not as individuals, but through data-points which 'make them up'. For Simon, Deleuze's societies of control operates as a model for a 'post-panoptic' visibility through technology:

> the 'dividual' is fundamental here, in societies of control the individual is doubled as code, as information, or as simulation such that the reference of the panoptic gaze is no longer the body but its double, and indeed this is no longer a matter of looking but rather one of data analysis.
>
> *(Simon 2005, 15)*

As Williamson (2014) has discussed, children come to be represented through their 'data doubles' or 'data doppelgangers' through a process of making education 'machine readable'. Data on children's progress and their attainment has become central to the governing of schooling so that primary children themselves become reduced to statistical pieces of data (Roberts-Holmes and Bradbury 2016, 11), which then 'fold back' onto identities in the classroom. As Lyon notes, in relation to surveillance:

> It 'makes up' the data double, Deleuze's 'dividual', and that entity then acts back on those with whom the data are associated, informing us who we are,

what we should desire or hope for, including who we should become. The algorithms grip us even as they follow us, producing ever more information to try to make the user data more effective. Users discover, one might say, that the price of our freedom in both political and consumer contexts is our shaping or conditioning by algorithms.

(Lyon 2014, 7)

This process of reduction through quantification is also present through the representation of students as test scores, as argued by Koyama and Menken (2013) in reference to bilingual children who are 'increasingly framed by numerical calculations' to become 'numerical liabilities' in the US accountability system. Various descriptions of this process have been found, such as a shift to students as 'textual things' (Law and Hetherington, 2003 cited in Koyama and Menken 2013, 87), 'retrievable identities' (Poster, 1996 cited in Lyon 2001, 335), or 'digital personae' (Clarke 1993 cited in Simon 2005). As mentioned above, Haggerty and Ericson (2000, 611) refer to 'decorporealized body, a "data double" of pure virtuality' in discussion of the 'surveillant assemblage'. Simon similarly refers to 'databased selves' as:

> stable representations of identity such as no visual enclosure could ever produce. The object of traditional disciplinary surveillance is the body but in dataveillance the object of control is simply the digital representation of the body.
>
> *(Simon 2005, 15/6)*

Furthermore, databases work to distance the data from the individual: following Poster, Lyon comments that, 'The subject is multiplied and decentred in the database, acted on by remote computers every time a record is automatically verified or checked against another, without ever referring to the individual concerned' (Lyon 2001, 335). This reductionism is the focus of Chapter 4, while in Chapter 3 we discuss the construction of individuals through data, using the phrase 'data doubles' for ease of reading.

Throughout this discussion we note the complex interplay of the individual as subject to discourse (and databases), and as having agency. As Butler argues, 'it would be a mistake to understand the operation of norms as deterministic' (2010, 4). Instead, discourse operates to constrain, while simultaneously allowing for other possibilities, 'giving rise to docile bodies "free" to act within the confines and limitations of dominant norms and discourse' (Lewis and Hardy 2015, 248). However, recognisability continues to relate to power; though subjects have discursive agency, powerful 'regimes of truth' delimit the bounds of intelligibility as 'good teachers' or 'good students'. As Foucault argues, 'there is no individual, no self, that is ontologically prior to power' (Ball 2013b, 126).

These concepts of performativity, visibility and 'data doubles' or *dividuals* help us to analyse the productive and reductive aspects of datafication, particularly the data-driven subjectivities we discuss in the following chapter. We now step back from this focus on the individual to sketch out the political context for our work.

Neoliberalism in education

In our analysis we draw on several perspectives arising from discussion of the neo-liberal education system. Modes of organisation associated with neoliberal thought have dominated many education systems worldwide over the last three decades (Apple 2006; Ball 2013a), particularly choice between schools, high-stakes tests as a method of accountability and schools operating in a market. This context is rel-evant for us here as data form an essential component of the comparison of schools, and are part of the neoliberal policy assemblage. 'Within the contemporary techno-cratic market regime of neoliberalism the relationships of truth and power are articulated and operationalizes more and more in terms of forms of performance, or outputs, and expressed in the reductive form of numbers' (Ball 2017, 43). Numbers have always been important in education (Goldstein and Moss 2014; Lawn 2013): through testing 'individuals were made calculable and subject to the "power of a single number"' (Ball 2013b, 72–73 citing Rose 1999, 214). However, data have particular functions within a specifically neoliberal education system, which we discuss here.

Of particular relevance is the shift in values associated with neoliberalism, towards the prioritisation of economics: neoliberalism has been described as the 'disenchantment of politics by economics' (Davies 2014, 4). Educational political projects of welfarism, community and equality become 'transformed' into those of market-place economics and calculation which are described as 'destructive of social cohesion' (Lazzarato 2009, 111). 'Under the logic of neo-liberalism's ideas, the social, and also the political, collapse into the economic, so that "all aspects of social behaviour are reconceptualised along economic lines" (Rose 1999, 141) and policies are depoliticised, reduced to economic calculation' (Moss 2014, 66). Here the market model of schooling within an 'enterprise society' (Lazzarato 2009, 109), based on competition, inequality and privileging the individual, has transformed the wider purposes of schooling from a benefit for the whole of society to com-peting individual schools, teachers and children. According to Moss (2014, 63) 'inequality is the basis, inherent and necessary. It is the heart of neoliberalism, not just some unfortunate by product'. Hence inequality of educational opportunity, resourcing and outcome becomes a central premise of neoliberalism. Lingard (2009, 18) notes that:

> We have seen a new individualism, with individuals now deemed responsible for their own 'self-capitalising' over their lifetimes. Common good and social protection concerns have been given less focus and the market valued over the state, with enhanced market or private sector involvement in the work-ings of the state.
>
> *(Cited in Ball 2012a, 2)*

Within this shift in values, data allow for the simplification of choices; complex, uncertain and ambiguous educational politics and ethics become simplified to quantitative economic indicators, ideally to 'a single number, as achieved by a market' (Davies 2014, 4). Websites such as the Australian 'My School', which colour codes schools by attainment to help parents make a choice, exemplify this trend towards reduction and abstraction (Hardy and Boyle 2011). Good attainment data become a property of the school, currency to be used within a competitive market: 'The public goods of pupil outcomes have become *private goods* for schools, owned *exclusively* by them for their own use and *rivalrous* in the way they are "consumed" in the service of the competitive market environment' (Pratt, 2016, 897). Rivalry, competition and a 'winner takes all' competitive logic pervades all sections of society including education so that 'the neo-liberal dream of competitive individualism ... guides our educational consciousness and sensibilities' (Slee 2011). As we have argued elsewhere (Roberts-Holmes and Bradbury 2016) this leads to 'a highly reductionist' policy and 'a comparative narrative about "who does better or worse" and thus constructs the need to improve test scores as the only sound basis for undertaking educational reform' (Lingard, Sellar and Savage 2014, 725). Educational rivalry, competition and the threat of losing and inequality generates apprehensions and anxieties and a 'micro-politics of little fears' (Lazzarato 2009). The fear of losing out to one's competitors motivates schools and families to constantly engage in ever more elaborate and thorough calculative practices to secure a winning place in this competition. Here neoliberal calculative economics 'incites and constrains each individual to become an entrepreneur of him/herself, to become "human capital"' (Lazzarato 2009, 120). As 'human capital' we supposedly become *homo-economicus*, that is, rational economic beings in constant pursuit of self-interest. Here the logic of business transforms schools, teachers and families as competition becomes naturalised, normalised and internalised by individuals. Such competition has 'made possible a "new type of individual", an individual formed within the logic of competition – a calculating, solipsistic, instrumentally driven, "enterprise man"' (Ball 2013b, 132). This enterprise man is a champion of self-responsibility 'who is flexible and high-performing' in this market economy (Lupton 2016). But perhaps more than that, the neoliberal project of homo-economicus 'reaches down into the deepest recesses of humanity to shape and govern our desires and fears, our expectations and hopes, our assumptions and understandings, our beliefs and values – our very sense of who we are' (Moss 2014, 70). Ranked numerical data for the purposes of management and control operate as a highly efficient neoliberal human technology to govern the entrepreneurial self. Indeed Lyon notes that, 'A neo-liberal logic of control fits neatly with the ways that individuals are "made up" by data' (2014, 6). Comparable and competitive data ontologically make sense within the neoliberal project and imaginary. As we will see throughout our analysis: 'powerful techniques to manipulate data, enabled by technological and economic developments, can be easily co-opted to serve the restrictive frameworks of hyper-controlling, managerial accountability' (Perrotta 2013, 116).

Neoliberal values in primary and early years education

Neoliberal market-place economics constructs the early years as a starting line for a broader global economic race in which young children are constructed through discourses of human capital as a fertile source for future employment; this is apparent in this policy document from the UK:

> If we want our children to succeed at school, go on to university or into an apprenticeship and thrive in later life, we must get it right in the early years. More great childcare is vital to ensuring we can compete in the global race, by helping parents back to work and readying children for school and, eventually, employment.
>
> *(DfE 2013a, 6)*

Here the purposes of early years (and implicitly, primary) education are deliberately and explicitly reduced to economic and industrial imperatives so that everything 'is quantified, costed and calculated, creating a constant calculus of profit and loss, costs and benefits, investments and returns in an endless flow of accountability' (Moss 2014, 65). Education is reduced to quantifiable, calculable rates of return, 'rendered into an input/output calculation' (Ball 2013b, 104). This economisation of early years and primary education fulfils neoliberalism's fantasy and desire to collapse the purposes of education into a market-based quantitative competition of winners and losers.

Within early childhood education Moss (2014) terms this the 'story of quality and high returns' such that if state invests and buys into young children at the correct time with the correct human technologies then there will be a high return on that investment in the form of improved education, employment and earnings and reduced social problems. This simple model can be represented as an equation:

'quality' + 'early intervention' ▶▶ ↑'human capital' + ↓dysfunction

This economic model for the justification and rationale of early years education is succinctly summed up, in a UK Government Report entitled 'Early Intervention: Smart Investment, Massive Savings' (Allen 2011). This report purports that early intervention investment has the potential to:

> make massive savings in public expenditure, reduce the costs of underachievement, drink and drug abuse, teenage pregnancy, vandalism and criminality, court and police costs, academic underachievement, lack of aspiration to work and the bills from lifetimes wasted while claiming benefits.
>
> *(Allen 2011, xiv)*

This necessity to efficiently increase the human capital of young children has spawned an entire early years and primary education industry of measurement, ranking and auditing in which the processes of accountancy and financial management dominate. As schooling changes to a model imported from business, educational practices have become increasingly financialised 'so that there is a calculable rate of return on any investment': the business language of 'assets, income, liability, opportunity costs, products, "input-output", overheads, revenue and return on investment' becomes naturalised and normalised within audited educational contexts (Moss 2014, 66). Schools become reshaped 'into ever-expanding systems of measuring, costing, monitoring and ranking and converts them into manageable and auditable entities' (Shore and Wright 2015, 25).

This monetarisation of primary education demands tightly regulated and managed pedagogical contexts within an increasingly competitive global race. The business model of education needs the state to interfere and intervene to maximise its competitive edge. 'Neo-liberalism calls for state intervention to further its aims and ensure its survival, while the state regulates markets and governs children and adults alike to further its aims' (Moss 2014, 73). So, within early years and primary education, the state insists upon tightly regulated and prescriptive curricula, accountability and inspection regimes with results leading to schools being designated 'requires improvement' or 'outstanding', and primary children who are either 'secondary-school ready' or not. The numerical standardisation of these pedagogical processes is thoroughly decontextualised so that schools, teachers and children become winners or losers in a ranked competitive system of league tables. Visualised data are a tool with which to enact competition as schools can constantly monitor and evaluate their performance relative to their competitors – for example, through their 'data dashboards' which compare attainment with similar schools (Williamson 2015a). These school digital dashboards enable government at a distance such that 'a network will enable power to be exercised over events and processes distant from oneself' (Rose 1999, 211). Children's percentage gains and losses are visualised on web-based platforms such as RAISEonline and are equated with overall school performance in a crude and simplistic conflation of individual children's progress with a school inspection grading such as 'outstanding' or 'requires improvement'. However, these numbers and the categories are themselves socially and culturally constructed as the data analysts make coding and algorithmic decisions so that the data 'are abstractions, subsuming a range of potential differences into a small number of indicators' (Goldstein and Moss 2014, 261). However, the validity and reliability of the data are unimportant in easy-to-read, decontextualised and popular tables of comparison. The point is the data can be appropriated to meet an immediate policy need: 'the statistical data strengthens confidence in policy choices, politicians have already made' (Goldstein and Moss 2014, 261). Within schools, the comparable datasets fulfil neoliberalism's need to encourage rivalry, competition and apprehension, and crucially at the same time, complex political and ethical considerations fade into the background.

Governing through numbers: surveillance and 'dataveillance'

As we have argued, within the educational system of the UK, and across the world, numerical data operate as an increasingly powerful and ubiquitous neoliberal technology, strongly governing schools and families. We see 'the active surveillance of people through the documents and databases they produce' (Apple 2010, 179). Schools' constant rendering and reading of themselves as numerical-laden spreadsheets, graphs and data-handling software, tracing the rise and fall of their performances, is analogous to business activity. Simplified numerical reductionism facilitates hierarchical comparison through its potential to rank and so data allow schools to constantly compare and contrast and to take action to *govern themselves* (Fenwick, Mangez and Ozga 2014, 9). The recent dramatic increase in the power and hegemony of governance *by and through numbers* has been facilitated by the recent extraordinary proliferation of data production in education (Ozga *et al.* 2011). Simplified and comparative numerical data have become *the* dominant technology of governing and key to the 'governance turn' (Fenwick, Mangez and Ozga 2014, 6). Datasets have become the dominant providers of information for teaching and learning so that 'data, coding and algorithms' lie at the heart of schools (Selwyn 2015).

Williamson (2015a) and Fenwick, Mangez and Ozga (2014) argue that digital data have become interwoven with the governance of education. We argue here that this increasingly applies to early years and primary education. Primary schools become reconstructed as entrepreneurial systems that must 'engage in self-reflection and acquire self-knowledge to take responsibility for their outcomes' (Lupton 2016, 47). Burgeoning comparable datasets incite these calculative and entrepreneurial schools to govern themselves through numbers and algorithms as they attempt to take responsibility for improving their competitive rank order in the datafied world of education. Rose argues that this is because schools 'must calculate about *themselves* in certain ways because they are calculated about in certain ways *by others*' (1999, 213, emphasis in original). Such self-calculating schools open up new spaces for private companies, and accompanying new flows of power: Hogan, Sellar and Lingard (2016) note that the proliferation of such comparable databases has led to a 'commercialization of comparison' in which datalabs with the technical expertise to visualise data are able to make a profit. The exponential demand for more data to provide further indicators and rankings is needed by the entrepreneurial and self-actualising schools, who must take responsibility to favourably position themselves within the ever-growing number of different league tables.

This ubiquitous visibility can be theorised in terms of surveillance, as we discussed above, as both discipline and control. Ozga has noted how data as a regime of numbers constitute a 'resource through which surveillance can be exercised' (Ozga 2008, 264 cited in Ball, Maguire and Braun 2012, 140). Within primary schools this data-based surveillance can be understood by coalescing the terms as 'dataveillance'. Dataveillance means that Foucault's (1977) description of Bentham's plan of a 'network of mechanisms that would be everywhere and always alert, running through society without interruption in space or in time' 'has become a reality for some primary and early years teachers' (Roberts-Holmes and Bradbury 2016, 610). The relationship between dataveillance and governmentality is made clear by Kitchin: 'Dataveillance is a mode of surveillance enacted through sorting and sifting datasets in order to identify, monitor, track, regulate, predict and prescribe … and is a key component of modern forms of governance and governmentality' (Kitchin 2014, 168). Here dataveillance is a powerful, constant and all-seeing monitoring and judging of children's, teachers' and institutional data. With reference to Foucault's panopticon discussed earlier, Tsapkou (2015, 114) notes the critical power of dataveillance is that 'whereas the Panopticon maintained an illusion of one being watched at all times, dataveillance makes possible an actual uninterrupted observation of every individual of interest'. The invisible and continuous nature of dataveillance means that it operates as a form of silent control. Thus, the continual monitoring and dataveillance of children's statistical data is an example of a move away from Foucault's *disciplinary* techniques within enclosures (such as the school) and towards the constant and mobile *control* of Deleuze's 'society of control', as discussed above.

A further key point in relation to visibility is that schools are not coerced into dataveillance of themselves and comparable others but willingly conform and comply, as Foucault noted:

> He who is subjected to a field of visibility, and who knows it, assumes responsibility for the constraints of power; he makes them play spontaneously upon himself; he inscribes in himself the power relation in which he simultaneously plays both roles; he becomes the principle of his own subjection.
>
> *(Foucault 1977, 202–203)*

Here, comparative data as a form of visibility becomes 'a trap' (Foucault 1977) to which schools voluntarily subject their calculating selves. The school's *will to know* and *the will to perform* (Ball 2016, 1130) demands ever more regulatory data as schools strive to hold their position or even move up the ranking. The numeric data encourage teachers to make pedagogic and strategic choices to improve scores. Such encouragement is understood as a form of 'soft governing' (Cheney-Lippold 2011), rather than coercion, to entice teachers to undertake improvement practices. This continual and urgent need to self-govern demands that schools are:

> permanently in need of information in order to position themselves and to improve their position … promoting a kind of self-government that includes a staging in the centre and where one submits oneself permanently, voluntarily and openly to the gaze of others.
>
> *(Simons 2014, 167)*

Dataveillance governs through what has been termed '360 degree comparative feedback' (Simons 2014) and can be represented as shown in Figure 2.1.

The above 360 degree dataveillance diagram illustrates how both Foucault's disciplinary power and Deleuze's society of control are useful tools of analysis here.

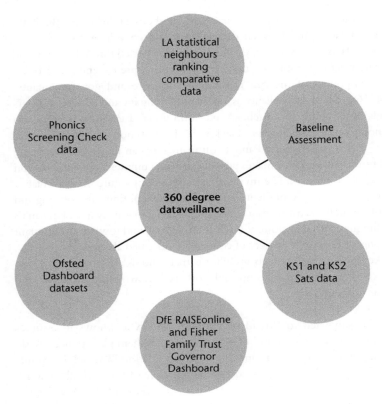

FIGURE 2.1 Diagram demonstrating 360 degree dataveillance (after Roberts-Holmes and Bradbury 2016, 609).

More formal state-mandated tests such as Year 2 and Year 6 children's Sats tests demonstrate Foucault's disciplinary power, while Deleuze's conception of a control society adds further to this disciplinary power through fluid and disparate web-based dataveillance, such that the Sats test results now become visible on any number of connected devices, by anybody, anywhere and at any time, hence the need for continual self-governance.

Indeed the nature of such liquid dataveillance is that it is continuous and relentless and operates as an 'indefinite discipline, an interrogation without end' (Foucault 1977, 227) and in this sense is a powerful development upon Foucault's panopticon. Indeed web-based school digital data, constantly updated and shifting, provide a precarity and uncertainty which is a 'fundamental condition of neoliberal society' (Ball 2013b, 134). This is because, within such liquid and ubiquitous datasets, a school's comparative positioning is constantly vulnerable, exposed and in danger.

Following this, we note that there is a tendency for some discussion of surveillance to sound alarmist – the academic equivalent of tabloid headlines about government 'snooping' – or, as, Taylor puts it, scholars 'quickly find themselves on the well-trodden path that ultimately leads to urban dystopia or totalitarian regime' (2013, 5). Also, there are strong arguments about the need for ethical practices in data collection (Bauman and Lyon 2013). The overwhelming nature of the volume and variety of data, often referred to as a 'data deluge', underlies some of this concern. As Lupton (2016) comments, the metaphors associated with data describe it as liquid, flowing and constantly changing; this brings with it the concomitant problem of data as 'potentially uncontained, out-of-control' (Lyon 2014, 9). This tone of alarm is associated, we would argue, with the affective dimensions of data and their role in neoliberal governance (Sellar 2015). While data can be essential in making disadvantage and discrimination visible, data also scare, provoke action and create uncertainty, so their very unpredictability and 'out-of-control-ness' are vital to neoliberal precarity and uncertainty. We write with an awareness of Foucault's maxim that not everything is bad, but everything is dangerous; we seek to apply his direction that critique does not involve labelling things as wrong, but the examination of the underlying assumptions, in this case about the neutrality and accuracy of data.

Data, policy and equality

As we have argued in previous work, assessment policy is invariably intertwined with issues of equality in primary and early years education (Bradbury 2011b). Data may be manipulated to fit with deficit discourses of a 'difficult intake' in inner city schools, in a cycle of low expectations and low results (Bradbury 2013c). Although our specific focus here is not on issues of 'race', class and gender, or other axes of difference, we remain aware of the potential for practices associated with data to reinforce and reinscribe disparities in attainment. Processes such as the targeting of borderline children (educational 'triage') are based on the use of data to predict outcomes (Gillborn and Youdell 2000); we have described this in recent work based in early years (Roberts-Holmes 2015). Data have a role in maintaining the categories of difference that permeate school discourses: terms used in data analysis such as 'summer-born', 'SEN' and 'EAL' define groups of children as problematic, more likely to experience 'underachievement'. The classification of children into these groups in databases makes the categories real, permanent and productive of certain subjectivities. As Ball notes following Foucault, historically statistics have been used to 'demarcate the valuable from the residual', a process which has become embedded in schooling:

> The dualities of totalization, division and exclusion articulated by this literature [on eugenics] became embedded in pedagogical practices and orderings – the lists, sets, 'tables', streams and bands, etc. – of schooling, and in the separation of 'special' from regular schooling, the demarcation of 'impossible learners'.
>
> *(Ball 2013b, 79–80)*

Within the current context, this use of classification to demarcate and exclude frequently relies on data, which identify the subjects of 'intervention'. Children's 'data doubles' (Williamson 2014) and their 'algorithmic identities' (Cheney-Lippold 2011) have material effects with primary schools, through sorting, labelling and setting children within 'ability' groups. Data provide an 'algorithmic authority' (Lupton 2016, 57) to such sorting, labelling and notions of fixed 'ability', a problematic discourse within early years education particularly (Bradbury 2013c). This may further disadvantage certain groups of children, shaping their life chances: 'Digital data and the algorithmic analytics that are used to interpret them and to make predictions and inferences about individuals and social groups are beginning to have determining effects on people's lives, influencing their life chances and opportunities' (Lupton 2016, 44). The power of prediction is especially problematic, as increasingly 'learning analytics' are developed which involve using children's previous performance (or the performance of other 'similar' children) to anticipate their future attainment. Children's data are used to connect the dots from previous performances to their future anticipated and predicted school performances as well as having the potential 'to individually customise and optimise their further educational experience' (Williamson 2015b, 263). Here Foucault's biopower 'renders bodies more visible and manageable' (Lupton 2016, 55) as children are physically ordered and separated into different 'groupings' based upon their data. Numbers, statistics and data are increasingly central to this 'governing of life' (Rabinow and Rose 2006) through data-based grouping, and the definition of who becomes an 'impossible body' (Youdell 2006a). The risk is that, for those with initial low attainment, predictive systems such as 'value added' measures reward continued underachievement; low expectations are set in stone and dramatic progress is required to move out of the 'below expected levels' category (Bradbury 2011a). As Taylor argues in relation to surveillance more generally, there is a predisposition to 'sort people into typologies based on abstracted profiles, which ultimately attracts discrimination' (2013, 5). Thus data and its associated processes and practices can be significant in reinforcing inequalities in education, as well as appearing to record them (Bradbury 2011b).

Through this discussion of the theoretical underpinnings and political context for the book, we have aimed to examine the rationale behind the use of data in education; the neoliberal logic that makes numbers attractive, essential and powerful. We have argued that data can be useful in highlighting social injustice within schools but we have also argued that data have an important function in terms of discipline, as they decide who to 'reward or punish' (Foucault 1977), but they also control, by encouraging the individual 'enterprise man' to engage in a constant process of self-improvement and reflection. We now turn to the research studies themselves, which provide the research data for the arguments that follow.

The research studies

The research data examined here were collected as part of two research projects during the period 2013–16. The first project (called here Project 1 for ease of reading) aimed to explore practices associated with assessment in a range of early years settings, following changes to assessment and funding policies under the Conservative–Liberal Democrat coalition government of 2010–15 (Roberts-Holmes and Bradbury 2016; Bradbury and Roberts-Holmes 2016a; Roberts-Holmes 2015). This was a small-scale exploratory project, which led to a more detailed focus on the use of data as the research progressed. Project 2 was a larger scale project focused on the introduction of a specific policy – Baseline Assessment. This project was funded and commissioned by two teachers' unions, the Association of Teachers and Lecturers (ATL) and the National Union of Teachers (NUT), and aimed to examine the operation and impact of Baseline Assessment as it was introduced in the autumn of 2015 (Bradbury and Roberts-Holmes 2016b).

Methods

Project 1 was a small-scale qualitative study into the impact of recent policy on the main types of early years state provision in England, involving a children's centre, Nursery and Reception classes in primary schools, and a combined nursery school and children's centre. We also interviewed a local authority (LA) early years advisor, to provide an alternative perspective on changing school practices. Access to the four different case study sites was identified through opportunistic sampling and existing research relationships from an earlier project. At each site, interviews with several staff, focus group discussions and some limited observations were conducted. Documentary data including anonymised Excel spreadsheets of assessment data were also collected. Across the sites, we interviewed headteachers, deputy headteachers, children's centre managers and early years teachers (a total of 13 interviews). In addition, we carried out a lengthy interview with the LA advisor, unconnected to any of the sites. In all interviews, semi-structured interview schedules which focused on the practices relating to assessment, the collection and processing of data, reporting of data to the LA and the role of Ofsted were used. After transcription the participants were provided with email copies of the salient points of each interview, which prompted further dialogue and correspondence. The email exchanges built upon and developed the themes identified in the earlier interviews and totalled 115 emails across the three sites.

Project 2 used a mixed-methods approach involving a nationwide survey and interviews at five case studies of primary schools. The survey was distributed via the NUT and ATL email databases using the Bristol Online Survey service, and was completed by 1131 people. Fifty per cent of respondents were Reception teachers, 38 per cent EYFS or phase leaders, 7 per cent senior leaders and the remainder support staff or other. Respondents were asked how long they had been teaching, where relevant, in order to analyse differences between teachers who had experienced a number of policy changes and newer teachers who had only worked with the EYFS Profile (which was also updated in 2012). Almost half of the respondents had been teaching prior to the introduction of the EYFS in 2003 (47 per cent) and a similar proportion had worked under the original EYFS (42 per cent). Newer teachers (under three years) comprised 11 per cent of the sample. The majority of respondents (80 per cent) worked in the standard form of school at primary level in

England, state-funded non-academy schools; 16 per cent worked in academies (state-funded schools independent from LA control). Most worked in schools graded by Ofsted as 'good' (63 per cent) or outstanding (21 per cent). The Baseline Assessment provider used by survey respondents reflected the proportions nationally: 76 per cent used Early Excellence, 10 per cent CEM and 11 per cent NFER. The remaining 3 per cent used a discontinued provider or had opted to do no Baseline Assessment (1.9 per cent). Results were analysed with these demographic data to see if there were differences in responses due to different school situations, roles, length of service and Baseline Assessment provider.

The survey involved a number of questions for teachers and school leaders on their views and experiences of Baseline Assessment. For some questions, respondents were asked if they 'agree a lot', 'agree a little', 'disagree a little' or 'disagree a lot' with key statements on Baseline Assessment. The survey was piloted with existing teachers before distribution. The data generated by the survey were conducted using the Bristol Online Survey service, and exported and analysed using SPSS, the quantitative data analysis software program. The majority of respondents answered all the questions. In cases where there were non-responses, we report percentages as a proportion of those that answered the question, rather than of the whole number. Written responses are included as quotes in Chapters 3–6, denoted by the letter W.

The five case study primary schools were located across England, as detailed below. A total of 36 people were interviewed, comprising of five headteachers; two assistant headteachers or EYFS coordinators; 13 Reception teachers; one Nursery teacher; and 15 parents. Purposive sampling ensured that the five case study schools represented different areas of England. At each school, Reception teachers, EYFS coordinators, headteachers and other school leaders, and parents were interviewed using standard semi-structured interview schedules focused on their experiences of using Baseline Assessment. The parents were interviewed as a group but all others were interviewed individually, with the exception of one interview with two teachers. Interviews were recorded and transcribed professionally for analysis. A summary is provided in Table 2.1.

TABLE 2.1 Case study schools

Region	Status	Most recent Ofsted category	Baseline Assessment chosen
London	Community	Good	Early Excellence
North	Community	Outstanding	Early Excellence
South	Community	Good	Early Excellence
South West	Community	Good	Early Excellence
West Midlands	Church of England Voluntary Controlled[1]	Good	Early Excellence

Note

1 Voluntary controlled schools in England are state-funded schools where a religious foundation has some involvement in the running of the school – for example, on the school's governing body.

The sample was limited in that we were unable to gain access to an academy school, and all of the case study schools had chosen the Early Excellence Baseline Assessment, reflecting the trend across the country. Our sample of parents was also limited in terms of gender and social diversity, as most respondents were white mothers; for this reason we do not explore parents' views in detail here. In order to protect their anonymity, the schools are referred to using pseudonyms and the region where they are based is not made explicit.

Research sites

In this section we provide a short description of each of the sites included in the two projects, beginning with the early years settings in Project 1. All names of schools and individuals are pseudonyms.

Project 1 research sites: early years settings

Westhill Children's Centre

Westhill Children's Centre was located in a deprived inner London borough. A wide range of activities took place at the centre, including Nursery classes, drop-in, 'stay and play' sessions, midwifery services and postnatal care. Westhill had two groups of children who regularly attended the centre, the two-year-olds and the Nursery class for three- to four-year-olds. The two-year-olds attended for 15 hours a week, three mornings a week, taking part in a range of activities inside and outside; in the Nursery class, some children attended for longer, 'topping up' their allocated hours by parents paying a fee. These 15 hours of education and care are provided free of charge for children whose parents qualified for a range of benefits, including income support (DfE 2014b) from the age of two. We interviewed the headteacher of the Children's Centre and her deputy, who also worked as a class teacher.

Easthorne Primary School

Easthorne was a primary school in another area of inner London where we conducted research with an EYFS Nursery class for three- and four-year-olds and the Reception class for four- and five-year-olds. We interviewed the headteacher, the deputy headteacher and two Reception teachers. As well as ongoing assessment, the EYFS teachers had responsibility for providing data for the EYFS Profile, the statutory assessment reported to the LA and parents at the end of Reception. The EYFS coordinator attended meetings within the primary school and LA to discuss the data, and met with the senior management team and LA early years advisors to scrutinise and compare the early years data with other comparable schools.

Northside Primary School

Northside Primary School was a community primary school in a different area of London with high levels of poverty and a significant ethnic minority population. We interviewed the Nursery and Reception teachers. As at Easthorne, the Reception teachers had responsibility for providing data for the EYFS Profile and both engaged in ongoing assessment.

Hopetown Nursery School and Children's Centre

Hopetown Nursery School and Children's Centre was located in a socially mixed area of a city in the south-west of England. In order to provide the 15 hours' free care for disadvantaged two-year-olds, the nursery school had recently opened a children's centre for this group on a separate site. We interviewed the headteacher, deputy headteacher, the Children's Centre manager, their assistant manager and a Reception teacher. Data were collected regularly on the children and their families, and these data flowed rapidly between the nursery school, the children's centre, the local primary schools and the LA.

The local authority advisor

As part of this project we also interviewed an LA early years advisor who was based in a separate borough in a diverse and deprived area of London. An experienced early years teacher and advisor, his role involved supporting both primary schools and private and voluntary settings within the borough, primarily with assessment and the collection of data. He described his role as 'support and challenge'. We interviewed the early years advisor using a similar interview schedule to the other participants, but with a greater focus on the 'statistical journey' of the data collected in early years settings. The advisor also provided additional documentation relating to the LA's role in collecting data.

Project 2 research sites: primary schools

Alder School

Alder School was a large, oversubscribed primary school which was highly regarded in the local area, with excellent league table results. The school was located within a comfortable area on the outskirts of a large city, made up of owner-occupied, semi-detached former council houses. The population was largely white working class with a very low level of ethnic diversity, but within the immediate area of the primary school there were also large detached homes, owned by professional middle-class parents, who largely contributed to the parents' discussion. There were three Reception classes. We interviewed the headteacher and three Reception teachers and conducted a focus group with a large group of parents.

Beech School

Beech School was an overwhelmingly middle-class school located in an expensive neighbourhood with very low ethnic diversity. It was smaller, with two-form entry, but with a large attached nursery for three-year-olds. Beech was a highly competitive school to gain entry to as it was also very well thought of locally, particularly as a creative, alternative school, priding itself on teaching the arts. It had extensive facilities, including large green fields and a wood. We interviewed the headteacher, two Reception teachers and one Nursery teacher, and conducted a focus group with parents.

Cedar School

Cedar School was a three-form entry primary in a deprived urban area. The immediate surroundings were a mixture of local authority housing and newly built apartment blocks. The large site catered for a school population which included many nationalities and a higher than average proportion of children receiving free school meals (FSM). The headteacher, EYFS leader and three Reception teachers were interviewed, along with one parent.

Damson School

Damson School was a very large primary in an urban conurbation, with four Reception classes. It was located in a traditional white working class neighbourhood experiencing increasing levels of diversity. The school was under a lot of pressure, partly financial, to join with a local academy chain, which was relevant as conducting Baseline had cost considerable money due to employing four supply teachers to allow the teachers to do the assessment. We interviewed the headteacher, deputy headteacher and four Reception teachers.

Elm School

Finally, Elm School was located in a quiet, affluent residential area of a small town and had two forms per year drawn from a large catchment area. The school population was almost entirely white and socially very mixed, but with a small proportion of children receiving FSM. We interviewed the headteacher, two Reception teachers and a small group of parents.

Ethical considerations

The research projects were conducted within the ethical guidelines provided by the British Education Research Association (BERA 2011) and the UCL Institute of Education. Care has been taken to ensure anonymity of all respondents and the security of data. In Project 2, schools were recompensed with funding for either a half day or a full day of teaching cover (depending on the number of interviews) in order to reduce the impact of the research on the children.

3

DATAFICATION IN THE CLASSROOM

The production of data-driven subjectivities

Introduction

In this chapter we begin to draw together the ways in which datafication is *productive*. Foucault writes about power as 'totalizing, individualizing and as productive' (Ball 2013b, 6–7); we argue here that data are an important part of the operation of power in education. We start the analysis of our research data with a deeper exploration of what 'datafication' looks like in schools and early years settings – its forms, practices, artefacts and values. This includes a detailed discussion of the ways in which data disrupt and challenge established pedagogical practices, and the tensions between the necessity for school performance data and young children's emotional well-being and learning. We then consider how data affect teachers' and students' every-day lives, their relationships to each other and their value within the school: the production of *data-driven subjectivities* in education.

The overriding prominence of data

The increasing use of data in education has been documented in various educational settings worldwide, though ours is the first detailed study of early years and primary schools in England. The spread of data has been described in terms of the three Vs of volume, velocity and variety (Laney, 2001 cited in Selwyn 2016a, 81). The issue of volume was the most prominent point in many of our interviews, with the problem of being overwhelmed a recurrent theme; some also mentioned the variety of data:

> The collection and analysing of data is just too overwhelming.
>
> *(Teacher, Easthorne)*

Where do you stop with it because there is so much of it! Health data, education data, family support data and well-being data and to be perfectly honest I just can't cope with that much data all the time!

(Headteacher, Hopetown)

Many of the data we discuss in this book are traditional forms of educational data: attainment results and formative assessments. However, at Hopetown they also collected various forms of data about parents and families as part of their monitoring systems. Elsewhere, it was not the variety of types of data that was surprising, but the volume and detail of these data. In all the settings and schools in both projects, a huge volume of data was collected on all aspects of the curriculum, at regular points through the school year, in order to show progress and make predictions:

We all do a baseline across all 17 strands of the Foundation stage curriculum and we will age band. [...] We would then repeat those assessments at Christmas and at Easter and then at the end of the year.

(Teacher 1, Alder)

We record how the children enter when they are two, so we have a baseline and then throughout the year we do three assessments with the children at set points and then compare them with each other to check that they are on track and are making progress. You have to show that you have made 'value added' by the time they reach the end of Reception. The LA are using that information to predict how two-year-olds are going to do at the end of FS, KS1 and KS2.

(Head, Hopetown)

The tracking begins from Nursery in the Prime Areas and right through to Year 6. If you are 'exceeding' at the end of Reception you have to show that you are 'exceeding' at the end of KS1 and if not then we are not doing our job.

(Deputy Head, Easthorne)

... when Ofsted come and ask to see the tracking data, I can show this child, at their baseline, then their first, second and third term and this is where they are now.

(Deputy Head, Westhill)

These quotes indicate the extent to which early years settings and primary schools have become part of an 'audit culture' (Apple, Kenway and Singh 2005; Biesta 2009), where teachers engage in data collection to show they are 'doing their jobs', to paraphrase the quote above; within this culture 'individuals and groups increasingly police themselves, and are seen to police themselves, in an effort to prove their worth' (Hardy and Boyle 2011, 214). At Westhill Children's Centre they were required to provide data on the two- and three-year-olds to the local authority every three months, and to the primary schools when the children moved on. We see in this quote how data recording and collection are a constant presence in these teachers' and school leaders' lives, whether they are working with two-year-old children or 11-year-olds. These quotes resonate with Deleuze's comment that 'in the societies of control one is never finished with anything' (1995a). Children are assessed and tracked through their school lives, from nursery or children's centre to the end of primary school. The language used – of 'tracking', 'checking' and 'value added' – is drawn from economic models of progression through pre-determined stages; this allows data to be used to predict outcomes, such as in the comment from the headteacher at Hopetown above. We can see evidence of Finn's 'atmospheres of progress' (2016, 30), 'spatially specific shared senses of progress making (or the lack of it) that are collective and yet also individualising'; while he uses the term to refer to secondary students and staff, here early years and primary teachers are engaging in atmospheres of progress in their references to constant tracking of children. Data are finalised or solidified at regular points, usually termly, but as we discuss in detail below, the process of collection through observation is constant and therefore the need for data is productive of certain forms of pedagogy.

The datafication of practices and pedagogy

Across the research sites, teachers' choices about how to teach, organise their classrooms, use their time and prioritise tasks were dominated by the need to produce data, both for one-off assessments such as Baseline and ongoing assessments such as the EYFS Profile. As one teacher commented:

> In this game, you gotta play the game. If you're being judged on a score – teach to it – you're a fool if you don't. You must teach to the test – that's the agenda.
>
> *(Teacher, Northside)*

'Playing the game' is the only option within this context, so that restricting the curriculum for the purposes of assessment is a 'must'. Arguments around the 'narrowing' of the early years and primary curriculum away from creativity and towards English and maths as a result of national standardised testing have been thoroughly rehearsed (Wyse and Torrance 2009; Alexander 2009; Wyse and Ferrari 2015). Many note that, ironically, testing such as Baseline Assessment has the effect of 'driving teaching in exactly the opposite direction to that which other research indicates will improve teaching, learning and attainment' (Wyse and Torrance 2009, 224). The pressures of high-stakes accountability are, for example, in danger of usurping the dedicated time, patience and insight needed to promote sustained shared thinking in the early years (Siraj-Blatchford 2010) and dialogic primary teaching (Mercer, Dawes and Staarman 2009), both of which are known to improve attainment.

In the schools using Baseline, we found significant changes to the curriculum provided as a result of the need to collect data. Several teachers explained how they had changed their activities in order to produce evidence which could be translated into Baseline data:

> This year it is very much a case of find our way through it I suppose, working out how to change our curriculum to meet the needs of what we need to do for Baseline. [...] We are having to do activities to find that information, so that has taken away from being able to get into the areas of provision and work with the children, and showing them what types of things they can do with the new resources they have got.
>
> (Teacher 1, Alder)

> [We] thought that actually we haven't really looked at that [some areas] so we had better do something about that, so we might put out a particular activity to almost cover those points.
>
> (Teacher 1, Beech)

> Rather than go with the children's interests – of what they were interested in – I have geared what I have been setting up in the class to try and help me gather information for the purpose of this assessment.
>
> (Teacher 3, Cedar)

> We assessed usually one activity by activity. So we set up an activity that we knew would fulfil the criteria for certain statements and then watched the children access it and then we just went down [the list of names] and said, yes they can do it.
>
> (Teacher 2, Elm)

Here the content of structured activities was determined by the need to provide observable learning for Baseline Assessment; thus the data collection process was not simply a record of what was happening in the classroom, but a determining factor. This is the prioritisation of what can be observed and measured, over what the children are interested in or need to know; what Souto-Otero and Beneito-Montagut refer to as 'alignment' (2016). This finding was reinforced by the nation-wide survey which showed that a majority of respondents (59 per cent) agreed that, 'The Baseline Assessment has disrupted the children's start to school' (33 per cent 'agree a little'; 26 per cent 'agree a lot'). This did not vary with length of time teaching or by provider.

The responses to the needs of Baseline were not uniform across the schools, however, suggesting a complex process of negotiation of a new policy as it is enacted (Braun, Maguire and Ball 2010). In one school, their reaction to Baseline was more dramatic: they took the decision to 'stop teaching' until the Baseline was complete, in order to provide a 'true baseline':

> We have stopped teaching. You know normally we would do very gently
> settling in, rules, all of that. But then we would start with some of the more
> formal teaching activities, you know a little bit of phonics, but we have not,
> we have held back because we don't want to influence judgements.
>
> *(Teacher 1, Alder)*

Here we see a significant commitment to the accuracy of results, drawn from a
discourse of measurable calculable learning gain; this teacher appears to believe that
children could be unaffected by their experience of school, so a 'true baseline' can
be measured. This practice was described by the teachers as being advised by Early
Excellence, the Baseline provider. It was seen positively in Elm School as a change
which allowed the teachers to focus on children's personal and emotional
development.

> I liked the way that they said that, that you have got to look for their well-
> being and involvement before you worry and you had the six weeks to do it.
> I mean we did try and do it before the six weeks was up because then we got
> into the whole debate of EExBA would say don't do direct teaching. I mean
> even though there is teaching going on with any interaction, there will be
> teaching. But in terms of like the phonics we didn't start until sort of three or
> four weeks in.
>
> *(Teacher 2, Elm)*

Thus the demands of data collection could also result in pedagogical change
which was seen as positive for children. The teachers at Elm School reworked the
advice of Early Excellence to fit with their values and used the need to collect
'pure' data as justification for the prioritisation of 'well-being and involvement'.
The range of different practices in response to Baseline also had an impact on the
data collected, as we discuss in later chapters. We also return to the practices
associated with datafication in terms of grouping and setting in the following
chapter.

Relationships

In the Project 2 schools, we found that the need to collect data for Baseline Assessment affected the establishment of relationships between teachers, support staff and
pupils. This is usually regarded as a key focus of the first few weeks of Reception,
as it may be some children's first experience of a formal educational setting. Similarly in the national survey, 32 per cent of respondents agreed there had been a
negative impact on the development of relationships between children and staff,
which is notable, although the most common response was to disagree with this
proposition.

Many comments, both from interviews and from the survey, focused on Baseline Assessment as a distraction:

I feel that the baseline assessment has to be completed too early in the year and means that teachers are madly trying to collect evidence, rather than concentrating on the welfare of their new pupils and helping to create a calm and relaxing environment which is vital for a positive start to their school life.

(W)

For some, this detrimental effect was linked directly to changes in the activities provided and the time taken:

You had to set it up so you could actually assess these things, which makes it very difficult to make, to start forming a relationship with the children, which is so important at this time of year.

(Teacher 2, Cedar)

It has had a negative impact on the children in Reception as their first few weeks are so important to establish routines, rules and relationships with staff and this was hugely impacted by the time it took to administer the assessment.

(W)

Although I agree with baseline in principle, the NFER package prevented us from building relationships with children at a crucial stage.

(W)

It has to be done as early as possible at the crucial time when you should be developing relationships with them not ignoring the majority and looking at a screen 1:1 with 1 child.

(W)

The reception teacher in our school found it impossible to administer the baseline test and teach a class of new reception children. A supply teacher had to be drafted in so that the tests could be carried out. The result was that our reception teacher was not able to work with her new class in setting expectations for behaviour, rules, routines or getting to know the children. The test caused a lot of disruption to learning and had a negative impact on relationship building.

(W)

As we see here, it is not only the observation-based Early Excellence Baseline Assessment which is seen as disruptive: the tablet-based NFER and CEM assessments were also seen as affecting the 'settling in' period. Sitting down with each child to administer a formal assessment took the teacher out of the classroom and limited their ability to establish routines and relationships. Thus the demands of data collection took priority over the normal practices of Reception; as Ball notes in his discussion of the 'tyranny of numbers': 'We come to make decisions about the value of activities and the investment of our time and effort in relation to measures and indexes and the symbolic and real rewards that might be generated from them' (Ball 2015, 299–300). For these teachers, and the school leaders who directed them, the rewards of doing Baseline outweighed the time lost in the classroom. This shift in priority had an affective impact on how some teachers felt about their role:

> It has taken away all the things I have always loved about the first six weeks of Reception, helping children settle.
>
> *(Teacher 3, Cedar)*

Unlike Finn's research (2016), which found that positive 'atmospheres of progress' were enabled through regular data-driven practices, we found that the one-time data collection of Baseline had a negative affective impact on Reception classrooms. It was not motivating (or shared with these much younger children), but seen as distancing the teacher from the children. This effect on relationships echoes Thompson and Cook's argument, based on research on the impact of high-stakes testing in Australia, that 'powerful interpersonal relationships with students become superseded by the simulatory and profiling machines deployed as a result of high-stakes testing' (2014, 140).

Ideological tensions

For many of the teachers, both in the primary schools and in the early years settings, there were significant tensions between their values and the demands of a data-driven education system. Thus datafication produced the need to negotiate complex ideological contradictions between requirements and beliefs. Internationally there have always been disagreements between practitioners and policy-makers in early years education in particular (Moss 2013, 2014), and this continues to be the case in England (Neaum 2016). The main debates centre on the efficacy of organising early education on a spectrum between child-centred and teacher-led pedagogy (Smith 2016; Graue 2008). Assessment has a complicated relationship to pedagogy in early years, as the majority of assessments are observation-based and therefore compatible with play-based, child-centred pedagogy (such as the EYFS Profile and the Early Excellence Baseline Assessment). Other assessments require children to sit a formal test in paper form or more recently on a tablet; this form goes against the ethos of informality and play promoted in much early years literature (Broadhead and Burt 2012; Fleer 2013; Samuelsson and Fleer 2009; Whitebread and Coltman 2015). It is, however, in keeping with the positivist, scientific principles of developmental psychology, which continue to dominate scholarship in early childhood education (Graue 2008). There is no simple split between the different paradigms of teacher- and child-led pedagogy, and the use or not of such assessments. This has led to combinations of discourses which are not easy bedfellows, such as the promotion of the Early Excellence Baseline Assessment as 'child-centred', although it is a summative assessment for the purposes of school accountability. This tension was noted in one of the parent interviews (quoted earlier in the Preface), where a mother commented that teachers had to ask themselves, 'Will I be there for the children or will I be there for the paperwork?'.

Furthermore, we see the complexity of these ideological tensions in the teachers' comments on choosing a Baseline Assessment which was 'early years friendly':

> EExBA baseline was our choice [...] it appeared to be the most in keeping with our daily practice.
>
> *(W)*

> We chose Early Excellence because it matched the way we currently assess in Early Years – through observation and teacher judgement, and we thought it would lead to the least disruption in what is a vital time for the children's personal, social, and emotional development.
>
> *(W)*

> EExBA was the best system for us as it was a holistic approach that had no detrimental effect on the children; we got to know them and observed and assessed as normal and then completed the questionnaires out of class.
>
> *(W)*

> I chose EExBA as I like the observation format. I would have made similar observations anyway. However I did feel that much of the first few weeks of school were spent on the iPad making observations instead of communicating and building relationships with the children.
>
> *(W)*

Thus the teachers engage with a traditional discourse of 'child-centred learning' while complying with a measure which is driven by neoliberal values of accountability. This is the strategy of 'making do around it' described as a form of resistance by Souto-Otero and Beneito-Montagut (2016); the fundamentals are not changed, but there are adaptations which make the process more acceptable. The issue of choice is discussed in more detail in Chapter 5.

There were some voices of resistance, however, which challenged the premise of a new assessment altogether; some teachers commented in the survey that their existing informal baseline assessments were more useful to them:

> My previous on entry assessments, created by me, were not time consuming and gave me all the necessary information I needed to know.
>
> *(W)*

Our pre-existing arrangements are more comprehensive than the EExBA assessment.

(W)

Our existing Baseline arrangements supplied all the information we need for showing next steps and progress in a manner which is sympathetic to the needs of very young children.

(W)

Our own baseline was much quicker, much more in depth and really enabled us to tailor individual learning.

(W)

Respondents saw the use of these existing baselines as more in keeping with the ethos of early years, or as evidence of their experience and expertise. Existing baselines were also more compatible with the EYFS Profile and other tracking systems, allowing their data to form part of the 'data machinery' of the school. Thus these teachers were able to combine their commitment to an 'early years ethos' with some forms of data collection, but resisted the formality of Baseline Assessment. In some ways this position chimes with Souto-Otero and Beneito-Montagut's description of 'rebellion' against data, 'various actions or inactions to lobby for the redefinition of the indicators used for commensuration, and the rejection of the inferences derived from the analysis of data that is not considered appropriate' (2016, 29). Comments which objected to the binary yes/no decisions required by the Early Excellence Baseline Assessment – which we discuss in more detail in the following chapter – chime with this desire for 'redefinition of the indicators'. These ideological tensions underpinned teachers' practical responses to Baseline and other assessment systems.

Data-driven subjectivities

Subjectivity is 'the possibility of lived experience within a context – political and economic' (Ball 2013b, 125). As discussed in the previous chapter, subjects are constituted through discourse, and although they have discursive agency, there are limits to the intelligibility of the subject (teacher, student or school leader) within regimes of truth that operate in a particular context. In relation to the current neoliberal education system, Ball and Olmedo argue that 'Neoliberalism requires and enacts a "new type of individual", that is a "new type of teacher and head teacher" forming within the logic of competition' (2013, 88). As Butler argues, 'categories, conventions and norms […] prepare or establish a subject for recognition' (Butler 2010, 5). We argue here that, within this overriding context of neoliberal values and priorities, datafication produces specific teacher and student subjectivities, bound up not only with the logic of competition, but also with competing definitions of worth, trust and value as demonstrated by data. These disputed definitions bring with them practices of resistance and rebellion, as 'subjectivity [is] the terrain of struggle, the terrain of resistance' (Ball and Olmedo 2013, 85). We aim to emphasise here the importance of data in the construction of teacher and student identities, through both internal and external gazes which produce self-regulation. Data are an incentive to work harder, to work on oneself, and to make others work differently. At the same time they are a record of what we have done and what we will be able to do, representing our roles and importance. To quote Ball, 'Measurement and numbers as techniques for reflection and representation play a particular role within the contemporary relationship between truth and power and the self that we call neo-liberalism' (Ball 2015, 299). We wish to emphasise the agency of individuals to resist subjectification, while recognising the power of certain truths to define acceptability. As Kitchin argues, individuals are 'both liberated and coerced simultaneously' by data as 'seemingly opposing outcomes are bound together' (Kitchin 2014, 164).

Teachers

As we have seen above, teachers are affected by datafication in multiple ways, in terms of practice, pedagogy, feelings and relationships. We argue that datafication produces specific teacher subjectivities – as data collector, organiser of data-producing environments, and professionally, as a personification of their children's attainment data. As Ball describes it, these teachers are 'subjected to numbers and numbered subjects', their worth defined by data (2015, 299; see also Pratt 2016). As one teacher at Easthorne described it, '*I feel a personal pressure* to make them pro-gress'. Internationally, there is concern that early years educators are increasingly subject to the pressures of performativity, resulting in great anxiety (Kilderry 2015). For teachers of young children, the shift towards more formal assessment is particu-larly difficult, as it goes against much of their training and often their beliefs about how children learn through play (Fleer 2013); this affects their feelings about being a professional. Our analysis builds on work such as Osgood (2006), who noted how primary teachers become self-governing professionals under the gaze of simplified governing data, and our own research into assessment and the collection of data in the sector (Bradbury 2012; Roberts-Holmes 2015).

The teachers we interviewed for Project 2 and in the survey saw Baseline Assess-ment as disruptive to their professional culture, and in some cases they felt deprofes-sionalised by collecting data for accountability rather than focusing upon the child's best interests. Often this deprofessionalising took the form of not feeling 'trusted':

> I am concerned that this will feed into a league table. I feel no longer trusted as a professional.
>
> *(W)*

> We deserve to be trusted as professionals to do what is best for our children's development ensuring their wellbeing is high and their love for learning is nurtured.
>
> *(W)*

> If I was sitting in the role play area talking to the children about what they are making and you know engaging with them in that way, I would have to say, 'Oh I have got to go and do some Baseline and assessment', it would make me feel guilty and it would just be this thing hanging over me and by the end of the six weeks I just thought, there it is. I handed it in and it was like enough was enough.
>
> *(Teacher 3, Cedar)*

This last teacher described how her sense of professionalism was affected by having to carry out Baseline Assessment, which took away her enjoyment of settling the children and made her feel 'fake'. She felt guilty about putting aside child-centred principles and instead had to attend to 'this thing hanging over me'. This teacher's experience demonstrates the tension between the need to complete Baseline Assessment for the purposes of school-based performativity and longer-held notions of professional skill. She has stopped 'engaging' in her words, and become a data collector: 'the teacher is not, as conventionally held, a transmitter of information [...] but a data producer and analyst who enrols the child as the same – as a social scientist of their own learning ability, achievements and life trajectory (Finn 2016, 37). This teacher thus removes herself from direct involvement with the children to collect data, a direct change in role. The pressures of performativity have thus become 'normalised' (Kilderry 2015), part of her every-day life.

However, there was resistance against the simplicity of some data collection, which was seen as undermining Reception teachers' professional status:

> As professionals we know there may be more about a child than yes/no. Nothing from the 'testing' told us anything we didn't already know or were learning (but had to rush the child to find out).
>
> *(W)*

> If you get to a statement and you are not sure and you are really like discussing it with your colleague or you are thinking, can she or can't she, 'err on the side of caution' and say no. We were told that on the training course. So if like with some particular children you are like, 'hmm, can they or can they not?', just 'err on the side of caution'.
>
> *(Teacher 3, Damson)*

This latter approach, which can be characterised as 'no reflection, no thinking, no dialogue' undermined teachers' sense of professionalism because it contradicted how they have been trained to operate (Fleer 2013; Samuelsson and Fleer 2009; Whitebread and Coltman 2015). Some respondents saw this lack of judgement as a benefit of the tablet-based options, however:

> [We] chose CEM as an assessment as it *would not require any practitioner judgement* and would not have any areas which we felt needed cross moderation.
>
> *(W, our emphasis)*

As Moss (2014) has argued, there is a risk that early years professionals are reduced to 'grey technicians' through the adoption of crude quantitative approaches. Assessments such as Baseline replace diversity, complexity and contingency with the solidity of 'facts' and numbers to demonstrate progress; for the teachers involved, this is a major shift in how they operate and the underlying principles of their profession, which, we argue, alters how they are constituted as subjects. The values on which they are judged are altered: to be a good teacher requires an alternative performance than before, one that involves less judgement and reflection and more definite decisions on set criteria.

This shift can be detected in the teachers' reactions to Baseline Assessment. Although many of the teachers saw Baseline Assessment as further eroding their professional control and autonomy, they 'begrudgingly accepted' it, in a similar fashion to the Australian secondary teachers in Selwyn, Henderson and Chao's research (2015).

> I can tell you, we headteachers just sighed, we just kind of had a group hug at the meeting, rolled our eyes, and thought here we go again.
>
> *(Head, Alder)*

> In the back of my mind I knew I had to do this Baseline and it wasn't really for my purpose it was for the government, so that kind of made me a bit anti to start with.
>
> *(Teacher 2, Cedar)*

> I have always taken the philosophy that as a teacher you know you have to do things you don't necessarily want to do or you might not see a purpose for but it is just one of those things that you have to do.
>
> *(Teacher 2, Alder)*

These teachers and school leaders are inured to the problems caused by continual changes to assessment systems, and therefore simply try to find a way to negotiate a new system. The failure of Baseline Assessment to provide useful information for their planning and the disruption to their professional expertise that this involved meant this negotiation was more challenging than with other policy changes. A comment from the survey summed up this feeling of frustration: 'Serves no other purpose than to give the government another tool with which to bash teachers' (W). Like the teachers in Pratt's research on the internal competition engendered by data in primary schools, we found the teachers were 'beaten over the head with facts and figures' (teacher respondent in Pratt 2016, 897). As Sellar comments, there is 'creative labour involved in producing new possibilities for data production and analysis' (2015, 135). Nonetheless, their professional identities are bound up with this process of constantly adapting to change; they simply 'sigh' and carry on, or see it 'as just one of those things'. They are ships buffeted by the latest storm; flexible, adaptable, willing, just as the neoliberal education system requires them to be, but also engaged in some 'care for themselves' through their reactions (Ball and Olmedo 2013). Research from secondary education has suggested the emergence of a 'post-performative' teacher who is neither compliant nor resistant, but who is able to reconcile the tensions between the pressures of accountability and professional autonomy (Wilkins 2011); the teachers in our research, we would argue, have not reached this balanced 'post-performative' state, but are still struggling with these tensions. They are, however, accepting of their new roles as they see they have little choice, even when this risks them becoming 'transparent but empty, unrecognizable to ourselves' (Ball and Olmedo 2013, 91).

Within these struggles, data have a role in encouraging these teachers to be self-governing:

> It [collection and analysing of data] makes you constantly think of how to improve it and what to do with this group and how to plug this hole and that one. I fill in trackers frequently and I feel a personal pressure to make them progress.
>
> *(Teacher, Easthorne)*

This teacher's response to the demands of data is to work *on herself*, to improve what she does with different groups to 'plug the hole' to 'make them progress'. Rather than challenging or subverting such regulation she is self-governed by intensifying her workload to demonstrate constant and uninterrupted progress and development for all children at all times; she is 'brought to work on [herself], under certain forms of authority' (Rabinow and Rose 2006). This teacher is 'burdened with the responsibility to perform' (Ball and Olmedo 2013, 88), as the data-driven school demands a new teacher subjectivity, within a new logic. Thompson and Cook argue, in relation to high-stakes testing in Australia:

> the statistically derived product of student's test scores represents a new, more intense, virtual (and fragmented) logic of schooling and teaching. When tests are fed into a machine that converts them to data-points aggregated via a computer program a pattern of data-points emerges that tells a story that is more powerful than that concerning how well this teacher enforces the time-table or uniform policy. [...] These teachers are rewarded or punished for the patterns they produce; not for anything they do in the classroom.
>
> *(2014, 133)*

The teacher above is self-governed by this 'powerful story', through which she is constituted as a good or bad teacher, capable or incompetent. While teachers collect data from children through observing them, at the same time they are themselves 'watched' through a comparative performance of the data they collect; they become 'watched watchers' (Taylor 2013, 11).

Overall, the research data suggest teachers feel they have lost control through the imposition of Baseline: they have become the 'data collectors', not trusted but important because of their role in the 'data journey'. Some teachers are disciplined by the process, where it is used directly to judge them as professionals:

> As a teacher I have no idea what the test involved as I was not allowed access, yet, I am being judged against it.
>
> *(W)*

> Having been pulled up on how our Literacy has come out higher than Communication & Language by SLT [Senior Leadership Team] & being treated like we don't know what we're doing on data being returned, it seems like a total waste of personal time for the Reception teachers in our school.
>
> *(W)*

For the first of these teachers, the negative impact of this judgement is aggravated by her lack of involvement in the conduct of the assessment, which only serves to further mystify the process. This is one of Ball's 'terrors of performativity': confusion over what one will be judged on, how and when (Ball 2003). This is similar to Jennings and Pallas' (2016) findings on the reaction of teachers in New York state to the introduction of value added measures; in their study one teacher described the scores as 'like the weather' in their unpredictability and distance from her practice. Despite this distance, the second teacher above has been criticised for producing the 'wrong' data, as the figures for one area have 'come out' higher than others. The implication is that the data collection process, and therefore the teacher, must be at fault; she feels her professional skills are questioned ('treated like we don't know what we're doing'), and rejects it as a 'waste of personal time'. This inclusion of 'personal' reminds us of the individualised pressure on teachers to engage with data production in the 'correct', most useful ways, despite their heavy workloads. This is again similar to research findings in relation to the EYFS Profile, where teachers felt great pressure to engage with an assessment they had little faith in, which they were told they 'got wrong' (Bradbury 2013c).

For some teachers, the connection between their production of data and their 'effectiveness' was made explicit:

> The baseline assessment was initially carried out by SLT, then I was suddenly given a host of tick statements to fill in, without really observing the children in these specific areas. I have now been told exactly what scores 'I' need to achieve at the end of the year to ensure I'm not an 'ineffective teacher'. A number on an assessment I've never seen, with children who are so young.
>
> *(W)*

As this teacher suggests by her use of inverted commas in the phrase 'what "I" need to achieve', the use of scores to judge an individual teacher and her effectiveness is problematic, particularly when she has had no control over the original assessment and the children are 'so young'. Baseline is something 'done to' this teacher, not something she has taken an active part in negotiating, as suggested by many of our respondents. Her status and professional worth are constituted through the data produced by SLT with 'an assessment I've never seen'; this is a data-driven teacher subjectivity, in extremis. Ball comments: 'The regime of numbers hails us in its terms, and to the extent we turn, acknowledge and engage, we are made recognizable and subject' (2017, 44). Thus this teacher is complicit, but questioning, of her constitution through data, as indicated by her use of quote marks for 'I'; this reflects her ambivalence about who exactly is 'achieving' the scores. There is no doubt, however, that they will be taken as an indicator of her worth as a teacher; this is the frame through which she is recognised. This emotive response chimes with Jennings and Pallas' (2016) findings, where one teacher commented, 'It has taken everything I've got not to brand my own self as a failing teacher in the face of my VAM [value added measure], and I haven't been successful yet'. As Sellar argues, performance data 'work affectively in schools and in interactions between school leaders, teachers and students' (2015, 142); they create feelings of pressure, guilt, failure and frustration. But they remain overridingly prominent in discourses of the 'good teacher', as 'a set of informational structures and performance indicators [...] become the principle of intelligibility of social relations' (Ball and Olmedo 2013, 90).

Datafication produces these changed relationships between teachers and their superiors, and between teachers themselves, who may be set up in competition with one another in an 'internal market' (Pratt 2016). It produces new data-driven teacher subjectivities, which in turn interact with a model of the student or learner, also shaped by data.

Children

This section explores the impact of datafication on students' (or perhaps, more appropriately, children's) subjectivities. Here we build on our own and others' work on the constitution of children as learners to varying degrees of success (Bradbury 2013c; Youdell 2006a), focusing particularly on the way in which data frame how learning is defined and who is successful.

Data are based on a series of norms – in the case of the Early Excellence Baseline, statements of capability – which are applied to children as student subjects. These norms work to define what is good learning, and therefore who is recognisable as a good learner, or 'high ability', or 'more developed' (Bradbury 2013c). In the case of Baseline, they work to identify who has more potential than others by defining different starting points in terms of 'readiness' for school. As we discuss in more detail in the following chapter, this process is based on subjective judgements in the case of Early Excellence, or a combination of tests and observations with CEM and NFER. These assessments rely on a model of what a child should be able to do on entry to school, which is by no means universally agreed, and some of the teacher respondents took issue with this system, particularly the limited content of the CEM assessment:

CEM doesn't take into account anything other than literacy and maths. What happened to 'the unique child'?

(W)

This teacher refers to the phrase 'the unique child' from the EYFS policy documentation (DCSF 2008); she emphasises the difference between this approach and the limited literacy and maths content of the CEM Baseline. For her, the shift between these two approaches is too dramatic and the loss of focus on the individual child is problematic. Another written response noted the CEM assessment 'in no way encompassed the whole child' (W).

Similarly, others felt the focus on assessment drew them away from the focus on the children's *individual* learning:

I felt like I spent half a term assessing rather than teaching. I would like to get back to my actual job of moving children's learning on!

(W)

As a teacher I would rather spend time supporting children settle in properly, talk to them, get to know them as individuals, use my experience to identify needs and interest, not just fill in more forms.

(W)

Here we see how children function in a data-obsessed system, no longer as individuals, but as data-points, and how the teachers resist this shift. Williamson describes children becoming their 'data doubles', 'decoded and disassembled into discrete units of data' (2014, 1). This fieldnote refers to this trend:

As we go through the interview questions, the Reception teacher shows me her results from Early Excellence. They are presented as a grid of coloured dots, indicating whether a child is above, expected, below or well below. Each child is a horizontal line of dots, while each area is a vertical line, so that she can see who has a lot of blue dots, for example, and which areas her class do well or badly in. It looks very attractive, like a Damien Hirst spot painting. She refers to children with 'lots of blues', meaning lots of 'well belows'.

(Interview Fieldnotes, Damson)

These coloured dots are an example of the results of making a child 'enumerable and machine readable' through the collection of data (Williamson 2014, 2). The child becomes defined by these judgements of 'above' or 'below', calculated through an algorithm elsewhere. This will in turn affect how the teacher teaches them (for example, through intervention for the child with lots of blue dots), as data are the basis for the targeting of resources. Relevant here is the warning from Bryce *et al.* (2010, 15) of a 'dehumanising, shift from social to informational ways of authoritative knowing, from reliance on rich narrative accounts about people to shallow database profiles'. There is a danger of over-simplification, so that the data become reductive as well as productive; children are categorised on the basis of simple analysis, leading them to different educational trajectories.

Deleuze's concept of *dividuals* is useful here in examining this shift towards children as a source of data. Data collection processes such as Baseline Assessment constitute children as *dividuals* rather than individuals; they become data to be mined, aggregated, analysed and acted upon. As Thompson and Cook argue, 'one of the logics of *dividuation* is the end of care for individuals' (2014, 138); instead there is 'a new logic in which care is not registered', to be replaced by a focus on the data. This loss of care as a fundamental organising principle of early years and primary education, a move towards what has been called a 'culture of carelessness, grounded in rationalism' in reference to other areas of education (Lynch, 2010, 54 cited in Urban 2015, 297), is apparent in the quotes from teachers above, and this quote from a headteacher:

> If you have got 60 young people coming in through the door and in six weeks' time you have got to tick 47 boxes about all of them, of course your mind is going to be on that rather than on talking to them about their nice shiny shoes and about their pet rabbit at home and all those things that give young people a sound, secure start to learning.
>
> *(Head, Beech)*

The teachers and school leaders attempted to resist this shift towards *dividuation*, but the pressure of producing the data overcomes that commitment to care. These teachers operate within a context where 'the policy debate has hardly begun to grapple with the notion of care as a public good that must be valued' (Urban 2015, 297); Baseline Assessment is a policy which prioritises data over caring for children. However, we found similar sentiments among teachers of younger children:

> I am now pushing information into three-year-olds rather than developing meaningful relationships. Even in the nursery I now feel that pressure. If a child doesn't recognize a number or a letter I go 'aggghhh' and hold my breath. I have to remind myself the child is three and not yet ready for it.
>
> *(Teacher, Easthorne)*

This teacher wrestles with the pressure of 'pushing information' into children in order to show progress, when he knows they are 'not yet ready' and would rather be developing 'meaningful relationships'. This is the contradiction between the idea of children as individuals to care about and as producers of data.

Comments on the emotional effects of the Baseline Assessment further indicate the tensions felt by teachers between caring and assessment:

> It took much too long for each child to complete the assessment and they often became tired and irritable. Also the children wanted to answer questions

directly themselves on the computer rather than the adult pushing the appropriate buttons.

(W)

Although we do not have detailed research data on children's affective responses to Baseline Assessment, these teachers' comments suggest that datafication has an impact on the constitution of children as student subjects, at least during the process of assessment. They no longer function as the 'unique child', but are instead reduced to units of data, or 'miniature centres of calculation' (Williamson 2014, 12).

This depersonalising effect was emphasised by a number of respondents who used analogies to describe how they felt children were being understood:

Where did learning through play and having fun disappear off to and get replaced by this extreme pressure of grading and assessing children like sausages in a factory?

(W)

Children are not sausages all made the same, let them be children and trust professionals to do their job.

(W)

Gaining this kind of information assumes that they will learn according to totally adult-directed process, akin to a factory model; the great conveyor belt of education.

(W)

Testing them makes them into data driven robots.

(W)

They are children and they are not robots, not machines, they are children.
(Teacher 3, Cedar)

We have constant meetings looking at the data. It has become very clinical and children have just become numbers...
(Teacher, Northside)

These descriptions of children as 'sausages' and 'robots' within the system relate to this new status as *dividuals*; not human, not unique, but unfeeling objects to be processed and moved along the 'conveyor belt of education'. This positioning of schools as 'exam factories' (Hutchings 2015) is contrasted with 'letting them be children'. Borrowing from Simon's analysis of databased selves, we can see how children can be repositioned as non-human data, which shifts over time and can be used for prediction:

Databased selves also exhibit the capacity for growth as new data is assimilated over time and by virtue of the systems in which they are embedded, they are capable of long-term memory, risk-assessment, and the anticipation of the future. What makes databased selves different from our actual selves is that databased selves are more easily accessible, observable, manageable and predictable than we are.

(Simon 2005, 16)

As children become constituted through their data, they are 'assessed and "valued", and invested in, as a resource for the school and indirectly the nation' (Ball 2013b, 105). They are rendered more manageable and predictable, and thus further distanced from the lived reality, becoming unthinking 'robots'. As Kelly, Downey and Rietdijk describe, the prioritisation of performance data turns 'schools into factories in a forlorn attempt to measure the immeasurable' (2010, 106).

The extreme analogies quoted above also reveal the affective impact for the teachers, who feel children's identities and emotions are being subsumed by the pressure to produce data. As we discuss further in our next section, the operation of power and control here is significant: children are powerless but important as the 'raw material' of data production, while power lies with those who control the data.

School leaders and data-based roles

In this final section on data-driven subjectivities, we consider the role of school leaders as managers and interpreters of data, and the new roles and reliance created by datafication. New flows of power (and capital) are created as the ability to analyse and process data becomes a key skill (Selwyn, Henderson and Chao 2015; Williamson 2016b).

As with any policy enactment, school leaders have a different role from classroom teachers: 'part of the role of headteachers […] is to join up disparate policies into an institutional narrative, a story about how the school works and what it does – ideally articulated through an "improvement" plot of some kind' (Ball *et al.* 2011a, 626). The headteachers and other school leaders we interviewed were similarly engaged in a process of interpreting the dominance of data, and attempting to translate it to fit with their school's ethos. This was done with varying degrees of resistance and rebellion, as we discuss in more detail in Chapter 5; here the job of data analysis is described as reducing time to support others:

I should be in classrooms supporting colleagues but I spend far too much time looking at assessment data and it is for proving to Ofsted that we are great. I'm an expert at speaking to Ofsted and tell them everything they want to know about data in our school. *But actually I would be far more effective if I were in class and the children would benefit more.*

(Deputy Headteacher, Easthorne; our emphasis)

As Manovich argues, hierarchies and divisions are produced between the 'data classes': those who can collect, process or analyse data (2012). Power and authority lie with the small number who can analyse – school leaders, but also outside agencies, as we discuss below. This deputy headteacher identifies being able to 'talk about data' as the skill she possesses with most value, although she accepts that the children would benefit more if she were in the classroom. Those teachers without these skills remain in the classroom, while the 'expert' prepares for the crucial event of speaking to Ofsted.

School leaders have power over the classroom teachers in how they interpret data, including affecting decisions on their salaries (DfE 2013b). As Pratt (2016) comments, regular meetings about 'my data' with the headteacher are a key feature of classroom teachers' lives. But at the same time senior teachers are also subject to demands from Ofsted and local authorities or multi-academy trusts, who scrutinise data.

> Schools currently do a baseline on entry to Year R, and send it to us and we carefully analyse the baseline and do a projected Good Level of Development. Schools use that in-depth analysis of the data as a support and *challenge to drive improvements forward*. We set a percentage projection but it is a very crude one – so they need to go back and check it and *drill right down into it to set challenges for themselves*.
>
> *(Local Authority Advisor)*

Here we see how data production, exchange and prediction have become central to the relationship between the LA and the school. The LA engages in a process of 'support and challenge' to 'drive improvement', (Roberts-Holmes 2015) based on their analysis of the data. They set up a prediction – albeit a 'crude one' – but encourage the school leaders to do further detailed analysis, in a process of 'constant self-evaluation' of performance (Fenwick, Mangez and Ozga 2014, 5).

Thus, the headteachers are in a difficult position in the chain of data production, controlling those below but subject to demands from above. The headteachers affected by Baseline Assessment described feeling it was part of an assemblage of policy that made them feel vulnerable, under attack and lost:

> As you know we were given six choices […] So I guess I went into headteacher defence mode and said we will do the quickest system that tells the least so then whoever is here in seven years will be least punished by it. […] We are bound down and broken by those judgements and the way people view us. […] I don't think I have ever come across a situation where heads feel so at sea. You know when levels came in nobody, if I am honest, nobody really liked it but having had the system for so many years and everybody knowing what it means, every teacher knows what it means, we are now back in a situation where nobody really knows what they are doing.
>
> *(Head, Damson)*

> It just feels like we have got a whole assessment pit at the moment that nobody is quite sure how we are all going to come out at the end of this year really. What that is going to look like, which is not good. [The situation] is not good. Especially when the stakes are so high and you are looking at how we are judged and all the Ofsted...
>
> *(Head, Cedar)*

As referred to in this first quote, the policy of 'assessment without levels', announced under the coalition government in 2013 and implemented in 2015, removed the familiarity of national curriculum levels. For some, this combination of removing an established system and introducing the uncertainties of Baseline Assessment was contradictory, and put them under additional pressure. For all these headteachers, there was a feeling that the situation is damaging – they feel 'punished', 'under the cosh', 'bound down and broken', 'at sea' and in a 'pit'. This emotive language reveals the affective impact of policy, which is seen as a tool with which to criticise schools; one headteacher referred to Baseline Assessment as 'giving us enough rope to hang ourselves' (Cedar). This description of intense pressure chimes with findings from recent research on other sectors of education and accountability (Hutchings 2015; Ehren, Jones and Perryman 2016).

The uncertainties of the future leave the headteachers feeling anxious and lost, particularly at a time when their support from the local authority has been reduced. As one headteacher commented, 'Once upon a time something new like this would have come in and the Local Authority would have solved the problem for us' (Head, Damson). The wider move of reducing LA funding and therefore support for schools exacerbates the problems of new policies by leaving individual schools to find appropriate solutions on their own. School leaders' response is to be defensive and reduce the threat as much as possible, as the quote above suggests, by finding the solution which will leave them 'least punished', thus limiting the potential damage caused. As Ball *et al.* argue, 'One of the peculiar features of current education policy in England is the extent to which policy must be seen to be done' (2011a, 629). The headteacher's role is to defend the school by producing data – making sure the policy is seen to be done – but to simultaneously limit the negative impact.

Given this vulnerability felt by school leaders, those who can 'solve the problem' in place of local authorities have great attraction – these are the elite of Manovich's 'data classes' (2012). Much of the attraction of private companies – as seen in the case of Baseline Assessment – rests in their ability to act like a school-based 'data guru' (Lingard and Sellar 2013). These 'data intermediaries' (Williamson 2016b), whether they be individuals or companies, have the ability to draw out key conclusions from the data. These conclusions may harm or benefit the school, and as such they hold great power; it is an 'expertocracy' (Grek 2013).

Productive data

In this chapter we have begun our analysis by drawing together several ways in which data are productive. Data are productive of particular pedagogies and practices, including those that prioritise some children over others, and some areas of the curriculum over those not included in assessments. Data collection affects relationships as teachers become data collectors rather than engage with individual children. Data-based practices create tensions, as other ideological positions on the purpose of education are forced out. Finally, and most significant, is the production of data-driven subjectivities, as teachers, children and school leaders are constituted through their relationship to the stages of data production and processing. Teachers are torn between their roles as carers and as producers of data which demonstrates that learning is happening; children are reduced to *dividuals*, inert blocks of data to be mined; and school leaders are simultaneously in control – of the analysis of the data and therefore the teachers that collect it – and under the control of outside actors such as the local authority and the private companies who can help them negotiate a policy terrain where they feel 'at sea'. Having focused on the *productive* elements of datafication, we turn in the following chapter to the ways in which data are *reductive*.

4

DATA, REDUCTIONISM AND THE PROBLEMS OF ASSESSING YOUNG CHILDREN

Introduction

This chapter examines the ways in which data collection processes simplify and abstract complex phenomena into numbers, a process of *reduction*. This aspect of data use in education is linked to a hyper-positivist scientific paradigm, in which 'reductionism is the name of the game' (Alexander, 2010, 812 cited in Moss, Dahlberg, Grieshaber *et al.* 2016). The multifaceted nature of learning and interaction is simplified to figures, labels such as 'below expected levels' or 'above', or into colour codes on a spreadsheet. In the case of Baseline Assessment, the DfE required that the end result be a single number, which summed up the child's attainment across all the areas of early learning, including emotional and physical development, literacy and mathematics. In reference to wider practices of reduction to single numbers or scores, Lingard, Martino and Rezai-Rashti comment: 'the single number hides the technical work that has gone into category creation, measurement, the creation of metrics, data collection and analysis' (2013, 546). For the children assessed through Baseline, the contingent nature of the assessment, which we detail here, further obscures the complex 'technical work' involved in designing these assessments. Official guidance for Baseline Assessment stated that 'each assessment item must require a single, objective, binary decision to be made by the scorer' (STA 2014, 1); thus even when teachers were involved in decision making (as opposed to scores being generated by tablet-based questions), their answers had to be simply either positive or negative.

In this chapter we explore this reduction by examining the effects and impacts of Baseline Assessment's use of simplified data in primary schools. We begin by considering the problematic nature of such reduction, and the problems of accuracy it creates. We also explore the negation of English as an additional language (EAL) children's competencies in their first language through the assessment; the further narrowing of the curriculum; and the problem of assessing children of different ages.

The inaccuracy of binary judgements

Baseline Assessment's hyper-positive scientific paradigm required the production of a single number, and that the three Baseline Assessment providers had to construct binary 'yes' or 'no' responses to a series of statements.

> It is a binary yes/no! And children aren't like that, children are more compli-cated than that ... those contradictions exist within the child and that is a true reflection of an individual, a unique child, who can be complicated.
>
> *(Teacher 2, Beech)*

This need for a binary judgement contrasted with Reception teachers' established 'best fit' approach using the Developmental Matters framework, which allowed teachers greater flexibility across a range of competency, skill and age charts to establish where children's cognitive and emotional development most accurately lay. This 'best fit' approach was seen as more accurate and reliable because it gave the teachers, in dialogue with others, the opportunity to record what the children were capable of within a series of complex paragraphs, and how their learning might be developed. However, with Baseline Assessment binaries, there was no room for subtlety:

> I guess with the yes or no there is no room for that is there? There is no wriggle room.
>
> *(Teacher 1, Beech)*

> With this, it is just a yes or no. Whereas we can show progress with Develop-ment Matters [...] But there is no way of doing that with EExBa, it is either yes or no.
>
> *(Teacher 2, Beech)*

> It is difficult to assess whether the child should achieve it or not (i.e. they may achieve part of the statement, but not another part of it, meaning the official answer is 'no') and so the data does not give the whole and true picture of a child's abilities in that aspect.
>
> *(W, Early Excellence user)*

These comments demonstrate the teachers' professional frustration as they attempted to navigate and negotiate the simplicity of either 'yes' or 'no'. As the comments above note, binary statements did not allow for the fact that a child may potentially have achieved at least part of a statement; hence binary statements negated and ignored what the child *could do*, leading to the generation of inaccurate information.

> Baseline does not support our knowledge of children, as it merely states whether or not they can independently do specific things; this does not provide information as to where the children ARE, simply where they are not.
>
> *(W, CEM user)*

This tendency towards a negative and deficit measurement system is even more problematic when we consider the temptation to keep results low, as we discuss in the following chapter.

In thinking about how Baseline Assessment operates in the classroom, we need to bear in mind MacNaughton's reminder that: 'the everyday language, ethics, routines, rituals, practices, expectations, ideas, documents and invocations of quality in early childhood services are formed through and motivated by *very particular understandings of children* and how best to educate them' (2005, 1 emphasis added). For these teachers, the particular understandings of children underlying their practices were based on the socio-cultural principles of the Early Years Foundation Stage (EYFS), and so they were used to more complex narrative assessments. Assessing the lived social practices of young children's learning includes being able to tune into their contextually specific multiple and diverse 'voices' in order to understand their meaning-making practices. Baseline Assessment's stark and de-contextualised reductionism stands in contrast to Reception teachers' contextually driven EYFS assessments, which are underpinned by Vygotsky's socio-cultural theoretical argument that children learn in sociable contexts. To ignore this can be 'disastrous':

> to fairly and truly judge what a person can do, you need to know how the talent (skill, knowledge) you are assessing is situated in – placed within – the lived social practices of the person as well as his or her interpretations of those practices … many a standardized test can be perfectly 'scientific' and useless at the same time; in a worst case scenario, it can be disastrous.
>
> *(Gee 2007, 364 cited in Moss, Dahlberg, Grieshaber et al. 2016)*

Within this a socio-cultural approach to teaching and learning is centred on a 'relationship between human mental functioning on the one hand, and the cultural, institutional, and historical situations in which this functioning occurs on the other' (Wertsch and Del Rio 1995, 3). Socio-cultural assessment is concerned with the participation of young children in meaningful contexts in collaboration with other children and adults. For example, within narrative-based learning stories teachers' long-term observations of children participating together in learning activities in a range of different meaningful contexts make visible what young children are capable of doing in collaboration with others (Fleer 2010; Broadhead 2006). Within socio-cultural assessments, authentic relationships are central:

> Assessment of early learning and development is informal, carried out over time, and in the context of the child's interactions with materials, objects and

other people. It is most effective when it is authentic in the sense that it takes place in real-life contexts where it is embedded in tasks that children see as significant, meaningful and worthwhile. Play is a key part of children's learning and development and thus an important part of the assessment process. Informal assessments, carried out as children engage in experiences they see as relevant and meaningful, are likely to produce the best and most comprehensive picture of early learning and development.

(Dunphy 2008, 4)

Crucially, such an approach is respectful of young children's multiple voices and ways of expressing what they are capable of doing, and allowed for the creative and imaginative 'One Hundred Languages of Children', which suggests that children are 'rich in potential, strong, powerful, competent and, most of all, connected to adults and other children' (Malaguzzi *et al.* 1996). In contrast, Baseline Assessment's approach can be seen as disrespectful to young children's competencies and abilities because it refused any notion of context, complexity and ambiguity, as it attempted to bring the allure of scientific authority and technical precision to the sociable complexity of young children's learning. This policy attempted to strip away the educational politics, ethics and complex lived realities of young children's learning, through a technical bureaucratic exercise representing an extreme form of educational reductionism (Moss, Dahlberg, Grieshaber *et al.* 2016). Baseline Assessment thus represented what Malaguzzi has termed 'nothing but a ridiculous simplification of knowledge and a robbing of meaning from individual histories' (cited in Moss, Dahlberg, Grieshaber *et al.* 2016, 344). Moreover, it must be noted that any assessment of children against set 'developmental' statements through observation is a 'disciplinary apparatus', which involves particular understandings of knowledge and what can be 'seen'; as one of the early years educators in MacNaughton's study comments, drawing on Foucault, 'I turn my gaze on the child expecting to know all of her' (2005, 58). Given Reception teachers' understandings of the socio-cultural principles of assessment and their concomitant professional desire to record children's competencies, it was no surprise that the teachers remained strongly against Baseline Assessment's simplistic binary reductionism; only 7.7 per cent of teachers in our survey agreed with the statement 'Baseline Assessment is a fair and accurate way to assess children'.

In contrast to the DfE's scientific desire for neutrality and objectivity, the teachers understood that making judgements about young children's complex, ambiguous and context-dependent learning was inevitably and unavoidably particular, individually determined and inevitably subjective. Making judgements about four-year-olds' complex and context-specific characteristics of effective learning, such as 'risk taking', 'curiosity' and 'persistence', were seen by one headteacher as 'rather crude and a bit silly' (Head, Beech). Another headteacher argued that individual teachers' different experiences, understandings and interpretations would inevitably lead to highly personalised judgements:

So look at this statement, 'Curiosity: shows curiosity about objects in the world around them and has particular interests'. That is open to such a wide range of interpretations! And also you are judging children according to what you think is typical, aren't you? You might be judging children according to the types of children you have had in the past or your own child – so you see how very vague it all is and how subjective.

(Head, Alder)

Clearly a teacher's understanding of children's curiosity is highly subjective, variable and context dependent. For this headteacher with 25 years of experience the assessment of four-year-olds produced 'wildly different judgements from school to school and teacher to teacher' because teachers' judgements were dependent upon different individual experiences and context-specific interpretations. Teachers' understandings that the judgements were inevitably open to subjective interpretation were reflected throughout the case study schools and the survey sample:

Observational assessments are subjective, they are only as good as the teachers' knowledge of what they are assessing.

(Teacher 2, Elm)

The interpretation of some statements and exemplifications are open to misinterpretation and have caused uneasiness among our reception team.

(W)

The statements are still open to interpretation which is why the data reports are not showing an entirely accurate picture of children.

(W)

There have still been huge inconsistencies about the practitioner expectations for judging how children have met the statements.

(W)

Here the teachers demonstrated their concerns about their colleagues' varied interpretations and inconsistencies, leading to inaccurate and misleading information. The idea that any assessment of young children can be simple is based on a misunderstanding of the complexity of children's learning at this age.

This is not to say that assessment is an impossible task with young children, only that we need to bear in mind the discourses underpinning assessment, because 'truth claims based on expertise, technology and management seek to impose consensus and to close down the contestability of subjects' (Dahlberg and Moss 2009, xiv). Reception teachers were experienced in making detailed long-term observational assessments and judgements about young children's learning for the professionally respected Early Years Foundation Stage Profile (Roberts-Holmes 2012). These judgements were based on a detailed long-term analysis of evidence and dialogue with other colleagues and parents; though, this assessment also has its associated problems of unreliability (Bradbury 2013c). Similarly, the internationally respected Early Childhood Environment Rating Scales (ECERS; Sylva and Taggart 2010) are methodologically centred upon 'inter-rater reliability', which is dependent upon teachers' collaborative dialogue, interpretations and evidence in professional decision making. Extensive international testing of the inter-rater reliability of the ECERS has shown that such dialogue between teachers coupled with intensive five-day training workshops is essential to the generation of accurately agreed observational scales (Sylva and Taggart 2010). For both the EYFS Profile and the ECERS scales, intensive training combined with teachers' professional dialogue contributed to more valid judgements and assessments.[1] Interestingly, despite Baseline Assessment not requiring such professional dialogue, many teachers did discuss their judgements with colleagues, thereby attempting at least some notion of 'inter-rater reliability'.

> So it is open to interpretation, as I say it would have been very hard to do without having another teacher to talk to and sort of sound off ideas.
>
> *(Teacher 1, Elm)*

Baseline Assessment, however, did not require formal evidence to support teachers' professional judgements and rather than encouraging professional dialogue and moderation, teachers were encouraged to 'err on the side of caution' when unsure about making particular judgements. Teachers saw this as a serious flaw:

> Well, the 'no evidence' to me makes it less solid, doesn't it? Because there is no evidence, it is just a practitioner's point of view.
>
> *(Head, Alder)*

> Having evidence to prove that is important, but something crude that is just yes and no, I don't know if that is any use long term or not.
>
> *(Teacher 2, Alder)*

Without sufficient detailed evidence to support their judgements these teachers doubted the reliability of Baseline Assessment; as a result, many planned to keep their existing baseline assessments. This production of 'shadow' data is indicative of the perceived difference between what Selwyn, Henderson and Chao (2015) term 'compliance data', produced to fulfil a commitment (usually policy based), and 'useful data', which aids learning. The teachers' continued use of their own baselines reflects Kelly and Downey's finding that teachers see 'internal' data as more trustworthy, more realistic, useful for tracking, more specific and better able to take into account other factors (2011, 158). Thus they have a strong preference for 'internal' data over 'external' data produced for the purposes of accountability. In this case, Baseline Assessment proved of little use in the teachers' planning for the year, remaining an exercise undertaken purely for other purposes.

The above inconsistencies around interpretation were exacerbated by the limited training teachers received because the DfE only paid for one teacher per school to attend a provider's training. Some of the primary schools paid for extra teachers to attend the training at the school's expense, demonstrating their professional desire to make Baseline Assessment as accurate as possible. However, even where staff did attend training, there were concerns about the consistency of the training being offered.

> Even though there has been training, not everybody has gone on the training ... and it would appear that not all the training has been cascaded to the practitioners and there seems to be quite a bit of confusion ... For some children the baseline is not being done until six weeks, for some it is done on week one or week two, and I am not sure of the validity of that.
>
> *(Assistant Head, Cedar)*

> Training needs to be consistent across the country!
>
> *(W)*

Schools attempted to address such inconsistencies by establishing moderation, even though this was not required by the DfE, again demonstrating that teachers attempted to ensure that their judgements were as accurate and fair as possible:

> I know we are not meant to moderate but I think there is a place for moderation if only to ensure that everybody is singing from the same sheet when they are doing the assessments.
>
> *(Assistant Head, Cedar)*

For these teachers, the need to produce 'accurate' data was more important than the instruction not to moderate and the sacrifice in terms of time. Even so, teachers realised that moderation itself was a process of interpretation: 'Having moderated between cluster schools it is still very subjective' (W). One headteacher was frustrated with the associated costs in terms of time and money especially when the teachers should be engaged in forming relationships with the children:

> How are you going to moderate it without wasting huge amounts of money and time? You know I could pay thousands of pounds to have all my Reception teachers spending a month moderating when really what they should be doing is nurturing the children and making sure that the children are settled and getting to know the children.
>
> *(Head, Alder)*

In these examples, we see the teachers' commitment to 'getting it right', even when they do not agree with the principle; similarly research on the EYFS Profile has suggested that teachers have a strong professional commitment to 'accuracy', despite questioning the idea of labelling children with a score at this age (Bradbury 2012).

These contradictions are part of Ball's 'terrors of performativity' (2003); being given impossible tasks, but attempting to do the best they can, has emotional costs.

Young children's emotional competencies

We now turn to the issue of age more generally, and the emotional impact of attempts to collect data about 'development' with young children. Children in England experience more testing than many of their counterparts internationally, and the associated stress may contribute to the low levels of well-being shown by children in the UK in international comparisons (Unicef 2011). Issues of mental health difficulties in response to testing and academic pressure are a particular concern because teachers argue that they have less time to focus on pupils' social and emotional development (Hutchings 2015). Whitebread and Bingham (2012) suggest that the development of young children's well-being and learning dispositions are more important and reliable predictors of later academic achievement than early gains in the narrow skills involved in literacy and mathematics. Elsewhere – for example, in Finland – early childhood education is focused upon health and well-being rather than cognitive achievement (Sahlberg 2014). The Scandinavian emphasis upon educative play until the children are six and seven, combined with very low rates of child poverty, at around 4 per cent, means that by the age of 11 Finnish children perform better than their English counterparts. Sahlberg (2014) notes that the success of Finnish schools is partly due to the absence of ranking of children according to educational success, hence student 'failure' is removed.

Regarding the Scandinavian model of early childhood education, one of the headteachers commented:

> I think doing any sort of reputable assessment of very young children is dodgy because the children are so young. You know if those children were in Denmark they wouldn't have had to pick up a pencil yet.
>
> *(Head, Damson)*

In England, the curriculum for early years (EYFS) emphasises the 'characteristics of effective learning', including resilience, motivation, creativity and emotional well-being. Baseline Assessment attempted to simplistically measure such learning dispositions when the children had not yet had the opportunity to develop them:

> I did have children that were crying and I just couldn't get anything out of them at all because they were too upset to do anything, even when I left it later on. Some children just refused or just weren't ready and I know they said you only assess them when they are ready, but some children, well, you got to the point where you had to assess them because it had to be done whether they were ready or not. And obviously then it is not accurate because they weren't at a stage when they wanted to say things.
>
> *(Teacher 1, Cedar)*

It's ridiculous. It's not a fair representation of children. Many young children are not yet confident enough to show their new teacher what they can do when put on the spot.

(W, Early Excellence user)

Some children looked at me and said 'I can't read' when asked to read parts of the assessment. It was heartbreaking to see their reaction to it and I spent a lot of time reassuring children.

(W, CEM user)

Trying to assess children who are not yet sufficiently emotionally competent is highly problematic, as it can lead to the establishment of low expectations for a child's whole educational career. This means that the assessment itself provides an inaccurate and detrimental measure, as well as an upsetting experience. Early Excellence's Baseline Assessment was aware of this problem in measuring young children before they were ready to show what they could achieve and hence attempted to use the widely known and respected early years Leuven Scales of Well Being and Involvement (Laevers, Declercq and Thomas 2010) to ascertain whether the child was 'settled'. Unfortunately, however, the strict DfE regulations meant that Baseline Assessment had to be carried out within six weeks of the children starting school regardless of whether or not the children had 'settled'. This lead not only to inaccurate data being generated but was ethically inappropriate and potentially damaging for children's developing self-confidence, self-esteem and learner identity, at the very beginning of their educational careers. Thus we see again how the prioritisation of data produces 'a new logic in which care is not registered' (Thompson and Cook 2014, 138).

There were further problems arising from the young age of the children involved: teachers pointed out that four-year-old children who have just started school tire easily and hence those assessed at the end of a long day were tired and would score lower than those assessed in the morning. This was particularly the case with the computer-based assessments.

Due to having to do one at a time, some children were assessed in the morning and others at the end of the day when they were tired and easily distracted.

(W, NFER user)

Similarly, respondents pointed out that if children were tested at different weeks then their computer test results and assessments would also be distorted because young children learn at a rapid rate in their first few weeks in Reception:

In addition one member of staff administered the whole test so those children who did it in the first week of starting generally had lower scores than children who did it in weeks 5 and 6 into the term.

(W, CEM user)

Here the basic daily management of teaching and learning with large numbers of young children and often few staff lend themselves against generating accurate and valid data. This is the 'messy' lived social reality and context in which such data were generated; it is not a scientific lab in which all the many variables have been accounted for. So, the problem here is that even 'objective' computer tests are in fact distorted, inaccurate and invalid due to the inherent multiplicity of testing variables in individual school contexts such as the ages of the children, timings and arrangements of the tests. Interestingly such concerns around the inaccuracy of Baseline Assessment have already been raised in one survey school during an Ofsted inspection:

> Our school's concern is that we don't feel the test reflects the actual level of children, i.e. the children in my school have always in our opinion been well above national average yet the test shows otherwise and that children are below the average. We had Ofsted in this week who queried the accuracy of our test results as they felt children were above average ... but we have simply followed the test.
>
> *(W, NFER user)*

Thus even the CEM and NFER computer-based tests, which it could be argued were more accurate since they were less reliant on teacher judgement (although they too have teacher observation sections), were equally perceived as inaccurate and invalid as the Early Excellence assessment. This is in keeping with the arguments that Baseline Assessment is located within a scientific paradigm that cannot accurately measure young children who are emotionally and cognitively highly varied depending upon a whole range of variables that are impossible to reduce, quantify and compare.

This lack of recognisability suggests too great a distance between the child and their 'data double'. Some teachers commented that they did not 'recognise' their classes in the data that were returned to them from Early Excellence, as children were placed differently from how they perceived them. We can conceptualise this distance as occurring at 'surveillance interfaces', where we see the 'interaction of the data doubles of databased selves with real bodies' (Simon 2005): 'These are the local, material sites where something like interpellation or attachment takes place; where the subject recognizes herself in her databased double' (2005, 18). Here the teacher does not recognise the child, and thus she resists the power of the database and algorithm to define what these children are. Althusser's concept of interpellation, where an individual is recognised as a subject through the call of another, can be used here to examine this disjuncture between real and databased selves. As Simon continues: 'Minimally, the subject must be able to recognize him or herself in their databased double for interpellation to function and failing this there must be some other means to attach material bodies to digital forms' (2005, 17). These teachers, acting on behalf of the children, do not recognise their pupils as subjects in the data because of the distance between database and material body; the data are, as in the quote above, not a 'reflection', but something created for the purposes of accountability.

Children with English as an additional language

We turn now to some groups of children who may be systematically disadvantaged by the use of data in education, particularly where they are used for prediction. As Selwyn notes, 'predictive' profiling:

> can lead to a variety of statistical discrimination, where individuals are reclassified in terms of their associations and linkages with others, and then included/excluded on the basis of the attributes of the groups and data segments that they belong to.
>
> *(Selwyn 2015, 74)*

Indeed, there is a history of using past attainment of pupils with similar demographic characteristics to predict attainment and measure comparative 'value added' in England (Bradbury 2011a). In the case of Baseline Assessment, the issue of inaccuracy leading to low expectations was particularly acute for one group of children: those who spoke English as an additional language (EAL). Unlike the EYFS Profile, Baseline Assessment had to be conducted only in English, rather than in home languages. This approach belies the positivist principle that 'everything can be reduced to a common outcome, standard and measure. What it cannot do is accommodate, let alone, welcome, diversity – of paradigm or theory, pedagogy or provision, childhood or culture' (Moss, Dahlberg, Grieshaber *et al.* 2016, 348). Such an intolerance of linguistic diversity negated EAL children's potential, by refusing to acknowledge what learning they could demonstrate in their home language. In England at least 19 per cent of primary school children have a first language other than English and in many areas the proportion is much higher (DfE 2014a; Strand 2016). Not surprisingly, when EAL children first start school in Reception class, where they may have had less exposure to English on average, they achieve lower outcomes (Andrews 2009). However, the association between EAL and achievement decreases markedly at the end of Key Stage 2 as they become more able to access the curriculum and assessments (Strand 2016). By insisting that Baseline be conducted in English, the DfE produced a policy which risked establishing low scores and therefore low expectations for all EAL children. The teachers we interviewed who taught many EAL children were concerned:

> The problem we have found this year is because we have to do it – it has to be conducted in English. I think that has impacted quite a bit. And normally for our on entry assessment we would – most of our support staff are bilingual and for the majority language here – so we would use that to inform our on entry assessments. Now with the Baseline having to be conducted in English I think it will impact on the results.
>
> *(Assistant Head, Cedar)*

EAL children it was disadvantaging wasn't it? Because you couldn't do it in another language, it had to be in English.

(Teacher 2, Elm)

It is important to note that not allowing the Baseline to be conducted in children's home languages meant that what these children were capable of doing and their understanding was not adequately accounted for. By not being able to assess EAL children's abilities, comprehension and achievements served to further undermine the accuracy of Baseline Assessment and its credibility as a measure of progress. This was the case both with observation-based assessments which rely on children speaking and the more formal computer-based assessments which may include instructions that EAL children cannot understand.

> Baseline must be fair for EAL children – I had 6 this year, 3 of whom achieved less with Baseline Assessment but did well in my own assessments as I allowed them to use their own language.
>
> *(W)*

> I come from an inner city school with very high numbers of EAL children. The prescriptive questions detailing what you can/can't say meant that some things I knew my children would be able to do with a simplified instruction, they couldn't do as part of the Baseline.
>
> *(W, NFER user)*

> Not having any opportunity to note children with EAL is a concern as this will clearly mark them lower than necessary.
>
> *(W)*

> Children who are EAL or didn't understand the question in a certain way were unable to answer questions correctly, affecting their scores.
>
> *(W)*

Even within a context of an education system with marked disparities in attainment by ethnic group (Gillborn 2008; Strand 2016), the enactment of a policy which systematically disadvantages EAL children (most of whom come from minoritised backgrounds) is still surprising. The reductive quality of Baseline here has a potentially serious detrimental effect on children's educational careers. There may be long-term consequences for these children, who may be seen as having made expected progress even when they have low attainment later in their school careers.

The importance of age

The issue of 'summer-born' children's attainment is frequently raised in primary education (for example, Weale 2016; NFER 2016). Under the existing EYFS

Profile, the proportion of summer-born children reaching the benchmark 'Good Level of Development' (who started school younger than their peers) is 59 per cent. This compares to 79 per cent of autumn-born children, who start school when they are almost five (DfE 2016a). The importance of age is often recognised in this phase through age-adjusted scores. However, within the government regulations for Baseline Assessment, there was no allowance made for a child's age, despite the rapid development which takes place between a child's fourth and fifth birthdays. The simple demands of Baseline Assessment were therefore unable to accurately reflect these large differences between young children's development. One parent we interviewed commented:

> I think the four to five gap is phenomenal. And so maybe assessing those who are all new to it and just four by a few days, maybe against kids who are five in a few days might be extremely different.
>
> *(Parent, Alder)*

The autumn-born children may have had an extra year of pre-school education, which would make them more amenable to a classroom setting.

> My son he has only just turned four [...] He is very young in his year so obviously he is going to be compared with children who are a bit older. It does seem very early. [...] He did go to nursery at the school here as well so he was used to some of the routines, but some of the children they may not have had that experience at all ... it might be all very new to them so it does seem quite an early time to be doing this.
>
> *(Parent, Beech)*

Reductionism, the curriculum and 'ability'

The guidelines for Baseline Assessment explicitly specified a narrow curriculum focus upon communication, English and mathematics progression between Reception and Key Stage 1:

> The clear majority of the content domain must be clearly linked to the learning and development requirements of the communication and language, literacy and mathematics areas of learning from the EYFS, appropriate for children's age and experience at the start of reception and must demonstrate a clear progression towards the key stage 1 national curriculum in English and mathematics.
>
> *(STA 2014, 1)*

Here Baseline Assessment's curriculum focus had a 'reductive effect on the provision and experiences of schooling ... as curriculum width is reduced to ensure the enhancement of test scores' (Lingard, Martino and Rezai-Rashti 2013, 553). The narrow emphasis upon formal literacy and mathematics was consistent with the ongoing school readiness agenda that has increasingly drawn early years and Reception children into the narrowed primary school national curriculum and has been dubbed the 'schoolification' of the early years. Here the early years is functionally reduced to that of preparation and delivery of children who are 'readied' for the rapid skills and knowledge acquisition needed in the primary school and later for their assigned pathways: 'If we want our children to succeed at school, go on to university or into an apprenticeship and thrive in later life, we must get it right in the early years' (DfE 2013a, 6). The focus on mathematics and literacy in Baseline was in keeping with the DfE's policy prioritisation of 'essential knowledge and concepts' and 'the essentials of English language and literature, core mathematical processes and science' (DfE 2010). This focus was found within the revised and 'slimmed down' EYFS curriculum (DfE 2012, 1), which stated that 'a good foundation in mathematics and literacy is crucial for later success, particularly in terms of children's readiness for school'. Such a reduction in the curriculum width has also been noted in US kindergartens, where there has been a reported increase in standardised testing upon academic subjects and a concomitant reduction in time spent on play and art activities (Bassok, Latham and Rorem 2016), leading some to ask, 'Is kindergarten the new first grade?'. Within the English EYFS Profile, the increased focus upon literacy and maths is evident in the raised thresholds for the EYFS maths and literacy Good Levels of Development (DfE 2012). As we have written elsewhere, in order to meet the increased demands of the reformed EYFS Profile, Reception teachers grouped children by 'ability', to strategically focus upon identified children who they attempted to move from 'emerging' to 'expected' (or ones to twos) (Roberts-Holmes 2015). The early years advisor explained:

> It's about who's going to achieve the GLD. So we say 'they're easily gonna make it, thank you very much'. And we say 'they're never going to make it so go over there and have a nice time' and we look to the middle group. We target these children because they are the ones who may make it. It's the same as Year 6 Sats. So you put all your effort and intervention into those that are just below and it's a very unfair system.
>
> *(Early Years Local Authority Advisor)*

This functional allocation of Reception children into three crude groups based upon predicted pupil progress data was similar to Gillborn and Youdell's (2000) 'educational triage' in secondary schools where identified children were given increased resources to ensure they achieved in the 'A–C economy' of GCSE exams. Gillborn and Youdell (2000) maintained that a focus on some children led to a neglect of others, with uneven access to teacher resources. In the US, Booher-Jennings (2005) noted a similar process of educational triage with seven-year-old children: in preparation for a literacy test, 'bubble kids' were identified who were then allocated extra resources in order to pass the test. Similarly, Vince's (2016) study demonstrated that 'cusp children' were identified in Pupil Progress Review meetings. These cusp children were allocated extra time with the teacher, who attempted to convert these identified children's Good Levels of Development from 'failing' ones into 'passing' twos.

Given that Reception classes were already using educational triage to group children by ability to achieve particular results, it was not surprising that Baseline Assessment scores were used in a similar manner to group children by some schools.

> Also there is no time given to these poor little children to settle in before they are assessed and in our school they are put into ability groups based on these results!
>
> *(W)*

> Baseline Assessment helps us to group the children in differentiated maths and phonics group.
>
> *(W)*

The Cambridge Primary Review Trust (2013) was very clear in their consultation response that 'notions of fixed ability would be exacerbated by a baseline test in reception that claimed to reliably predict future attainment'. This is because with any assessment there was a tendency for children to be 'sucked up' as objectified and quantified data (Selwyn 2015; Williamson 2014), which is then used to rank and ascribe children into particular 'ability' groups. The plan to judge schools' performance based on the Baseline results compared to Key Stage 2 tests exacerbates this tendency towards ability grouping, as it suggest that children's attainment can be predicted from their score on entry. Predictions across seven years were to be made using algorithms (mathematical calculations); although these were not available to the schools, the idea that children have a set ability or potential which can be predicted reinforces practices of 'ability' grouping, setting and streaming.

Baseline Assessment data here provide 'actionable intelligence' (Williamson 2015a) and underpin predictive pedagogical decision making and choices, such as ability grouping and setting. Wrigley (2015), however, states that it is not valid to attempt to extrapolate progress expectations in such a hyper-positivist scientific and linear fashion from the early years to the end of Key Stage 2, especially given the serious reservations of the accuracy of the starting point. This, he suggests, is not a 'criticism of the competence of the organisations providing baseline assessment but of this deeply flawed government policy'. The DfE requirement to make predictions across seven years was particularly problematic given that two of the three providers had no data linking particular pupils' performance in their assessments with how the child does later in KS1 or KS2. For example, even CEM, arguably the most statistically experienced of the three providers, claimed that its Baseline Assessment test provided 'excellent predictive validity' with correlations of around 0.7, meaning that predictions from Baseline are likely to be correct about four times out of ten (Wrigley 2015). This was based upon relating scores at the end of Reception to KS1 results in reading; Baseline Assessments taken at the start of Reception and extending to KS2 are likely to be even less reliable. So, studies mapping previous early years scores to later attainment have found that even the strongest correlations mean that no more than half the children will later attain the anticipated score, and the spread of later attainment is very wide. This level of predictive inaccuracy invalidates the Baseline policy as it was supposed to provide a firm basis to *compare* different schools' 'value added' across the seven years. The fact that schools might be held to account on faulty predictive data is problematic for the school itself. The teachers were very wary of Baseline and did not believe that Baseline Assessment provided statistically valid or reliable information and hence had serious reservations about making any such predictions based upon such invalid and unreliable starting points.

> I find the awarding of a point score to four and five-year-olds unhelpful and fail to see how it can be an accurate predictor of future performance.
>
> *(W)*

The potentially damaging effect of Baseline Assessment is identified here: that for children with low scores ('below typical'), even if they make good progress, it will be seen as acceptable for them to remain low-attaining at age 11. This is a problem inherent in any 'value added' measure where the baseline is known and is more likely to affect those groups who are lower attaining within the system in general, such as ethnic minorities, children receiving free school meals, children with SEN and EAL and some summer-born children (Bradbury 2011a). Despite these teachers' reservations, the language used to describe Baseline Assessment surrounds these false predictions and low expectations with an aura of science, reinforcing dividing up children on the basis of fixed 'ability'. This low scoring within Baseline Assessment was problematic because research into ability grouping has demonstrated that: 'a lack of fluidity in ability-grouping systems often means that a child's initial group placement is highly significant, giving or restricting access to particular learning opportunities, creating and fixing educational outcomes and life chances at a young age' (Marks 2016, 9). Thus, even though the data produced through Baseline were flawed and subjective, they may have a long-lasting effect on children's school careers.

Conclusion

As we have argued in the previous chapter, data on children's progress and their attainment have become central to the governing of schooling so that there is a sense that primary children themselves become reduced to statistical pieces of data. Indeed, Williamson (2014, 12) has suggested that databases *reinvent* teachers and children such that they become reduced to 'miniature centres of calculation'. Using the business model metaphor, children as pieces of reduced data are then tracked, mined and exploited for the school's maximum productivity gains. The hidden, yet powerful code and algorithms, that generate each child's single baseline metric, effectively 'make up' children into 'data resources to be collected, collated and calculated into comparable governing knowledge' (Williamson 2014, 22). These digital data are then used to track and monitor children in a relentless pursuit for school 'improvement' in which children become reduced to data in 'exam factories' (Hutchings 2015).

This re-configuration of children as data is, however, not benign but has social impacts and consequences in that children's 'data doubles' or 'algorithmic identities' have increasing material effects within primary schools – for example, through sorting, labelling and setting children within ability groups. Neopositivism, the renewed belief in numbers as a way of 'knowing' the world, is 'a scientific language game that has very real material consequences' (St. Pierre 2012, 499). The social and political problem is that such data, despite their evident inaccuracy, provide an 'algorithmic authority' to sorting, labelling and notions of fixed 'ability' which may further disadvantage certain groups of children and shape their life chances. 'Digital data and the algorithmic analytics that are used to interpret them and to make predictions and inferences about individuals and social groups are beginning to have determining effects on people's lives, influencing their life chances and opportunities' (Lupton 2016, 44). The use of such data-based techniques to support pedagogical decisions and judgements is sometimes known as 'learning analytics'. Learning analytics originated from business intelligence and involves the analysis of children's past data to model and predict their future potential success (Selwyn 2015). The reality of the dangers associated with such predictive modelling was exemplified during the Baseline Assessment trial in which Early Excellence had to apologise to over 12,000 schools for inaccuracies resulting from a 'few anomalies' in its highly simplified literacy judgements (Camden 2015). Baseline and other forms of statutory data collection are positioned and justified by policy-makers through a reductionist lens as being practical, technical and efficient (Moss, Dahlberg, Grieshaber *et al.* 2016). Here we have argued that they are none of these things. The reductive nature of data – in terms of both reducing complexity to single numbers and reducing children's complex potential to set expectations – is dangerous in terms of equality, and ultimately based on a political decision to view education in technical terms. We turn in the following chapter to the responses of schools to this model of education.

Note

1 We note that these assessments are still based on a model of education which relies on regular summative assessment; nonetheless, they represent a more appropriate way to engage in such a process.

5

SCHOOLS' RESPONSES TO DATAFICATION AND THE VISIBILITY OF PERFORMANCE

Introduction

In this chapter we examine how data make educational performance more visible, and how this increased visibility results in strategic responses from school leaders and teachers. We focus mainly on research data from our second project relating to whole-school responses to datafication, considering the range of reactions to a new policy, and processes of resistance, compliance and manipulation. These processes began with choosing a Baseline provider, based on the potential impact, but also include manipulation (or 'gaming') and the rejection of results – these are 'perverse effects' of data (Lingard and Sellar 2013) at the level of the school. Here we focus on data *abuse*, which is where data use in an accountability system can cause 'problematic consequences', which is distinct from data *misuse*, meaning the incorrect interpretation of data and the resulting inappropriate responses (Silliman 2015, 8). The aim here is to consider the ways in which datafication produces new strategies and approaches, and also new tensions. Performance is rendered more visible through data, and schools respond to this in different ways. As Beer argues: 'As people are subject to these forms of measurement they will produce different responses and outcomes, knowing, as they often will, what is coming and the way that their performance will become visible' (2015, 10). Building on our discussion of data-driven subjectivities, we consider how the teachers engage in the complex negotiation of new policy; this is a mixture of acceptance, resistance, attempted disruption and resignation. Throughout, we see the teachers as constrained by policy imperatives – the 'tyranny of transparency' (Lewis and Hardy 2015); as in our previous work, we fully acknowledge the limits to teachers' power to subvert policy, but also recognise their agency in enacting developments such as Baseline in their classrooms (Ball *et al.* 2011a). Throughout, we use Foucault's suggestion that 'visibility is a trap' (Foucault 1977) and Deleuze's argument for more diffuse forms of control to frame our discussion.

We also consider in the later part of this chapter how the 'reification of progress' demands different forms of data alongside summative assessment data, and the relationship between progress and prediction. This leads us onto further discussion of our concerns about social justice in relation to data.

The power of visibility

We begin our discussion with a reminder of the power of visibility in neoliberal forms of governance, as summed up in Lewis and Hardy's phrase, the 'tyranny of transparency' (2015). The introduction of Baseline Assessment is part of an international trend towards high-stakes testing and public accountability for schools. The idea of measuring progress across the primary school years and using this to hold schools to account is the latest step in a process of making 'performance' visible to parents and policy-makers. Primary schools' results at Key Stage 2 (age 11) are already publicly available and compared in league tables in England. Similarly in Australia, the My School website allows parents to compare schools' results (Hardy and Boyle 2011). In England, teachers are reluctant to collect data for these purposes:

> There is considerable negative feeling about current reasons for collecting pupil data, specifically: to tick boxes; to be used as a stick to beat teachers and schools; to set ever-increasing targets; to encourage competition between schools; and because the government does not trust teachers to be professional.
>
> *(Kelly, Downey and Rietdijk 2010, 8)*

As Selwyn describes, 'key performance indicators' and other data are posted publicly with the intention that families, employers and other 'consumers' of education will make more 'informed' choices and decisions' (2016a, 84); however, teachers see this as 'a stick to beat teachers and schools'. This visibility of performance and the subsequent media reporting of 'failing schools' has 'encouraged systems to become more cynical and to focus on the comparative representation of performance over and above substantive improvement' (Lingard and Sellar 2013, 645). The 'audit culture' (Apple, Kenway and Singh 2005; Biesta 2009) demands performance to be visible, in the form of attainment data in league tables, or grades in Ofsted reports. This process of being constantly 'knowable' through data can be seen as 'dataveillance' – the surveillance of schools not physically, but *through numbers*. Simons describes 'a kind of self-government that includes a staging in the centre and where one submits oneself permanently, voluntary and openly to the gaze of others' (2014, 167). We use the term dataveillance to emphasise the disciplinary nature of visibility, drawing on Foucault and studies of surveillance based on his work:

> the disciplinary thesis reveals a completely different meaning of being seen and watched: no longer recognition, but subjugation, imposition of conducts,

means of control. In the disciplinary society, visibility means disempowerment. Namely, 'visibility is a trap' (Foucault, 1977). The mere fact of being aware of one's own visibility status — and not the fact of being under actual control — effectively influences one's behaviour.

(Brighenti 2007, 336)

However, as discussed in earlier chapters, we conceptualise control as operating in more fluid terms beyond institutions and particular events (such as Ofsted inspections), as per Deleuze's 'societies of control', while simultaneously more traditional forms of power are exercised from above (Lyon 2014). For example, school data dashboards, which compare a school's results with 'statistical neighbours', serve 'as a reward or punishment' (Foucault 1977), disciplining schools through competitive performances with each other. This information is not freely available, but works on the basis of 'self-evaluation', so that the school is encouraged to *improve itself*. Ofsted continues to wield power, but the effects operate constantly. For example, in the name of self-evaluation, schools engage in the analysis of further visualisations of data, such as those produced by the Fischer Family Trust. These display success or failure (green or red) in simple terms, without the complications of statistical nuances, just as international data are presented to policy-makers (Gorur 2014).

We argue that surveillance is a central tool in producing schools' own governance and subjection. The fear of disciplinary neoliberalism combined with a willing and calculative compliance to engage in 'the conduct of conduct' (Foucault 1977) ensures that schools relentlessly govern themselves through data. Taking responsibility for one's comparable positioning through 'quantifying the self' (Lupton 2016) becomes privileged and expected. The political and moral environment means that the self-quantifying school is involved in a relentless institutionalised dataveillance of themselves and their competitors.

These processes of making performance visible are affective, designed to engender emotions in order to motivate, reward or punish. Competition and its associated inequalities 'sharpen appetites, instincts and minds, driving individuals to rivalries' (Lazzarato 2009, 117), as we see in this description of 'naming and shaming' practices from the LA advisor:

> We '*name and shame*' by showing all the school names [on the data sheet]. Some schools didn't have any children at 'working above the expected level' so you say 'Well, your statistical neighbour has this percentage, so how come you haven't?' And they think 'I'd better go back and *have another look* at that' [...] It does challenge them and that's why we do it. It's accepted and I've not had any adverse comments. It was agreed by the heads that they wanted that.
>
> *(Local Authority Advisor)*

This disciplinary process had the effect of getting Reception teachers to 'go back and have another look', such that comparative data are essential in the process of governing through data. This process of 'naming and shaming' is reported as being accepted and even desired by the headteachers because they want to know where they are in comparison with similar schools.

Schools are expected to constantly review their data, and make changes in response. As one school leader noted, 'Nobody's allowed to fall behind' (Deputy Head, Easthorne). The reflexive primary school headteacher regularly monitors and tracks their own and others' datasets in an attempt to be 'responsible'. The 'disempowering effects of visibility' (Brighenti 2007) mean that school leaders are subject to the power of those who collate and analyse the data; it is these external actors who produce their 'Ofsted story' (Bradbury and Roberts-Holmes 2016a). Thus, as Kelly and Downey found in their research, when school leaders receive data that are also made available to the public in league tables, leaders feel the 'story' gets 'out of control' (2011, 46), creating feelings of anxiety.

This self-quantifying and self-auditing demands that all aspects of primary schools are metricised and 'datafied' as they engage in a process of responsibilisation. Several of the respondents to our survey on Baseline commented that they needed a form of baseline to provide a 'starting point' – for example, 'We have always assessed our children's starting points to plan and measure progress' (W) – but did not want this to be formalised. Thus these teachers engaged with the idea of data on young children as part of self-improvement. The encouragements provided by dataveillance operate as 'powerful steering mechanisms' that have the effect of keeping primary teachers in a constant state of 'competitive self-improvement' (Simons 2014, 159). This affective basis for government is central to the neoliberal form in education: 'At its most visceral and intimate neoliberalism involves the transformation of social relations and practices into calculabilities and exchanges, that is into the market form – with the effect of commodifying educational practice and experience' (Ball 2013b, 132). Thus the transformation of children's learning into 'calculabilities', or their role as 'miniature centres of calculation' as Willliamson describes (2014) – as discussed in earlier chapters – sits alongside the 'visceral and intimate' effect on teachers of making their conduct and performance constantly visible. The affective dimension of visibility, particularly the anxiety provoked by constant measurement, reflects Deleuze's societies of control, where 'he predicted a new way of controlling people from the inside, so to speak, instead of as earlier, disciplining them from the outside into sanctioned behaviours' (Olsson 2009, 61). Throughout the following discussion, we can see the power of 'governing through emotion', whereby 'the approach to governing tries to create emotional dispositions or relations through which governing might work more effectively' (Grek, Lindgren and Clarke 2015, 118). We turn now to exploring how teachers and school leaders respond to such visibility – through acceptance, resistance and manipulation.

Choosing a Baseline provider: resistance and acceptance

The imposition of Baseline as a new form of *visibility through data* provides a case study of schools' responses to an additional burden of performance, particularly as the comments about choice of Baseline revealed a complex mix of acceptance and resistance. Nationally, the majority of schools chose Early Excellence, and all of our case study schools did the same, as well as 76 per cent of our survey respondents. Participants commented that they hoped that using Early Excellence would avoid the stringent 'testing' nature of the policy:

> For me it wasn't really much of a decision because we wanted to go with the EExBA because it was the ethos that we already follow. It wasn't a particular change from practice that we already do.
>
> *(Assistant Head, Cedar)*

> EExBA was chosen as it is reflective of our existing Baseline Assessment methods – in line with EYFS principles, although Baseline Assessment reflects ALL profile areas, not those limited by the Government.
>
> *(W)*

> I am happy I chose EExBA as we were able to decide the most appropriate activities and observations in order to gather information towards the statements.
>
> *(W)*

This idea that Early Excellence could be adapted and coalesce with existing practice allowed these teachers to accept the policy, even though they disagreed with some aspects, such as the content (Roberts-Holmes and Bradbury 2017). It allowed for continuity with informal baselines and the EYFS Profile, so that it was more useful. Moreover, many respondents framed this choice in terms of resisting the principles of the policy, or 'getting around' the problem of having to do Baseline by choosing an observation-based provider.

> Our response then as responsible practitioners for young people is that we must choose the one that we think is better in terms of application and rounded in terms of practice, and my understanding is that is the one that is least linked to tests and is more about practitioner type judgement.
>
> *(Head, Beech)*

While the headteachers felt they needed to engage with the policy even though it was still voluntary at the time, they tried to use the agency afforded them through choice of provider to reduce the impact on the children. At Alder School, this took the form of selecting a quick and 'non-damaging' Baseline:

> [We] selected another provider because we saw it as quick, quite simple. It was a kind of a little bit of a laptop based [...] It was click on a few buttons, it was very oral, it had been devised by Speech and Language Therapists for young children. It wasn't going to damage anyone and it was going to be fairly quick and fun to do. Because we were typically thinking 'Why are we doing this?'
>
> *(Head, Alder)*

While at Beech School the headteacher wanted to choose the system which would be most beneficial to the children, at Alder School, the head wanted to limit the damage caused by choosing a 'quick, quite simple' assessment. This headteacher went on to explain her rationale further: she commented that since they were already doing a baseline and the results were only for the DfE, she thought 'let's do it in the easiest, less onerous, cost effective way of doing it'. This is 'cynical compliance', a phrase used originally by Ball (2003) in relation to inspections, which we have used elsewhere to describe 'tokenistic, half-hearted and tactical adherence of some teachers to the requirements of [assessment], [...] undertaken in a situation where teachers feel they have very little power to resist' (Bradbury 2012, 183). The headteacher above comments that she does not understand the purpose of the policy, so she only wants to make it 'quick and fun to do'. However, following a presentation by the local authority which heavily promoted Early Excellence, she felt under pressure to choose Early Excellence:

> By that time busy, busy heads, early years coordinators who like to make decisions in groups ... The wave was, you know there was this wave of early years, Early Excellence, and you almost felt like if you were going with somebody else you know you were a traitor to good early years pedagogy.
>
> *(Head, Alder)*

The success of Early Excellence in presenting themselves as 'early years friendly' is obvious here (Roberts-Holmes and Bradbury 2017); picking another provider became traitorous to the dominant early years ideology. Despite this pressure, this headteacher decided to stick with her earlier choice. However, she was only to find that the provider had been removed due to low take-up; then, she commented, 'I was absolutely exhausted by it all but I just thought fair enough, we will just do the Early Excellence'. This reflected the 'begrudging acceptance' (Selwyn, Henderson and Chao 2015) discussed in Chapter 3; she has a moment of resistance against the trend towards Early Excellence, but does not have the energy to continue this battle.

At Damson School, a similar tension arose between the headteacher's desire to minimise disruption – to cynically comply – and the early years teachers' need for something 'meaningful':

> So as you know we were given six choices. I will be honest I wanted to go for the computerised one, it was pretty quick. [...] The Reception team felt that if they were going to do it they wanted to do something that was meaningful to them. Which I can fully understand, so they have gone with the system that was recommended by early years as being a meaningful assessment.
>
> *(Head, Damson)*

This head, unlike the early years teachers, also viewed the choice as being one driven by time constraints, but was happy to concede to the teachers conducting the assessment. The choice here is presented as between 'quick' and 'meaningful', or limiting the impact versus providing useful information. This reveals the extent to which data collection has become a task disconnected from educational realities; two of the headteachers we interviewed intended to engage in the production of data in a way which complied with the requirements but did not necessarily provide the teachers with anything useful. Their priority instead was to limit the damage. This tension might have arisen due to the differences in training and experience between school leaders (who were not early years teachers originally) and Reception teachers. One comment in the survey noted:

> In schools where headteachers are not as clued into reception I fear a test will be chosen as it appears easier to somebody who doesn't truly know how to work with and assess this unique age group.
>
> *(W)*

Nonetheless it reveals an interesting strategic response on the part of school leaders to another form of making their school's performance visible.

These comments reflect the problematic nature of an assessment which only serves the purpose of accountability, rather than providing useful information for teachers. The selection of Early Excellence as more 'early yearsy', as they promoted themselves, proved extremely popular, even though the results are used for the same purpose as the other assessments from CEM and NFER. This depiction of Early Excellence obscures the fact that it also produces numerical scores for children which will be used to measure progress. It may appear more useful or 'meaningful' in that the format is familiar to teachers, but is not actually intended to be a guide for planning. There are also limits to its usefulness, as discussed in earlier chapters, because it is not consistent with the EYFS Profile or compatible with data tracking systems, and does not provide more information than existing baselines. However, much of this appeared to be overlooked in favour of choosing a system which resisted the discourse of 'testing'. While these teachers engaged fully with the policy, they also felt they were resisting it.

The fact of having a choice of provider – a principle in keeping with neoliberal concepts of choice and markets, and private involvement in education – was seen by some as a method of making the policy more palatable for an intransigent profession; at Elm School, the headteacher described himself as 'cynical' about it:

> I imagine their intention is to make us feel we have got some control over it and some sort of ownership. And I guess if it goes the way of Early Excellence which is the one we feel is quite good then we will be quite happy. [...] But if they go with another one then we won't be quite so happy. [...] I think people have appreciated the ability to choose one system and try what they think is the best way to match our own practice.
>
> *(Head, Elm)*

This headteacher's comments show how choice as a process helps to make the policy more acceptable (as we discuss in more detail in Chapter 6). The provision of an option (Early Excellence) which they feel comfortable with means they do not question the fundamentals of the policy. We turn now to responses to conducting Baseline Assessment.

Fabricating Baseline

As Kitchin has noted, in any data-based system 'people start to game the system in rational, self-interested but often unpredictable ways to subvert metrics, algorithms, and automated decision-making processes' (2014, 127). In Australia, the responses of some states to comparisons of test results are described as 'perverse effects' (Lingard and Sellar 2013). These include 'gaming' and goal displacement; the latter describing a shift to practices which improve the data, such as 'teaching to the test' (already discussed in Chapter 3). In this section, we examine how 'gaming' or manipulation operates at the school level, following on from our other work on 'fabrication' in early years (Bradbury 2011b).

A wide range of literature from many countries has identified the strategic responses of schools to control measures such as inspections and performance tables (de Wolf and Janssens 2007; Mansell 2007; Ehren, Jones and Perryman 2016). These responses range from what is clearly 'cheating', such as changing pupils' answers on a test, as noted in various US cases – see, for example, Judd (2012) and Gilliom (2010) – to more subtle forms, such as improving displays before an inspection. With this literature in mind, we approach this topic with an awareness that 'gaming' is 'a rational and attractive option' (Lingard and Sellar 2013, 646) in particular policy contexts. We argue that measures of progress such as Baseline, or value added, are more vulnerable to such strategic responses. Indeed, one of the concerns raised in the DfE's own research into Baseline Assessment, before the 2015 cycle began, related to the temptation to deliberately deflate results in order to increase progress measures, referred to as 'gaming' (DfE 2015b). This temptation was present in the Reception classrooms in Bradbury's research (2011b, 2013c), where EYFS Profile results were deliberately lowered in order to show more progress as children progressed through the school. This is strategic manipulation, as demanded by the policy imperatives. In a survey of teachers in England, Kelly, Downey and Rietdijk found that teachers were willing to admit they 'played games' with their data, because the system rewarded this (2010, 8). Thompson and Cook argue, with reference to the Australian context, that 'manipulating the data is a regrettable but logical response to manifestations of teaching where only the data counts' (2014, 129). They describe the 'dividuated teacher', based on Deleuzian theory of societies of control, as overlaying old models of the 'good teacher'. What is known as 'cheating' becomes more important than other ethics because data need to be manipulated to 'tell a truer story'. While we feel the word 'cheating' is inappropriate in this context (where there is no suggestion that children's responses were changed, for example, as in cheating scandals), we discuss here how a decision to attempt to deflate results, or *fabricate* the Baseline, is a logical response to measures of progress which appear distanced from every-day teaching.

We use the term fabrication in line with Ball's description:

> Fabrications conceal as much as they reveal. They are ways of measuring oneself within particular registers of meaning, within a particular economy of meaning in which only certain possibilities of being have value. However, such fabrications are deeply paradoxical [...] Fabrications are both resistance *and* capitulation. They are a betrayal even, a giving up of claims to authenticity and commitment, an investment in plasticity.
>
> *(Ball 2003, 225, emphasis in original)*

This conceptualisation of fabrication, we would argue, affords the teacher more sympathy in relation to their situation, by recognising the 'particular economy of meaning' in which they find themselves. It also allows for the simultaneous feelings of resistance and acceptance which we discussed above in relation to choice, and which are evident in our discussion below. Ball and Olmedo discuss how teachers can engage in 'care for the self' through forms of resistance, including 'deciphering, understanding, unravelling and retranslating' (2013, 93); similarly, we view these actions of manipulations, and discussions of the possibility even, as practices of self-preservation or survival within an unforgiving context. They indicate 'the courage displayed in refusing the mundane' (Ball and Olmedo 2013, 94).

Our respondents, both in the survey (though we did not ask about 'gaming') and in interviews, presented some form of manipulation as 'rational and attractive' (Lingard and Sellar 2013, 646):

> Schools want their baseline scores to be low in order to maximise the progress they can show. This means there should be some moderation in place in order to ensure schools are being accurate with the data they submit. Headteachers' wishes for low baseline scores also mean that we are beginning the year looking for the negatives in children – what they can't do and how low they can be scored in order to make our scores low. This is the very antithesis of the philosophy behind the EYFS, which makes me very uneasy about completing such an assessment.
>
> *(W)*

> This pilot has shown that individuals have manipulated scores in their favour, for example, marking children lower than they are so that more progress will be shown.
>
> *(W)*

> I agree that there needs to be standardisation as some schools inaccurately score children as significantly below on entry to inflate progress but a test is not the answer.
>
> *(W)*

[At the meeting about providers] there was a sort of tongue in cheek response from headteachers that if it is going to be linked to progress perhaps we should choose the most difficult one.

(Head, Beech)

Obviously you are not going to shoot yourself in the foot, okay, if you are assessing a child with Baseline and it is a simple yes or no and we all know that there is a lot of grey in the middle of yes and no. Are you really going to tick the yes box if you are in any doubt? You are going to tick the no box, aren't you?

(Head, Alder)

Here teachers describe how deliberately keeping Baseline results low is a logical response if they are going to be used to measure progress; to do otherwise would be to 'shoot yourself in the foot'. Here, in line with many discussions of 'high-stakes' testing, we see evidence of 'Campbell's law', which states that the more you use a quantitative measure, the more people will corrupt it (1976, 49 cited in Ehren, Jones and Perryman 2016, 88). However, these responses all note disapproval of this practice and some recommend standardisation processes to prevent it. Similarly, the headteachers we interviewed argued they themselves would not engage in manipulation of results:

You have got to be honest, again you will really shoot yourself in the foot if you are working in a very leafy lane middle class school with highly educated parents and the children are coming in, you know broadly in line with national averages or slightly above and suddenly you are publishing data that you would expect to see in a slightly different type of school.

(Head, Alder)

Although we are bound down and broken by those judgements and the way people view us we believe in what we do and hopefully we will get good results by doing what we do, which we think is right, so we don't play those games. I know a lot of schools are forced to do that, particularly schools that are in trouble.

(Head, Damson)

[There is] this tongue in cheek idea of headteachers saying let's choose the most difficult system that the children are more likely to fail on. So you do have those moments cross your head because there is the pressure there, of course there is pressure there, it is hugely high stakes and yet you have to do this job with a very strong moral compass.

(Head, Beech)

These headteachers commented that they had not manipulated results for a range of reasons, including the moral imperative to 'get it right', the resulting uselessness of the data and the danger of 'coming unstuck' when compared to other similar schools. They did, however, recognise the temptation to 'play those games' due to the 'pressure' of high-stakes assessments.

Discussions about manipulating results were more prevalent in those schools that were visited later in the Baseline process, as they had access to the Early Excellence national results. These showed almost 50 per cent of children had been graded as 'below typical' or 'well below typical' nationally, according to our participants. This was seen as evidence of others misguidedly engaging in 'gaming'. These results may have been due to the instruction from Early Excellence to 'err on the side of caution', which was mentioned by many of the teachers interviewed.

> They said if you are umming and ahing and if you are not sure it is a no.
>
> *(Teacher 1, Elm)*

> I have said to the staff, say no [if you're not sure], because in one sense it is – I feel it is better to say no, because when you are then looking at that as part of assessment to inform your planning, it is better to say no and go over something again than say yes and shelve it and move on when the children might not be there yet.
>
> *(Assistant Head, Cedar)*

> It is all this pressure going on instead of just saying, the children are here and they are going to make the progress that is expected or slightly better. But everybody is so stressed about it all and so people start erring on the side of caution because they are worried.
>
> *(Teacher 2, Elm)*

> But it does seem like people pushing results down in order to maximise progress. Which is obviously a temptation. [But] if you suppress them, push them down a little bit then when Ofsted come and look at it and say, well this is rubbish for this sort of school, they can see the type of school, the type of area. So then they will say that your assessment isn't valid really.
>
> *(Head, Elm)*

This practice of always saying 'no' if there is any doubt a child can achieve a point facilitates the deliberate deflation of results, and even legitimises the low scores that schools have produced with the Early Excellence Baseline. However, as the final comment indicates, there remains pressure from Ofsted to show results appropriate for 'this sort of school'; it remains important to produce realistic, intelligible data which relate to the intake of the school. Similarly, research on the EYFS Profile has suggested teachers in schools with a 'difficult intake' feel pressure to produce results which are 'realistic' for that cohort (Bradbury 2013c).

Some comments suggested that headteachers had strongly advised their teachers to assess in a particular way, which minimised scores:

[Teachers] may feel that they are under pressure for the children to appear more able and developed than they actually are, because there is that natural thing to want to do well in assessments and tests isn't there? We don't normally go into assessments and tests wanting to fail them, we normally want to go in them to shine and to celebrate where we are at. What I have explained is that if it is as crude as 'yes you can or no you can't' and you would only say 'yes you can' if that child actually could. If they nearly can you say no, that is the shooting yourself in the foot. Because we are all very positive people and I don't know, if one of the statements is 'Can recognise all letters of the alphabet', and you sit down with a child and they miss one, there is this natural feeling to say, 'Oh yes they can'. But actually that is shooting yourself in the foot, because technically they can't.

(Head, Alder)

This headteacher argues that, although it is against the natural inclination of early years teachers to be negative about what children can do, they should be cautious in order to avoid 'shooting themselves in the foot' when the children reach Key Stage 2 Sats. Thus these teachers are advised to choose 'no' if there is any doubt, resulting in a deliberately negative picture of what children can achieve. The results of a Baseline conducted with this in mind are a *fabrication*, a 'giving up of claims to authenticity and commitment' (Ball 2003).

It is important to note that we do not wish to imply criticism of the teachers and school leaders involved. As Thompson and Cook argue:

the latest form of high-stakes testing, with its emphasis on data-points, datasets and databases, disconnects the disciplinary space of the classroom so that moralising judgement of teachers' manipulation of the data cannot account for the space in which teaching is constructed.

(2014, 132)

For them, the 'dividuated teacher' responds logically to their context, even when this response involves 'cheating'. As noted, this term does not seem appropriate here, but the deliberate deflation of results is similarly evidence of teachers simply responding to a data-driven context; Baseline is, to use Beer's term, a 'productive measure' (2015), in that it produces particular responses and subjectivities.

Interestingly, there was some awareness among our respondents that such tactical responses might drive the policy further towards more formal forms of testing:

Well, it [manipulation] worries us slightly but on the other hand it runs the great risk of the whole thing being rubbished by Nicky Morgan[1] or whoever, who is going to say look this isn't worth the paper it is written on because clearly schools are not assessing it properly. Or they are going to bring in some sort of strict test regime because they will say this is too subjective, because that could be the criticism of the Early Excellence one, it is fairly subjective, it relies entirely on the professionalism and the viewpoint of individual practitioners. So she might want to bring in something that we don't really agree with, more of a yes/no test type of thing because she feels that she can't trust people to do it honestly.

(Head, Elm)

This concern is in keeping with the feeling that Baseline Assessment is another 'tool to bash teachers' with; for many teachers, Baseline Assessment is part of a game which teachers cannot win, whichever provider they pick and whatever tactical approach they take. The fact that, nationally, more than 50 per cent of children were labelled by the Early Excellence Baseline as 'below' or 'well below' expected levels suggests that many teachers decided to err on the side of caution in this first attempt at Baseline Assessment, in order to 'play safe'. In the follow-up report on the comparability of the different providers, this issue was not mentioned (STA 2016). However, the lack of comparability between providers was given as a justification when the policy was withdrawn, or 'paused', before proposals for a new iteration of Baseline were announced in April 2017 (Ward 2016; DfE 2017c).

As we saw in the schools we interviewed for our first project, the ideal for many teachers is 'freedom' – from inspections and testing – and this can be 'bought' by getting it right, albeit temporarily:

We're totally data driven. If the data is good Ofsted leave us alone but if the data is poor they drill right down into everything. We'll be punished if we have poor data, so obviously it's a huge, huge pressure to get the data looking good. Ofsted take the data from Year 6 and work back and see where they were in Year 2 and Reception. So it has really influenced thinking.

(Deputy Head, Eastside Easthorne)

You're only as good as your last year's results across the whole school. Get the data right and you buy five years of freedom.

(Head, Northside)

For the teachers and leaders using Baseline, the aim was to ensure they continue to be 'free' by not setting themselves too difficult targets for the future, a strategic response to the demands of a policy which prioritises progress. Again, we see the power of 'governing through emotion' (Grek, Lindgren and Clarke 2015) where teachers' priorities are driven by the need to focus on progress, to limit the damage of an accountability-based system. We now turn to the wider importance of this shift, which we have termed the 'reification of progress' (Bradbury and Roberts-Holmes 2016a).

Progress and value added measures

One important shift in values associated with datafication is the reification of progress over absolute attainment. As the early years advisor we interviewed concluded, 'schools are led by progress data and are judged by progress data'. This turn to progress is both fuelled by the production of data and in turn produces more data. The purpose of Baseline Assessment was to add to the 'audit culture' of schools (Apple, Kenway and Singh 2005; Biesta 2009) by providing another point of assessment which would complement the existing structure of Key Stage 2 Sats by showing 'progress' over seven years. In this case, the progress measure is 'simple progress', which does not take into account contextual factors such as pupil characteristics. The end-point Key Stage 2 tests are well established as the main measure of primary schools' performance, and as such subject to much scrutiny in terms of their impact on the curriculum and pedagogy (Stobart 2008). Moreover, although Baseline was new, the idea of measuring progress has a long history in education. There have been various attempts to measure progress or 'value added', with or without contextual factors, in the education system in the UK, including the introduction in 2016 of 'Progress 8' for secondary schools (Perry 2016; Leckie and Goldstein 2017). Similarly, in the United States, value added measures are used to judge teachers' performance (Jennings and Pallas 2016).

Frequently, using value added is seen as more sympathetic to schools where children arrive with lower levels of attainment (Bradbury 2011a). Indeed, one survey respondent commented that Baseline enabled her school to show 'impact':

> At my school many children arrive at school with very low levels and a baseline assessment enables the school to demonstrate the impact we have and the progress that children have made, particularly in KS1. We have used PIPs[2] throughout the school for many years for this reason.
>
> *(W)*

The idea of measuring progress is based on the principle that there is such a thing as *expected* progress, or that you can predict what a child will be able to do in the future based on what they can do now. This suggests that children learn at similar rates in a linear fashion, a technical, instrumental view of education which is contested, particularly in early childhood studies (Moss, Dahlberg, Olssen *et al.* 2016). Nonetheless, the idea of prediction is increasingly powerful in education: 'We have entered the era of "big data" where computer capacity and the "datafication" of the world have seen an emergent epistemological shift from concerns with causality and understanding to concerns of correlation and predictability' (Lingard, Martino and Rezai-Rashti 2013, 542). This concern with predictability – rather than concern over the structural, societal or systemic factors, for example, that might affect attainment – drives policy such as Baseline Assessment, which is not concerned with 'causality and understanding'. This is part of an international shift, Ozga and Segerholm argue, towards a belief in the power of knowledge and planning, using data to 'govern the future [...] to reduce risk' (2015).

This reification of progress and attendant belief in predictability has spread through the education system, even into areas which are not required to record progress data. In our first project, we found that a 'baseline' was being established for children at age two:

We record how the children enter when they are two, so we have a baseline and then throughout the year we do three assessments with the children at set points and then compare them with each other to check they are making progress. We have a system which shows where the children should be with where they are so we can see if they are on track.

(Deputy Head, Hopetown)

This concept of establishing a baseline and measuring against it at a later point is based on the idea that learning is an objective and linear process that can be predicted. It also facilitates a model of assessment which 'checks' everyone is progressing, a medical model also seen with the Phonics Screening Check at age six (Bradbury 2013b). In the case of the official Baseline Assessment, participants expressed serious doubts about the underlying principle of measuring progress from Reception to Year 6, based on an objection to the 'learning as a measurable process' discourse.

I don't think you should [use it to measure progress], I don't think you can, because they are children and they are not robots, not machines, they are children. You don't know what influences they have got from outside, what is going to happen in those seven years, so I think it is ridiculous.

(Teacher 3, Cedar)

I am very concerned that it will be used as a way to predict the children's KS2 attainment and assess their progress. I feel that is a great pressure on us.

(W)

So much can happen in a child's life between EYFS and the end of KS2.

(W)

You can't basically put a kid in a box when they are four and say because you did quite well on your baseline you will be a high achiever when you are eleven. It is too young to say. Or because you didn't do so well on your baseline that's it, you are disadvantaged, you are not going to achieve.

(Head, Alder)

It is damaging that this score will stay with the four year olds for the rest of their primary schooling. It labels the pupils and also creates pressure on staff to push children who aren't ready/are plateauing which is normal in academic progress. It will lead to inflation of scores further along the line.

(W)

Here we see concern that outside influences will render the data inaccurate as a measure of the 'value added' by a school, and progress measures will cause additional pressure. Additionally, problems with children moving between schools were mentioned as a key issue. Only 6.7 per cent of respondents to the survey agreed it was 'a good way to measure schools' performance'. Although value added/ progress measures are depicted as sympathetic to the needs of different cohorts of children entering schools, there are also serious concerns as to the impact on lower attaining groups, as discussed earlier.

There were also concerns about the underlying principle of tracking progress from age four to eleven, given that previously it had been a well-established idea that EYFS scores could not be used to predict Key Stage 1 results:

> Ofsted have never judged progress from Reception to Key Stage 1 or from Reception to Key Stage 2, because all the research showed that there was no correlation between a very young child's development and attainment at age five to where they would be at age seven or age eleven ... All of a sudden that has changed. [...] So where has that research come from? Why has somebody changed their mind? Was it the DfE?
>
> *(Head, Alder)*

> Not long ago the idea of any kind of formal assessment for Reception age children was considered unacceptable. How can it suddenly be OK?
>
> *(W)*

> Any educator knows, any parent knows, young people's journeys from the age of four and five can have huge ups and downs ... if we have a Baseline Assessment that it is looking at, or attempting to look holistically at the skills of a child and we link that to a Key Stage 2 assessment that is looking at SPAG, reading, writing and maths, how do the two correlate?
>
> *(Head, Beech)*

> We don't learn in a linear way. Learning is stepped. You know we learn a bit, we stop, we learn a bit, we stop. So it doesn't necessarily mean that these children are all going to be in a linear line, the same as they are now when they get to Year 6 [...] You are sort of setting from now a goal that they are going to achieve in Year 6, I think that is a bit harsh actually.
>
> *(Teacher 2, Elm)*

Baseline attempted to construct a linear relationship for progress from age four to age eleven, even though the content of the assessments is different, as the Key Stage 2 tests include only literacy and mathematics. School leaders were concerned that they were now being unambiguously told that there was such a relationship between the early years and Year 6 and they questioned why this had suddenly become possible when previously it had been dismissed. Furthermore, the variation between children and their rates of progress meant that a simple correlation between Reception and Key Stage 2 was impossible.

Here Lyotard's comments on data and performativity, as cited by Sellar, are highly relevant:

> The best performativity cannot consist in obtaining additional information ... it comes rather from arranging the data in a new way ... this new arrangement is usually achieved by connecting together series of data that were previously held to be independent.
>
> *(1984, 52 cited in Sellar 2015, 134)*

This 'imagination', the practice of connecting data that were previously regarded as independent, here draws an imaginary line between what children can do in their first six weeks of school in a range of curriculum areas to their attainment in literacy and mathematics seven years later. Our respondents felt this was simply unfair, as there were too many variations between the two assessments:

> Children's progress is going to be judged against how far they have gone in seven years. Now to my mind that is an almost impossible thing to do because you can't test children at eleven about the same things you were testing them at four. It just doesn't make sense.
>
> *(Head, Damson)*

Because of these doubts about the principle of tracking and prediction from Baseline Assessment data, there were also concerns raised about the future use of data by Ofsted and the publication of the data online. These developments were seen as inevitable: as one survey comment put it: 'It is certain to be used as yet another stick with which to beat schools by the likes of Ofsted.'

Concerns about the impact of data on social justice

As discussed, there were serious concerns about the potential labelling effect of Baseline and resulting low expectations, particularly for English as an additional language (EAL) and summer-born children. There were additional concerns raised about the potential for a measure like Baseline to encourage the 'coaching' of young children by some parents, with the result of widening gaps in attainment:

> If parents, like the parents you have spoken to this morning, pick up on the fact that this is happening every year there is the likelihood that some parents will be spending the whole summer holidays teaching, you know getting hold of this baseline assessment, looking at the criteria. Because there is this natural need for your child to pass tests you will be coaching them to pass the test. Another parent won't, so that is not a narrowing of the gap; that is an immediate widening of the gap that we already have.
>
> *(Head, Alder)*

This concern arises from a context where socio-economic status is a reliable indicator of attainment in the EYFS Profile. Data from 2015–16 using deprivation indices (Figure 5.1) show that children from more deprived areas are less likely to achieve the benchmark 'Good Level of Development' (DfE 2016a) and achieve lower scores on average (Figure 5.2).

The EYFS Profile is an assessment which parents cannot directly coach children for, as it is conducted through long-term observation. Children could be prepared for Baseline, however, as the content areas are public and it can be a one-off test. Thus the headteacher's concern above is a very real one in terms of equity. Children whose parents have the capital to prepare children for Baseline will produce higher scores, which set their children up with high expectations; those who do not will end up with low expectations. This problem arises from the underlying principle of measuring and establishing what this headteacher called 'limiting judgements':

> You know you don't want limiting judgements at this point. Because obviously what you are looking to do is open potential up, and I know that sometimes by measuring that and saying you could have issues here it might enable you to do that, but actually it can lead to low expectations as well. So obviously what we are in the business of trying to do is identify the needs as early as possible, but what you are *not* wanting to do is to say 'This is happening

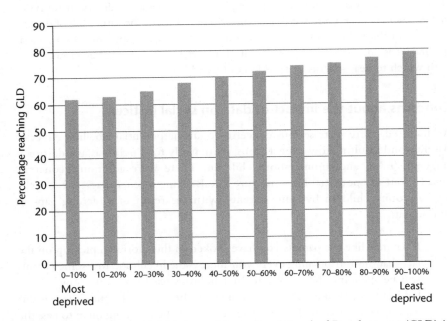

FIGURE 5.1 Percentage of children reaching a Good Level of Development (GLD) in England, 2015–16, by Deprivation Index decile.

Source: DfE (2016a).

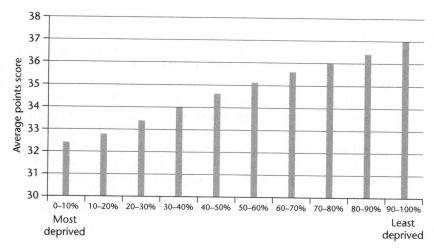

FIGURE 5.2   Average points score in EYFS Profile, England, 2015–16, by Deprivation Index decile.

Source: DfE (2016a).

here, therefore this is what we expect of you here'; that might be too low. But actually that worries me, I think there has been a real issue around target-setting in terms of lower expectations, actually. Because you have hit your target you don't need to go higher, that somehow people don't work beyond that. [...] If you are looking at staff in schools and expectations of children, yes, I just have questions around that kind of information setting expectations for the future at that very early stage.

(Head, Cedar)

The potentially damaging effect of Baseline Assessment is identified here: that for children with low scores ('below typical'), even if they make good progress, it will be seen as acceptable for them to remain low-attaining at age 11. This is a problem inherent in any 'value added' measure where the baseline is known, and is more likely to affect those groups who are lower attaining within the system in general, such as ethnic minorities, children receiving free school meals, children with SEN and EAL and summer-born children (Bradbury 2011a). Although schools were not being advised to set targets or make predictions based on Baseline Assessment, the form of the assessment makes this inevitable; one of the major frustrations that teachers noted was that data from Baseline Assessment did not fit into existing 'tracking' software. The nature of this software encourages the use of predictions based on expected progress, and thus the danger of low expectations. Therefore, the risk of particular groups of children being systematically under-assessed in Baseline Assessment is significant for their long-term educational trajectories. Although there is no official advice to set expectations based on Baseline, the culture of prediction is embedded within much data analysis in schools, under the guise of 'target-setting'. For example, the well-respected Fischer Family Trust, who provide 'data and analyses' to all schools and local authorities in England and Wales, comments that their analyses are used to 'inform the setting of ambitious and aspirational targets for students'. They offer: 'A personalised approach to pupil progress – whether you're setting targets for individual pupils, subjects, departments or your whole school, our target-setting system has been designed to allow the setting, recording and reviewing of aspirational targets for students' (Fischer Family Trust 2017). This established culture of prediction and target-setting means that any data on children will be used for 'tracking' as they progress through the school, at least; the Baseline data, which are built on the presumption that attainment can be predicted, are thus likely to be used for setting targets. This makes the problems of underassessment for EAL children, those less well prepared and summer-born children, and the problems of accuracy, serious concerns in terms of equality.

Conclusion

Lingard and Sellar argue, in relation to Australian states, that readings and representations of data 'give rise to feelings of anxiousness and nervousness among policymakers in response to media and political pressures for their system to be "seen" as improving and achieving at a high standard in comparison with other systems' (2013, 639). We would argue that a similar 'feeling of anxiousness and nervousness' is present in schools, local authorities and all levels where performance is compared. The culture of visible comparison is evident in school websites, for example, where 'successful' schools prominently place links to their data dashboard statistics, so that parents can locate the information on their good position; they take advantage of visibility to attract students. This is responsible and enterprising behaviour, just as taking action to improve scores and therefore position is a logical, expected response to the visibility of performance. Schools engage in this 'game' in numerous ways, framed by expectation and context. One response is to 'play with the numbers', to fabricate or manipulate the data, as we have discussed here.

Silliman (2015) argues that both 'data misuse' and, our focus here, 'data abuse', where data use can cause 'problematic consequences' in an accountability system, are caused by lack of trust and capacity. In contrast, we would argue that schools' responses to data-driven policy are instead framed by the complex operation of power implicated in accountability systems. Policies such as Baseline Assessment make schools' performance visible within set economies of meaning, where 'good' or 'outstanding' means children have got higher scores than expected, or a high proportion have crossed the line. This generates pressure to perform in particular ways; teachers are subject to the demands of the system. Thus they choose a baseline even when they are aware it is not 'meaningful', or they 'err on the side of caution' to make sure they do not set themselves up for failure at a later date. They have agency, of course, and use this to resist in small ways, by choosing the provider which 'limits the damage'; indeed, manipulating results or engaging in fabrication is itself 'both resistance and capitulation' (Ball, 2003). Furthermore, they are critical of developments which reverse established and agreed rules, such as the idea that progress can be directly predicted from early years to Key Stage 1 or 2. But their role, as data-driven subjects, is to produce and engage with the data in the ways the system demands; as such, the whole-school responses we see here show the power of data practices in shaping how teachers and school leaders think about fundamental ideas such as 'success' and 'good teaching'.

Notes

1 The Secretary of State for Education at the time.
2 PIPs is a form of non-statutory baseline assessment provided by CEM, in use for several years.

6

INTERNATIONAL DATAFICATION AND BUSINESS OPPORTUNITIES

Introduction

This chapter takes a step back from the context of schools in England to consider some of the wider international governance issues relating to data and education. This allows us to place the examples we have discussed thus far into a wider context of an international trend towards reliance on data in education and the development of a 'global measurement industry' (Biesta 2017). We begin by considering the power of the Programme for International Student Assessment (PISA) as a data source in international comparisons, and the plans to expand this to include younger children within the Organisation for Economic Co-operation and Development (OECD)'s proposed 'pre-school PISA' (Moss, Dahlberg, Grieshaber *et al.* 2016). This International Early Learning Study (IELS) involves tests for five-year-old children. Throughout this discussion of international datafication we are cognizant of Ball's caution that the UK is used as a neoliberal 'reform laboratory' (Ball 2012a, 12) for trying out experimental and controversial reform agendas. The language used in the OECD description of IELS establishes it as the latest development in the dominant narrative of early childhood, which Moss titles 'the story of quality and high returns' (2015) based on a neoliberal vision of early childhood as a site of investment. In the following section, we look at the broader international significance of the role of private companies in processes of datafication. We end with a discussion of the roles of different interests in the data and education 'game', and how they provoke, facilitate and expediate policy.

The Organisation for Economic Co-operation and Development, international governance and datafication

Much of the literature in the field of data and education focuses on the role of data in governance, particularly the use of data to compare schools', areas' and even countries' educational 'performance' (Fenwick, Mangez and Ozga 2014; Ozga 2009; Ozga et al. 2011; Sellar and Lingard 2013). Here data are an important part of the shift from government to *governance* both at national and increasingly at international levels: 'the shift towards governance rather than government in education [...] is intimately connected with the growth of data, and the increase in possibilities for monitoring, targeting and shifting cultures and behaviour that data apparently produce' (Ozga, Segerholm and Simola 2011, 85). Within this context of international datafication and governance, it is important to critique the OECD's global standardised tests known as the Programme for International Student Assessment (PISA). As Moss states, the OECD is 'an extremely powerful organisation, applying extremely powerful "human technologies"' (Moss 2016). PISA, for example, produces international comparable ranking scores for 15-year-olds in mathematics, science and reading across approximately 60 countries, and is now arguably so powerful that 'we are seeing the constitution of a global policy field in education created through numbers, statistics and data' (Sellar and Lingard 2014, 923). Here, at the international policy level, we see the governing power of the processes of datafication directly influencing policy itself. Ball refers to relationships such as between the OECD PISA datasets and national policy as global assemblages beyond national boundaries: 'The relationships involved here cross and erase national boundaries and form the basis for new kinds of *global assemblages*' (Ball 2012a, 11, emphasis in original). With PISA, the assemblage here is driven and centred by the comparison and ranking of national datasets against each other in a form of internationalised programme of datafication. As regards such an international datafication, Meyer and Zahedi argue that 'PISA has contributed to an escalation in such (nationalized standardized) testing and a dramatically increased reliance on quantitative measures' (2014; also Ozga and Segerholm 2015). Indeed, according to Sellar and Lingard, 'the Organization has also promoted arguments for the *necessity* of international comparative data as a basis for national policy-making and as a complement to national testing programmes' (2014, 930, emphasis added). In other words, it could be argued that the OECD is deliberately promoting the need for standardised testing and international comparable ranked datasets to fuel its own global hegemonic position in the need to provide yet more comparative numerical data. Regarding the OECD creating the spiralling requirement for yet more data to provide ever more accurate 'truths' and 'facts' to guide policy, Sellar and Lingard note that: 'Expanding the scope, scale and explanatory power of PISA is helping to create new modalities of governance for the OECD in education, both globally and nationally, with comparative data being very important in this respect' (2014, 931).

Within the context of our discussion of the datafication of primary and early years education, this critique of the expansion of PISA is timely and appropriate because, as we write, the OECD is establishing an international system of comparison of five-year-old children, known as the International Early Learning Study (IELS). The OECD's rationale for IELS is the production of further comparative data to encourage competition within a globalised neoliberal approach to education: 'internationally comparable data would enable countries to compare the relative strengths and areas for development in their own ECEC [early childhood education and care] systems with those in other jurisdictions' (OECD 2015, 103). Interestingly, as regards this OECD rationale impacting upon English early years policy, the DfE is quite clear that the IELS: 'will enable the department to robustly compare our policies and performance to other countries … and will facilitate our assessment and development of early years policy' (DfE 2017a, 1). Here we see the governing power of international datafication and dataveillance drilling down into effecting national governments' policy-making. Indeed Sellar and Lingard have noted that 'the OECD has promoted arguments for the necessity of international comparative data as a basis for national policy making' (Sellar and Lingard 2014, 923). Reflecting these OECD arguments, the DfE state that, regarding IELS data, 'countries need valid and comparable data to help facilitate these improvements to children's early learning' (DfE 2017a, 2). Here the use of decontextualised international standardised testing and subsequent ranking of results are justified by the DfE as an effective policy-making tool. Hence the proposed IELS is an explicit example of the power of data in challenging governments to adjust their internal policies according to their positioning within international comparative datasets. Here all the arguments noted about Baseline Assessment changing schools' curricula, pedagogy and 'teaching to the test' become ratcheted up to an international level where countries' performances are compared and ranked. This international performance ranking then affects national policy, which in turn is cascaded down to schools as curricular, pedagogical and assessment reforms. For Urban and Swadener, this 'abandonment of meaningful contextualized evaluation in order to create *comparability* in turn renders possible findings largely meaningless' (2016, 11) In its rush towards global uniformity of simplistic comparable data such as IELS, the OECD has tacitly adopted a 'hyper-positivistic' paradigm that, as seen with the technical reductionism of Baseline Assessment, 'values objectivity, universality, predictability and what can be measured' (Moss, Dahlberg, Grieshaber *et al.* 2016, 346). In New Zealand, IELS is seen as a threat to the unique bicultural and sociocultural *Te Whariki* early childhood curriculum. Mackey, Hill and Vocht (2016, 448) state it 'will shift the emphasis away from pedagogies which focus on that which is meaningful and relevant in children's lives and their learning, to an emphasis on achieving assessment results that fit a universal framework'. Such global governance and uniformity threatens the diversity of national early childhood education systems so that:

> when the government of the day becomes anxious about the costs of funding early childhood, it may be tempted to call on the apparent precision of numbers to prescribe and measure context-free and curriculum-free internationally developed and validated outcomes over time – and to use those numbers as a benchmark.

> *(Carr, Mitchell and Rameka 2016, 453)*

Hence there is concern that any future international comparison study in early years may be used to rationalise and potentially eradicate local policy in times of austerity.

IELS and Baseline Assessment

IELS was first proposed in 2012 and, at the time of writing (2017), is reaching the piloting stage in three countries, including England. The proposed IELS pilot will assess children aged 4.5 and 5.5 years of age, in Reception classes. The pilot sample will involve 'a stratified cluster sample of 3000 children, composed of 15 children per school in at least 200 schools' and will assess children in 'social and emotional skills as well as their cognitive abilities' in four 'early learning domains' (DfE 2017a, 2):

- Executive function, i.e. early self-regulation and attention;
- Emergent literacy, language and verbal skills;
- Numeracy and mathematics; and
- Empathy and trust.

Similarly to the CEM and NFER Baseline Assessments, it is proposed that the IELS will be conducted via a tablet, taking 15–20 minutes for each domain. The stated aim is to 'gain a better understanding' of:

- children's early learning and development in a broad range of domains, including social and emotional as well as cognitive skills;
- the relationship between children's early learning and children's participation in ECEC;
- the role of other contextual factors, including children's characteristics and their home backgrounds and experiences;
- benchmarking the dual roles of childcare and education in early years provision.

(DfE 2017a, 2)

While IELS is at an early stage of development, and the relationship to Baseline Assessment is not yet clear, it is interesting to note that they are both situated within the same hyperpositivist, comparative paradigm; they measure the same domains and have a remarkably similar methodology of assessment. It is interesting to note that, as with Baseline Assessment, the OECD is clear that prediction is central to the justification of IELS. However, whereas Baseline Assessment attempted to predict across seven years of schooling (age 4–11), IELS attempts to predict across ten years of schooling (age 5–15):

> In time, the information can also provide information on the trajectory between early learning outcomes and those at age 15, as measured by PISA.

> In this way, countries can have an earlier and more specific indication of how
> to lift the skills and other capabilities of its young people.
>
> *(OECD, 2015, 103; Moss, Dahlberg, Grieshaber et al. 2016, 345)*

Here, once again, as with Baseline Assessment, we see the desire to use mathematical algorithms to predict, track and mine children's data but not just across primary school but also across secondary school. As we argued earlier, the current neoliberal competitive conditions encourage the use of such data both nationally and internationally. While policy in England remains at the vanguard of testing young children (Bradbury 2014), it may be that within the current 'policy assemblage' in Europe there might be some form of 'policy transfer ... as policy knowledge circulates globally' (Ball 2012a, 10). Given neoliberalism's demand for new forms of governance in response to turbulent political and economic conditions, it is possible that some Reception children in England could be assessed three times: through a school's own baseline, a national DfE baseline *and* an OECD IELS test.

As argued elsewhere in this book, OECD's PISA represents the collapse of politics, ethics and culture to functional economics, leading Sellar and Lingard to state that 'nations now demand data on comparative schooling performance as a surrogate measure of their global economic competitiveness' (2014, 930). Indeed, the relationship between education and economy is so strong that 'the rise of the OECD's education work is linked to the "economization" of education policy and what we might see as the simultaneous "educationizing" of economic policy' (Sellar and Lingard 2014, 923). Such a relationship exists not only between economy and policy but IELS and Baseline themselves constitute economic opportunities, as we discuss in the next section.

Datafication business opportunities

The role of private companies in state education systems has come under much scrutiny as it has expanded (Ball 2012a). The 'increasing blurring of the welfare state demarcations between the state and market, public and private, government and business' (Junemann and Ball 2013, 423) is evident as data proliferates in schools – for example, in schools' reliance on private external consultants to manage their data, but also in wider terms as private interests become involved in the delivery of policy.

> To carry out PISA and a host of follow-up services, OECD has embraced 'public-private partnerships' and entered into alliances with multi-national for-profit companies, which stand to gain financially from any deficits – real or perceived – unearthed by PISA. Some of these companies provide educational services to American schools and school districts on a massive, for-profit basis, while also pursuing plans to develop for-profit elementary education in Africa, where OECD is now planning to introduce the PISA program.
>
> *(Meyer and Zahedi 2014)*

[IELS] raises the question whether political and corporate profit interests are being privileged over valid research, children's rights and meaningful evaluation.

(Urban and Swadener 2016, 7)

However, Ball argues that the 'retailing of policy solutions' is one of the forms of privatisation of education that has received insufficient critical attention (Ball 2012b, 94). Here we aim to redress this balance, in a small way, by drawing specific attention to the business opportunities that arise from reforms which encourage the collection of data. It is argued that standardised assessments such as Baseline and IELS provide business opportunities for the generation of considerable profit to whichever corporations, innovation labs or social enterprise institutions can secure these national and international contracts; this is evidenced by the growth of investment in education businesses (Williamson 2016d). Indeed, within the US context, the IELS pilot tender is explicitly packaged as a business opportunity on its FedBizOpps.com website (Urban and Swadener 2016, 11). From 2018, the PISA tests will be conducted by the large education company. Pearson's global position means that it is able to both influence education policy *and* provide 'solutions for the problems which it identifies ... creating opportunities for further profit-making interventions' (Unwin and Yandell 2016, 43, cited in Urban and Swadener 2016, 10). For international education companies such as Pearson, PISA and IELS can be understood as part of 'the market processes of capital growth and expansion and the search by business for new opportunities for profit' (Ball 2012a, 11). Within the early childhood context, IELS poses further risks, because so much of the early years sector is privatised; this market will provide a strong incentive to 'teach to the test' (Stobart 2008) with a competition agenda of 'We teach the international OECD programme' and a compliance mindset (Carr, Mitchell and Rameka 2016, 452)

Here we see the centrality of comparable datasets fuelling competition and inciting and driving actors at all levels – from countries to individual institutions – to compete with each other. At a local level in the competitive business environment where early childhood centres such as private nurseries carefully brand themselves to compete for consumers, the temptation to use such marketing would be compelling. Given the already fierce competitive advertising engaged in by early years providers, as exemplified by prominent Ofsted grading signs on both real and virtual nursery sites, it is quite conceivable that nurseries will use Baseline Assessment and IELS in a similar manner.

Moreover, when considering the role of private companies, we are cognizant of the fact that large datasets, such as those produced through Baseline Assessment and IELS, are of considerable commercial interest (Kitchin 2014; Lupton 2016; Williamson 2015a). The construction of such new 'big data'-driven knowledge can be understood as part of the knowledge economy of 'soft and knowing capitalism' (Thrift 2005) that produces data for 'soft' comparison. For example, there were several applications from private companies for access to the National Pupil Database, which includes information on attainment, exclusions and pupil demographics, in 2016–17, as well as from research organisations (DfE 2017b). The large education company Pearson Education Ltd. sought access in order to 'identify the main trends of learner progression from KS3 to Higher Education', while other applications came from Action Tutoring, Cambridge Assessment, Julian Clarke Enterprises Ltd. and GL Assessment. Clearly these data have a commercial use, for tailoring products and services particularly.

We have argued that within primary schools a digital knowledge economy has developed that relies on the production of children's data. Within this knowledge economy, knowledge itself becomes intertwined with the analysis of data so that data have become central to the constitution and exploitation of knowledge (Lupton 2016). Data breed more data, in the search for more knowledge and possibilities for profit. For instance, Early Excellence requested access to the National Pupil Database, as their application states:

> For research to establish potential links/predictors between EExBA Baseline Assessment and EYFS Profile Outcomes.
>
> To identify patterns in the linked cases between the EExBA Baseline Assessment and the EYFS Profile Outcomes.
>
> To examine the performance of specific groups of children, especially those defined as 'disadvantaged'.
>
> *(DfE 2017b)*

Their access to this huge dataset is requested in order to establish the possibilities of tracking between Baseline and the EYFS Profile, thus further demonstrating the usefulness of their product. This delicate interdependence between data, knowledge and economy is also noted by Hogan, Sellar and Lingard (2016, 245). In this context, it is important to remember the costs of Baseline, which were estimated to be between £3.5 and £4.5 million excluding teacher supply cover in 2015–16 (Heavey 2016); this is a large amount of money to be spent via commercial organisations. Within the context of high-stakes accountability, the confusion, apprehension and uncertainty around the new policy can be interpreted by some edu-businesses as a golden opportunity or even 'capitalising on disaster' (Saltman 2015; see also Ball 2012a). These business opportunities included the research and development and subsequent marketing of assessments, the selling of pre-and post-training, data analysis packages, 'improvement' packages and 'add-ons' such as assessments for younger year groups. These opportunities result from new policy contexts, such as the emphasis on data in inspection, but are also a space where other new possibilities for profit can be created; through their marketing these organisations generate and construct new knowledge about young children that enable them to produce new 'essential' products. For example:

> Sig+ is the complete school data company. Our services will equip you with the knowledge, skills and systems required to make the best use of your data and to take your school to the next level. Our aim is to help you understand

your school's data better than anyone else and to ensure there are no surprises.... During inspections schools can contact us for help and, as long as
the school has an online system, we can log in remotely to help produce
essential data for Ofsted, day or night. View us as your emergency data
service.

(Sig+ 2017)

Within a system which is 'governed by inspection' (Grek and Lindgren 2014),
schools do not want any surprises and so are encouraged to buy the 'emergency
data service' to reduce this risk. This is an example of the 'saviour discourse' which
has become apparent as such companies have proliferated; this discourse: 'promises
to deliver schools, leaders and teachers and students from failure, from the terrors
of uncertainty and from the confusions of policy and from themselves – their own
weaknesses' (Ball 2012a, 97). In the data-driven school, the 'weakness' felt by
school leaders is frequently the time and technical expertise to manage the volume,
range and complexity of data production, visualisation and analysis required by the
current policy context. We return to this issue of vulnerability in relation to Baseline below.

As an aside, it is important to note that data in education are big business around
the world, not just in neoliberal states which provoke anxiety, as companies seek to
use technology to improve education systems and generate profit. Less economic-
ally developed countries are an expanding market for such enterprises, which seek
to capitalise on the enthusiasm for 'big data' (Ball, Junemann and Santori 2017). As
an example, 'Report Bee', based in Chennai in India, is one such company. Their
homepage scrolls through slogans:

Harness the power of data: Measure, Analyse and Act
Intelligent Grade Books: A child's growth story told like never before.

(Report Bee 2017)

On their website, the word 'Data' is at the centre of a diagram, surrounded by Collect,
Analyse, Report, Communicate, with each in turn surrounded by names of products.
One product they offer is the 'Thinking Health Card', which allows a teacher to
record whether a child has 'well maintained hair', 'clean shoes' and 'tidy uniform'.
This form of data resonates with Foucault's arguments regarding control of populations
and impositions on the body through biopower (Rabinow and Rose 2006). The collection of data such as these on large populations can indeed be seen as a 'deluge',
which could result in significant profits for these companies. We recognise that the use
of data in education beyond the global north is an area for further research.

Emerging uses of data in education

When thinking about the impact of private data companies on education, we can
speculate about the extent of future use of data-based technologies, based on emerging

uses. Some argue that it is possible to see a fantasised and imagined future where complex political, ethical and social problems find solutions in an online digital world supposedly free of inequality, poverty and discrimination (Kitchin 2014; Williamson 2016d). 'New knowledges' from neuroscience, behavioural economics or psychology (McGimpsey, Bradbury and Santori 2016) combine with digital technology to create new business opportunities within an 'algorithmic imaginary' (Williamson 2016d) capable of disrupting education. Williamson (2017) cites the example of ClassDojo, a free mobile app which, it is claimed, is used globally by over 3 million primary and early years teachers and 35 million children. ClassDojo is theoretically underpinned by Dweck's theory of positive psychological 'growth mindsets', which has growing traction in education internationally (Rustin 2016). For example, the OECD (2015, 3 cited in Williamson 2017, 3) states that 'social and emotional skills can be measured meaningfully' and that 'such measures can be instrumental to help decision makers better assess children's current skill sets and their future needs'. This app enables a digitalised inculcation and assessment of neoliberal subjectivities such as flexibility, hard work, grit and perseverance. The teacher awards points to a child's on-screen monster avatar for desirable behaviour, such as helping others, staying on task, participating, working hard and showing persistence, grit and team work. By choosing to make the 'right' personal, social and emotional choices, children gain or lose points throughout the school day, which can then be shared with parents on their ClassDojo smartphone or computer app. Some teachers display the children's Dojo avatar and their points on the classroom whiteboard during the day. Through ClassDojo, children's compliant subjectivities are promoted through graphic visualisation, while competition is encouraged between children. The data can be displayed as points or as percentages and can be compared over time and with other classes within the school and across schools, thus enabling 'children to be surveilled, valued and made amenable to behaviour modification through persuasive technologies on a global scale' (Williamson 2017, 10). Thus currently fashionable practices based on a 'new knowledge' are being delivered through technology. Williamson argues ClassDojo's 'close alignment with emerging governmental priorities regarding children's social and emotional lives represents a contemporary entanglement of psychological expertise, commercial ed-tech, and policy priorities' (2017). The relevance for us of this analysis is that apps such as ClassDojo collect huge amounts of data about children's behaviour and attitudes, which have been areas previously less affected by data, with the exception of the early years, where 'personal, social and emotional development' has been assessed for a number of years. Thus the constraining systems of measuring 'character' as an individualised quality which can be blamed for success or failure within a neoliberal framework are spreading, through technology, upwards through the education system. We can see the use of such technology to produce desirable personal and character attributes as a form of 'gamified' dataveillance which both disciplines and controls. It operates within the enclosure of the classroom disciplining children into particular behaviours through reward and punishment, but also makes visible children's success in producing these behaviours to other teachers and their parents beyond the classroom, in real time.

The growth of apps such as ClassDojo provides a further example of datafication as an international phenomenon, operating beyond national policy. The app is used around the world, with local adaptations, in an international project of altering 'mindsets': 'This development appears to make ClassDojo's 30 million child users into research subjects in a massive experiment in mindset modification ... emphasizing the pursuit of individual improvement while ignoring the societal structures that impact on children's education' (Williamson 2017, 8). This trend is reflected in the OECD's support for measuring social and emotional skills, as quoted above, which is a manifestation of their positivist, technocratic approach to education, combined with their interests in measurement, accountability and ed-tech business possibilities. In this, the OECD is attempting to position itself within a 'sociotechnical imaginary' in which 'there are publically performed visions of desirable futures that are animated by shared understandings of forms of social life and social order and made attainable through the design of technological projects' (Williamson 2016d, 5).

Baseline as business

In the case of Baseline Assessment in England, the DfE, through its policy regulatory power, established such a business framework for competing edu-businesses to tender for the contract to provide the assessment. The DfE established a set of requirements and a number of organisations responded to the tender, with three organisations making a final list as 'approved' providers: Early Excellence, the Centre for Evaluation and Monitoring at Durham University (CEM) and the National Foundation for Educational Research (NFER). Some other providers were initially approved but had insufficient market share to be approved in the final stage. At the same time as the tendering process, the DfE ensured what Harvey calls 'maximum entrepreneurial freedoms ... and unencumbered markets' (2007, 22) by making the EYFS Profile, the only other existing accountability measure, non-mandatory and voluntary, thereby clearing away the state's potentially competing early years accountability measure. As we have argued elsewhere, 'Not only did making the EYFS Profile non-mandatory strengthen the importance of baseline, but it also had the effect of undermining and marginalizing the central role of Local Authority (LA) early years data profile management and organization' (Roberts-Holmes and Bradbury 2017).

Through this dual process of regulating for Baseline and removing market obstacles, the DfE maximised the opportunities of Baseline providers while the DfE's role became reduced to that of the technical organisation of privatised Baseline contracts and tenders. Thus we argue Baseline represented a further move from hierarchical government to heterarchical governance and as 'a decisive move from a system of state education to a system of state-funded education networks' (Ball and Junemann 2012, 142). The state's role here becomes reduced to that of the technical organisation of private contracts and tenders, while providing the funding. This heterarchical model of technical governance can be diagrammatically represented as shown in Figure 6.1.

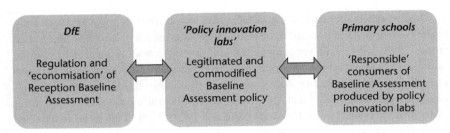

FIGURE 6.1   Heterarchical governance of Baseline Assessment showing network flows between the DfE, public policy labs and primary schools (Roberts-Holmes and Bradbury 2017).

The tendering process for contracts to become a DfE-accredited provider can be considered as part of the neoliberal blurring of boundaries and distinctions between the state, edu-businesses, datalabs and third-sector not-for-profit research-based organisations (Ball 2012b). Williamson (2015b, 252) refers to such hybridised organisations as 'policy innovation labs' that straddle both the public and the private sectors. Here the traditional binary categorisations of the state and private sector are no longer useful or applicable as: 'traditional lines and demarcations, public and private, market and state, are being breached and blended in all of this and are no longer useful analytically as free-standing descriptors' (Ball 2012a, 86). These diverse cross-sectoral organisations with their multiple allegiances and affiliations are able to 'face both ways' towards the public and private sectors (Higham 2014, 417). By being located at the interstitial space between the public and private sectors such 'policy innovation labs can operate as socially responsible philanthropic research based organizations *and* as profitable social entrepreneurial edu-businesses at the same time' (Roberts-Holmes and Bradbury 2017). Hogan, Sellar and Lingard (2016, 244) refer to such companies as being 'neo-social', that is, they are able to both meet their social responsibilities and make a profit. In the case of Baseline Assessment, it can be argued that such neo-social public policy labs had the aim: 'of trying things out, getting things done, changing things, and avoiding established public sector lobbies and interests, in an attempt to 'routinise innovation' and incubate creative possibilities' (Ball 2012a, 105). The removal of the local authorities' trusted advice and expertise and at the same time the increased use of policy innovation labs was deeply unsettling for the headteachers. Their uncertainties about the future were exacerbated and compounded because the local authority's traditional support and advice had been reduced, leaving individual schools to find solutions on their own.

Two of the headteachers we interviewed about Baseline identified this vulnerability:

> I don't think I have ever come across a situation where heads feel so at sea … nobody really knows what they are doing … If I am sitting here as a headteacher with over 20 years' experience saying I don't really know what

to do, even I am vulnerable for somebody to come in and say, 'I can solve this problem for you' ... There is a lot of money sloshing around and you know as whenever that happens you have got some very reputable and very capable people but you have also got some people who just see the pound signs first and don't have educational value at the top of their list. So it is worrying times. I think it creates even more scope for people to actually make a buck out of this whole thing if I'm honest.

(Head, Damson)

I feel extremely concerned about the increased use of private companies in the entire education world, but also within assessment at the moment. I feel that by removing and taking away all the known assessments and I am not saying they were great, but taking away all of those, what has happened is we have been opened up to a completely free market and we are being bombarded with sales pitches. And actually that is very hard when what you are trying to do is focus in on what you are doing for children. [...] I think that the companies at the moment can really capitalise on the fear factor in schools and with headteachers and it is not healthy really.

(Head, Cedar)

Here the headteachers stated how frustrated, apprehensive and exploited they felt by the intense marketisation of Baseline Assessment by the different companies vying for their Baseline data business. Private organisations and policy innovation labs have therefore been able to meet this data demand and have positioned themselves 'at the centre of how public education is funded, organised and delivered' (Selwyn 2016a, 107). Given the 'terrors of uncertainty' and the consequences of inspection failure, sometimes determined by the school data, such providers are indeed able to offer a crisis solution.

In the following interview, the headteacher describes how he attempted to stay as an 'ordinary old-fashioned school' within the strictures, demands and agonies of the market place that left him feeling 'vulnerable' and 'exploited':

Once upon a time something new like this would have come in and the local authority would have solved the problem for us and they would have got us all together and said 'This is what –'. Because they had the staff, they had the personnel, they had the expertise. They would have solved that problem for us and said 'This is what we are going to do as a local authority. It doesn't matter what the one next door is going to do; this is what we are going to do'. That doesn't happen now because the local authority has been so cut back that there isn't the level of expertise or people with the time to actually solve these problems so it is down to us. ... And of course in our authority we have got a high number of academies anyway that are all parts of different chains, so you have got chain A solving it one way, chain B solving it another way and maybe they have got people to help a smaller group of schools and

> then the rest of us are just left to our own devices, which does make schools vulnerable in so many ways, in terms of Ofsted, in terms of exploitation and in terms of actually doing your job properly. ... I mean with the breakdown of the education system, your academisation, your free schools, and then ordinary old-fashioned schools like us.
>
> *(Head, Damson)*

Within this ontological crisis, this headteacher was suspicious of the motives of the DfE-accredited providers but nevertheless felt the fear and threat of academisation if he made the incorrect 'market' decisions in trying to remain an ordinary old-fashioned school. The removal of the local education authority advice provides an example of the 'reluctant state' in which the headteacher was struggling with a 're-grounding of social relations in the economic rationality of the market' (Ball 2012b, 101). Baseline Assessment attempted to bypass the local authority and the EYFS Profile while ensuring that the DfE-accredited provider was able to analyse the data. Here the state (expensively) produced the data, but then was removed from its subsequent analysis, in favour of the policy innovation labs. As one headteacher succinctly put it, 'You are paying the private sector for the joy of delivering your own assessment' (Head, Alder).

Headteachers commented on the extra costs involved in Baseline, beyond what was provided by the DfE, mainly relating to training and cover to allow teachers to moderate and input data.

> Yes, I think we have spent £420 on a one-day training course for our early years lead teacher. I literally couldn't afford to send all three. So she has been on the course and rolled it out and I think there is another training event for headteachers and coordinators to go along – that will have a cost and then the actual materials.
>
> *(Head, Alder)*

> It has taken a ridiculous amount of time to complete – and also has cost the school a lot of money in terms of getting supply teachers to cover classes whilst the Baseline Assessment was undertaken. This is not value for money for schools – even if the government paid for the test itself.
>
> *(W)*

The cost of training appeared to be a particular issue, which resulted in many Reception teachers receiving training only from the one teacher who had attended the course, leading to further confusion over how to assess the children. There were also concerns about the costs of additional materials, and the fact that those who went on training were only allowed one manual, which they were instructed not to photocopy. One deputy headteacher stated that the early years teachers were about to 'explode' with the increase in their workload caused by Baseline so employed four supply teachers to help in the process of managing the Baseline collection. These problems of cost seemed to be a particular issue at a time when budgets are being reduced in general at school and local authority levels. Again, the issue of usefulness was a key part of value for money.

> This Baseline Assessment has told us no more than the profile and our own assessment systems. So, a waste of money.
>
> *(W)*

This perception that Baseline is a 'waste of money' was an important part of the devaluing of the policy among school staff and made Baseline particularly unacceptable to teachers and school leaders when other budgets were being reduced. Teachers felt frustrated, disrespected and undermined as they 'lost control' of the data they collected as it was submitted online to the providers. They were unsure about what would happen to their Baseline judgements, how they would be analysed and what they were expected to do next.

> It does feel a bit odd that you have given something away having no idea of how it is to be used.
>
> *(Head, Cedar)*

> There are so many unanswered questions about what is going to happen, what it is going to look like, what it is going to be used for?
>
> *(Teacher 1, Alder)*

These early years teachers felt that they had become reduced to data gatherers and 'grey technicians', harvesting data to be sent out to the providers to be recycled back to them as governing tools. In this sense, they experienced a professional 'democratic deficit' (Ball and Junemann 2012; Hogan, Sellar and Lingard 2016).

The importance of policy 'translators'

As argued elsewhere, the process of policy from conception to enactment is complex, and where policy is in some way controversial or unpopular, this journey can be aided by a number of different actors, including third parties (McGimpsey, Bradbury and Santori 2016; Ball 2012a). We argue here that the Baseline providers facilitated the implementation of Baseline as a policy by 'translating' it into something more acceptable to the educators involved. We note that this is a slightly different use of 'translation' from that used in McGimpsey, Bradbury and Santori (2016), which describes how new academic fields are 'translated' into policy; and different from Ball *et al.*'s use of 'policy translators' (2011b); however there are commonalities in our arguments. We argue here that the three DfE-accredited providers each had a role in delivering, and making palatable, a policy which was deeply unpopular with many educational organisations (BWB 2015). Early Excellence was by far the most popular, with 12,500 schools. These organisations variously portrayed themselves as 'inspiring learning' and providing 'an expert view on policy and practice for the reception year' (Early Excellence 2016):

> The overwhelming take-up of our version of the baseline test, EExBA, was entirely due to the fact that it was a practitioner led, non-invasive observational assessment, that used the Leuven Scales of wellbeing and involvement to ascertain whether the child was settled and used the characteristics of effective learning alongside the areas of learning and development to derive the – albeit numerical – outcome … by choosing to re-register for EExBA in 2016 we are building momentum around practitioner-led assessment and helping to ensure that the government's next move is shaped by best practice.
>
> *(Early Excellence 2016)*

Here the careful use of targeted early years terminology and child-centred rhetoric and approaches functioned as highly effective niche branding and marketing for this public policy lab and enabled it to rapidly capture 70 per cent of the market share. By centrally engaging with the early years discourse and language of 'child centred observational assessment', alongside 'well-being and the characteristics of effective learning' helped it to mobilise the early years constituency for whom such principles and values are central, as we saw in the data relating to how baselines were chosen in the previous chapter. The webpage for EExBA is professionally designed and encapsulates both early years principles of a young child physically engaged in her own learning and a professionally developed video.

A particular feature of the Early Excellence webpages was its association with established early years academics such as Professor Ferre Laevers and his respected Leuven Scales of Well-Being. As we have argued elsewhere:

> Such branding helps to present the company as a legitimate and 'responsible' actor whilst at the same time ensuring its market dominance and profit. By presenting itself as child-centred, it effectively 'moralizes' the baseline to the early years community. This 'economisation of morality' (Hogan *et al.*, 2016) further built the Early Excellence brand. Such 'responsible' and 'moral marketing' not only engendered early years consensus building but also limited the emergence of refusal or resistance to the policy.
>
> *(Roberts-Holmes and Bradbury 2017)*

The Early Excellence webpage states:

> The Early Excellence Baseline (EExBA) offers a principled approach to on-entry assessment. It does not include any predetermined tasks or tests and will not disrupt settling in routines. Instead, as part of their everyday practice, practitioners build their knowledge of each child through their observations, interactions and every day activities. They use this professional knowledge to

make a series of judgements about each child based on a clear set of assessment criteria.

(Early Excellence 2016)

Such niche marketing may appear to make Baseline more useful or 'meaningful' in that the format is familiar to teachers – a process we can see as 'translating' the policy into the specific context of early years – but like all of the providers, Early Excellence had to abide strictly by the DfE's requirement for 'yes' or 'no' binary statements on individual children. Crucially such marketing serves to obscure the fact that, along with all the other providers, it produces a highly reductionist single numerical score, tacitly acknowledged in the last sentence of the above Early Excellence website statement. When in 2017 the government announced a consultation on replacing Baseline with a single new 'robust' assessment, the national director of Early Excellence, Jan Dubiel, expressed his 'surprise', commenting, 'It is weird the Department for Education seems to want to do the same thing again, but not take into account … the clear and overwhelming rejection of a test-based approach' (Camden 2017). Obviously there are commercial reasons why Early Excellence would favour a system which allows schools to choose, but his comments further underline our argument that Early Excellence positioned itself in an intermediary role, *translating* policy for the early years community.

The promotional webpage for the Centre for Evaluation and Monitoring (CEM) at Durham University focused on their long-established reputation as providers of assessments for young children in their marketing of their Baseline. CEM's webpages emphasised that they were a university-based research assessment specialist, which they emphasise to establish credibility:

Used by education professionals for over 30 years in over 70 countries, CEM is one of the largest and longest established research groups providing learning assessment for children of all ages … CEM's methods are research-based, evidence driven and market-tested, built on a foundation of non-commercial academic practice with the School of Education at Durham University. Based on over 20 years' research, with over 3.6 million reception baseline assessments carried out, BASE will assess literacy, numeracy, communication, and PSED★ – combining objective and observation-based assessment to enhance ongoing assessment practice.

(CEM 2017)

CEM's detailed and thorough suite of webpages boast an extensive collection of case studies, promotional videos, pricing options and advice for different stakeholders as to their benefits.

In contrast to Early Excellence's subjective observation, CEM's central marketing focus was to provide 'a quick and easy-to-use baseline assessment' and the objectivity of its tablet-based assessments. The speed of the assessment combined with its computer objectivity is emphasised on its webpages as one of its central features and is in contrast to the longer time taken for the Early Excellence assessment.

> The reception baseline assessment takes approximately 20 minutes with each child (you can stop and restart if needed), and there is no teacher marking or data to input … Objective assessment can offer insight beyond observation, telling you things that are hard to observe and giving you information as a teacher that you would not otherwise easily get – it should be used alongside other forms of assessment as part of a holistic assessment approach.
>
> *(CEM 2017)*

As with Early Excellence, CEM's Baseline webpage was highly professional in its marketisation of its long-running expertise and experience while at the same time appealed to the early years community through its use of the base insect cartoon-like character.

Like Early Excellence and CEM, the third provider, the National Foundation for Educational Research (NFER), also carried a promotional video on its front webpage along with a raft of information tabs.

NFER states that it is a national not-for-profit charitable independent foundation for education research. As with CEM, and in contrast to Early Excellence, it promotes itself as 'quick and easy to administer with no additional training required', taking around 30 minutes per child with a tablet-based assessment. In their marketing materials, all three policy innovation labs can be seen as having softened the hard bureaucratic power of centralised government policy through 'the techniques of attraction, seduction, persuasion and the cultivation of support and shared interest' (Williamson 2016c, 38). By engaging with the language of early years, particularly in the case of Early Excellence, they position themselves as ethically aligned with the educators rather than policy-makers, thus limiting resistance to the policy, and as suggested in the quote from Ball above, 'getting things done'.

Overall we can see the use of these organisations as part of the shift from government to 'polycentric' governance, as described by Junemann and Ball: 'A contrast is drawn here between government as accomplished through hierarchies, within administrations and by bureaucratic methods, and governance as carried out through the more flexible and "informal authority" (Rhodes 1997) of diverse networks' (2013, 425). The involvement of this diverse range of organisations in the delivery of Baseline policy reflects this 'shift to polycentrism', as policy is being done in spaces beyond state organisations with the involvement of new networks of actors. Policy labs become critically important and significant as government policy carriers since they are able to expertly 'legitimate and naturalise policy "narratives" such as the controversial baseline, that might otherwise have been previously unthinkable' (Roberts-Holmes and Bradbury 2017). With Baseline Assessment, the use of policy innovation labs to get such difficult and controversial accountability policy done enabled the government 'to try out' new, creative and alternative ways of producing reductive comparable data in the early years. These partnerships brought in 'new voices within policy conversations and new conduits through which policy discourses enter policy thinking' (Ball 2012a, 9). By bringing in policy innovation, entrepreneurs who had a blend of early years knowledge and the technical expertise of analysing large datasets enabled a new 'policy conversation' to be started around the possibilities and extent to which a national standardised Baseline Assessment was possible. It can be argued that by introducing such a range of new early years digital entrepreneurs the DfE hoped that 'these might serve to "short-circuit" or displace existing policy blockages' (Ball 2012a, 105). Such 'policy blockages' might be seen as including an early years professional community that was perceived to be resistant to the reductionism of an assessment resulting in a single number.

Conclusion

Datafication is an international development in education, operating differently in different places, but raising similar questions about what data 'do to' teachers and children. We would argue that Baseline Assessment and IELS are examples of early years assessments being used inappropriately with young children. Measuring children, and similarly financial profit, between two decontextualised points seems simple, logical and linear but this model cannot be readily transposed onto the complexity of learning and interaction in the early years. Nonetheless, the concept of such simplistic progress remains a priority for many governments, as evidenced by the popularity of PISA.

This international aspect of datafication reflects a wider shift in how policy is produced, translated and enacted, which relies on private and philanthropic organisations (Ball, Junemann and Santori 2017). Important emerging actors include 'public policy labs' (Williamson 2015b), whether they be small scale such as Early Excellence or large scale such as OECD's PISA. Private companies are a driving force for datafication, which operates beyond national borders, combining with current trends in education to produce products which appear essential. Thus, as Biesta argues, it makes sense to talk of a global measurement *industry*, which has:

> managed to bring a wide range of actors with significantly different interests into one network, including researchers, academics, national governments, commercial publishers and supra-national organisations such as the OECD and the World Bank, thus creating as Latour (1987) has called it, a strong *asymmetry* between those who are inside the network and who are outside of it. This makes it significantly more difficult, more expensive, and more energy- and time-consuming to interrupt and oppose this network with meaningful alternatives.
>
> *(Biesta 2017, 316, emphasis in original)*

We turn in our final chapter to a discussion of these meaningful alternatives, with an awareness of the difficulties of challenging the international phenomenon of datafication.

7

DATAFIED LEARNER IDENTITIES

Towards an understanding of the future of data in education

Introduction

In this book we have sought to question taken-for-granted assumptions about data and to ask critical questions about what data do in education, to practice and to people. In this concluding chapter, we bring together our key arguments and discuss the significance of data for education in the 'age of measurement' (Biesta 2009). In asking the question 'Why does any of this matter?' we hope to reinforce what we see as the important issues, concerns and principles that are implicated in our findings in relation to datafication. We emphasise that this is not simply a matter for academic discussion, but a real phenomenon which affects the every-day lives of teachers, school leaders and, of course, children.[1] It is also indicative of wider epistemological shifts in education, which prioritise data as a form of knowledge and method of governance. In a final section, with the aim of ending on a positive note, we set out possibilities of alternatives within early years and primary education through the postmodern 'discourse of meaning making', which is set in contrast to the 'discourse of quality' (Dahlberg, Moss and Pence 2007, 86). We hope that this discussion of alternative ways of thinking about education and data will provoke further critical reflection on this topic.

Key arguments

Educational data can have important and useful functions at a number of levels; governing through data can include monitoring, highlighting and challenging disadvantage, inequality and social injustice throughout the education system. Data systems can allow us to connect different forms of information, and 'democratise decision-making processes' through increased transparency and making 'elite actors more "accountable" for their actions' (Selwyn 2015, 66). At a classroom level, clearly some collection of information is useful to teachers and helps parents understand what their children are doing and need help with. Moreover, we must remember that 'there are no intrinsic, "essential" qualities to data which, in absolute terms, will bring about troubling consequences' (Perrotta 2013, 119). But we argue that the disciplining governmentality of data warrants critical scrutiny and examination, which we hope to have achieved here.

We have argued through this book that early years settings and primary schools are undergoing a process of 'datafication'. This is not happening consistently in different places and times perhaps, but we argue there has been in recent years an overall shift in practices and values which represent a 'turn to data', and this is likely to continue. New technologies of monitoring and tracking enable vast quantities of primary school data to be easily collected, analysed, visualised and, importantly, compared. Within neoliberal schooling there is 'an increasing fetishisation of statistical measurement and competitive ranking' (Shore and Wright 2015, 22) purporting to offer reliable and valid calculations of largely qualitative processes. Data have important functions at a number of levels, but also label the individual four-year-old as 'above' or 'below' their expected level. Here we have focused mainly on the operation of data *within* schools – the impact on practice and pedagogy, subjectivities and strategic responses – but with an awareness that the 'statistical journey' of the data in question continues on to government. Our examples, from early years settings recording the 'progress' of two-year-olds, to the England-wide use of Baseline Assessment, provide case studies (or perhaps more accurately, cautionary tales) of how data can operate in education. Recent developments such as the OECD's International Early Learning Study, or 'mini-PISA', which we discuss in Chapter 6, make this examination of the role of data more pressing. There is a need to define and examine datafication, as it evolves in different contexts around the world. One limitation of this work is our focus on England and the similarities with practices elsewhere in Europe and in the United States and Australia, as data are used in a multitude of different ways in different parts of the world.

We have argued that data are productive *and* reductive. Data are, in Beer's term, 'productive measures' in the context of 'everyday neoliberalism' (2015), 'making up' new subjectivities for teachers as data collectors, and children as they become their data doubles, or Deleuze's *dividuals*. We have argued that the current fixation on numerical data is productive and generative of neoliberal child and teacher subjectivities that are: 'flexible, competitive, entrepreneurial, choice-loving and autonomous, able to thrive in markets; and it requires considerable management to produce this subject – starting from the earliest age' (Fielding and Moss 2011, 23). Thus data are a key part of the production of the 'neoliberal subject' in early years, building on the production of this subjectivity through the content of the EYFS (Bradbury 2013a). Through combining together ever greater numbers of datasets, such as Baseline, phonics, Sats and even possibly IELS, the datafied child with potentially limited pre-determined goals, expectations and pathways becomes a possibility. Within this, datafied children:

are configured as algorithmic assemblages as the result of these practices, with the possibility that their complexities, potentialities and opportunities may be circumscribed. They are encouraged to view and compare themselves with others using these assemblages from very early in the lifespans.

(Lupton and Williamson 2017, 787)

Once objectified as data it is relatively straightforward to classify and rank and ascribe particular values to children, such as 'talented' or 'irredeemable'. These data may be used by children and teachers to construct 'stories' of their 'ability', potentially affecting their self-esteem and limiting their potential. Using algorithms, children's data doubles are then used to make predictions about future tracking and attainment possibilities. These can then be acted against pre-emptively in primary school organisation – for example, through forward planning 'ability' grouping, setting and streaming. Here data are used as 'actionable intelligence' (Williamson 2015b) in much the same way that business uses data to predict risk, loss and potential profit.

We have also argued that data produce new expectations and flows of power between individuals in education, within data-based hierarchies based on relationships to data (Manovich 2012; Selwyn, Nemorin and Johnson 2016). They are essential to the 'quotidian, mundane neoliberalisations' of school life (Ball and Olmedo 2013, 85), vital to the 'little neoliberalism' of the every-day, demanding and expecting self-government and improvement within a performative culture. Through dataveillance, teachers and children are disciplined, in Foucault's terms, through visibility; but this power operates, as suggested by Deleuze, in increasingly fluid and mobile ways beyond traditional 'enclosures' of the school and in-between formal 'moments of exposure' (Thompson and Cook 2017, 34), such as formal observations and inspections. Moreover, data are a powerful means of control which delineate what knowledge is important, who is successful and what we can expect from children. While they appear to be a neutral construction, behind the categories, content and analyses of data in spreadsheets and databases lie particular 'regimes of truth' which govern young children and the people who work with them. Sometimes these are hidden from us, but we remain subject to 'problematic data manipulations performed "under the hood" on remote servers' (Perrotta 2013, 118). Data-based registers of meaning are in turn further solidified by the actions we take in response to data: putting children into 'ability' groups, selecting the subjects of interventions or deciding which teachers deserve to be paid more.

However, data are simultaneously also *reductive*, reducing the complexities and messy realities of young children to numbers, codes or colours, which fail to recognise or respect the multiplicities of learning that occur in early years and primary education.

In many approaches to the datafication and dataveillance of children, the embodied and subjective voices of children are displaced by the supposed impartial objectivity provided by the technological mouthpieces of data. Data are positioned to provide a more detailed and manageable account of who children really are, free from the messiness of dialogic deliberation and freedom of expression.

(Lupton and Williamson 2017, 790)

This reductionism can have damaging effects – over-simplifying, limiting expectations, as well as reducing teachers to processors of numbers. Simplistic data serve to conceal any local 'irregularities, histories and struggles over the meaning of data' (Ozga *et al.* 2011, 87). Instead, 'data assemblages … speak on their behalf' (Lupton and Williamson 2017, 791). Similarly complex pedagogical discussion and reflection becomes substituted by a technical, economic discourse of 'what works' as schools strive to maintain their competitive edge over each other. For many, the most fitting analogy for the school has become the factory, in its attempt to 'process' identical inputs and outputs, like sausages. This dehumanising conception of education operates in tension with an ethic of care, with emotional and professional costs for the teachers involved.

We have noted the serious concerns about the reliability of collecting data on young children, particularly with one-off assessments which do not take into account age or first language, and the potentially serious implications in terms of social justice. Although we recognise the use of data in highlighting inequalities, we also wish to emphasise the ways in which datafication may serve to reinforce rather than challenge inequality. Our critical analysis of Baseline Assessment has highlighted the datafication processes which label the individual four- or five-year-old as 'above' or 'below' their expected level, which in turn sets up expectations for the future; similarly, tracking systems in nurseries and children's centres may mean children are labelled as 'behind' before they even start school. This is important in a context where data offer an easy policy seduction so that not only can complex social problems such as inequality and poverty be ignored but, so it is claimed, be solved through digital computation (Kitchin 2014). Furthermore, a focus on data can limit thinking about equity (Lingard, Sellar and Savage 2014), as well as reveal inequalities. We argue, as elsewhere, that inequalities can be reproduced and reinforced through data in a productive cycle of systematic disadvantage (Bradbury 2013c) and emphasise how important the early years become in terms of resisting marginalisation in this context.

We have discussed the role of data in the visibility of performance, at various levels. Datafication has intensified processes of performativity, creating a hyper-performative atmosphere where everything must be quantified and accounted for. Data are key to self-government; as one teacher commented: 'we have to show they are making progress or we're not doing our job'. It produces new strategic responses, or 'perverse effects' (Lingard and Sellar 2013), including the tendency to keep Baseline scores low in order to maximise future progress, and to select a Baseline which is seen either as resisting 'testing culture' or as limiting the damage. The reification of progress allows learning to be predicted, anticipated, and attainment to be measured against these targets to ascertain failure or success. Whether we conceive of these developments as disciplinary power or a society of control, the impact on teachers and children is clear: data production, analysis and processing now form a key part of the school lives of these individuals, whether they are aware or not. They shape our notions of the 'good teacher' – even when this means one who 'plays with the numbers' – and our notions of the 'good pupil'.

One of our central arguments has been that policy such as Baseline Assessment is representative of the key neoliberal concept of economism, which 'is the reduction of everything to economic values ends' (Fielding and Moss 2011, 19). Attempts to use measurements of young children's learning to judge schools reflect the 'numericisation of politics' (Legg 2005, 143 cited in Ball 2017, 43); the desire to quantify for the purposes of assessing effectiveness. We have critiqued Baseline Assessment as based on a crude pseudo-business model requiring simplified children's input data in Reception to be compared with output data seven years later at the end of primary school. Within this, we argue that children's families and the local school context and complexity are stripped away, and that this process was happening with young children in their first six weeks of schooling was a form of hyper-governmentality.

We have focused mainly on the operation of data within schools – on their impact on practice and pedagogy, subjectivities and strategic responses – but with an awareness that the 'statistical journey' of the data in question continues through onto government comparative websites, such as RAISEonline, that are central to inspection outcomes. Data are political and ethical in both their construction and use, and far from objective. We have argued that the power of dataveillance is used to ever more tightly discipline, govern and control school populations both in the present and through predictive algorithms in the future.

These school-level developments occur in an international context where education systems are increasingly 'governed by numbers', both through the OECD's PISA tests, potentially the early years equivalent, IELS, and through national systems of inspection, monitoring and comparison underpinned by market imperatives. This international form of datafication has clear links with other distinctly neoliberal forms in education, especially the involvement of private companies whose expertise is required to analyse the data and manage the 'data deluge'. Both small businesses and huge corporations – the myriad of small data-analysing businesses available to schools; the dedicated sector companies such as Early Excellence; the international edu-businesses such as Pearson – all play an increasingly important role as the technological knowledge required for high-stakes datafication becomes ever more complicated. At every level, there are business opportunities as ever stronger and more complex governing webs of data are wrapped around a datafied child, teacher and school. Third-sector and private organisations, including 'policy innovation labs' (Williamson 2015b), thus facilitate the turn to data, both by providing services and by translating unpalatable policy into acceptable forms (Roberts-Holmes and Bradbury 2017). This development has been in part enabled by 'major global technology companies and venture capital investment firms that have begun to concentrate significant technical and financial resources in education in recent years' (Williamson 2016d, 1). For example, an estimated 1.6 billion dollars were invested in such 'ed-tech' companies in 2015 (Wan and McNally, 2015 cited in Williamson 2016d, 1). These ed-tech companies enable vast quantities of school data to be easily collected, analysed, visualised and competitively compared. We would tentatively suggest that Baseline Assessment in England represents a minor, localised policy skirmish into such 'a technocratic and algorithmically imagined' future (Williamson 2016d, 13). It could be argued that the UK Department for Education's unprecedented privatisation of early years assessment was a faltering flirtation with 'an algorithmic imaginary' acting as a catalyst to demonstrate potential to possible future investors. Indeed Baseline policy can be understood as an early prototype 'philanthropic governance' (Olmedo 2014) seeking to re-orientate government and the public sector 'to embrace the model of venture philanthropy from the private sector' (Williamson 2016d, 3). Ed-tech development and investment in Silicon Valley start-ups such as ClassDojo that have now become global businesses suggest that such venture capital investment can be lucrative.

Why does any of this matter?

One of the key reasons why this matters is that issues relating to datafication challenge the fundamental principles on which education systems are based. Hardy and Boyle argue that 'the abstraction and quantification of education' – for them epitomised by school comparison websites – challenges our conception of education (2011, 213). Reliance on quantification 'produces knowledge separate from those engaged in a particular practice' (2011, 213); this distancing of 'knowledge' from the reality which produces it calls into question what it means to learn, to assess and to be a professional teacher. Data are vital to the dominant discourse in early childhood education of 'the story of quality and high returns', which Moss describes as 'instrumental, economistic and technical in character, focused intently on the predictability, certainty and closure of predetermined goals achieved' (Moss 2015, 236). It is important to reflect on why reduction is attractive, and seductive. One position is that in the uncertainties of a 'late neoliberal' world (McGimpsey 2017) there is comfort in the apparent solidity of numbers, or what Biesta calls the 'pseudo-security of numbers' (2017, 317). We have seen in our research data how pedagogical decision making becomes reduced to improving comparative scores in an attempt to manage and replace the uncertainty and precarity of 'liquid modernity' (Bauman 2000) with the solidity of 'facts' and numbers that purport to demonstrate economic 'impact' and therefore worth. We would argue that much of the power/attraction of datafication lies in its ability to predict; to render the future knowable, as suggested by the hype around 'big data' and the ability to predict flu epidemics (Eynon 2013; Kitchin 2014). Risk management through carefully calculated and predicted data becomes a central management tool to generate predictable outcomes and alleviate fears and apprehensions of losing; the 'measurement industry is fuelled by a fear of risk and a concomitant desire for control' (Biesta 2017, 317).

Simplistic algorithms and data bring the allure of scientific authority and technical precision to the otherwise imprecise and unpredictable early years and primary education. Schools become transformed into 'data platforms' (Williamson 2015a) for incessant and urgent calculations of profit and loss. In this context, 'it becomes increasingly difficult not to look at the data [...] The availability of data ... is seductive and difficult to resist' (Biesta 2017, 324). However, the production of data does not reduce the anxiety, but generates further necessities – are we collecting the right data? Do we have the right story to tell about our data? What can we do to improve 'our data'? The affective dimension of data is significant in driving self-governance: as Ball and Olmedo argue, 'neoliberalism is experienced and perceived in the classroom and in the soul' (2013, 90). Professional judgement and autonomy becomes transformed into financial rationality so that:

> [teachers] calculate their actions not in the esoteric languages of their own expertise but by translating them into costs and benefits that can be given an accounting value ... the terms of that accountability were not professional but those of accounting. They were reorganised, transformed into aggregations of accountable spaces, reshaped into cost-centres ... rendered calculable in financial terms.
>
> *(Rose 1999, 152)*

This neoliberal rationality is pervasive, making children into data doubles, assessed for their potential to bring gains or losses to the school's performance. But prediction is a dangerous concept in education, which cannot be simply transferred from other fields. The rise of big data, led by private business and 'future orientated analytics' has been inappropriately applied to the unpredictable world of education, so that the 'ability' of a four-year-old is distilled into a single number which they will be measured against seven years later. This is a form of 'actionable intelligence' where algorithms are used to predict 'bumps in the road' or potential problems in the future. But the dangers of using algorithms within the cultural, political and ethical sphere of education are clear; their use is highly problematic even within the seemingly scientific and objective banking sector. Cathy O'Neil, a former hedge fund manager on Wall Street in New York, noted that algorithmic models:

> encoded human prejudice, misunderstanding and bias into the software systems that increasingly managed our lives. Like gods, these mathematical models were opaque, their workings invisible to all but the highest priests in their domain: mathematicians and computer scientists. Their verdicts, even when wrong or harmful, were beyond dispute or appeal.
>
> *(O'Neil 2016, 3)*

Even within the entirely different context of Baseline Assessment, the effects of algorithms cast an aura of scientific certainty and methodological rigor onto a Baseline score. However, as we have demonstrated, the opposite is largely true as

Baseline generated scores that were seen as incomparable, flawed and subjective. But within a data-based frame of value, that is unimportant because algorithms 'define their own reality and use it to justify their results. This type of model is self-perpetuating, highly destructive and very common' (O'Neil 2016, 7). So, for example, Baseline algorithms allocated low scores to children who were then incorrectly sorted, classified and ranked, including into contestable 'ability' groups. Ability grouping has been shown to impact on resources and reduce aspirations, often leading to low attainment (Francis *et al.* 2015). This model of education as something quantifiable is intrinsically linked with the continued normalisation of 'ability' as a fixed notion. This conception of 'ability' as permanent and measurable (which requires much further discussion than we have space here) is inherent to practices of prediction; more complex understandings of human possibilities make predictions meaningless. Thus datafication is significant because it reveals how the ways in which we think about education are changing, while in turn it has an impact on practices and subjectivities – what we do and who we are – which is surely something that matters.

In this book, we have highlighted the detailed evidence of the 'gathering momentum' (Selwyn 2016b, 66) of datafication occurring within early years and primary schools by focusing in particular on Baseline Assessment in England. We have argued that Baseline Assessment sits firmly within a hyper-positivistic paradigm which attempts to provide a universally reductionist, governing and economistic approach to early years and primary education. This hyper-governing, paradigmatic approach reflects a neoliberal regime which 'de-politicises':

> It acts as if there are no alternatives, either to its own utopian and totalising project of a world constituted by calculative market relationships or to the conditions needed for its practice, including a particular approach to education. The ends of education are taken-for-granted, ensuring neoliberal subjects. The only question is about means, 'what works?', a question to which experts can supply the one right answer. Education is thus reduced to a supremely technical practice, requiring no democratic deliberation about critical or political questions.
>
> *(Moss 2015, 231)*

Teaching, learning and understanding are essentially political and ethical relationships imbued with power; assessments such as Baseline draw children out of their complex, diverse and distinct cultural backgrounds through a universal 'technique of normalisation' (Dahlberg, Moss and Pence 2007, 32). Reductionist assessments are ignorant of and even disrespectful to the localised relationships within which teaching and learning occurs. The practice of reducing a four- or five-year-old's subtle and complex learning relationships to an algorithm 'hammers complexity into simplicity' producing 'crude proxies' (O'Neil 2016, 208), including those which label the majority of children as 'below expectations', as claimed in relation to Early Excellence. We have argued that Baseline policy was not driven by a concern to listen to children (or teachers) but rather that it was driven by an economistic approach so that: 'Politics and ethics are drained, leaving economics: education as an economic commodity, education as a source of private profit, economic performance as education's primary goal' (Fielding and Moss 2011, 23). This economistic approach continues in policy, although Baseline in this form was withdrawn in 2016. The government was under huge pressure to change tack, in an example of what has been called the 'mediatization of education policy' (Lingard and Rawolle 2004 cited in Lingard and Sellar 2013, 647). At the time of writing, the future of primary and early years assessment is uncertain as the government is consulting on a replacement baseline for Reception, providing an example of the continued 'reification of progress' as a measure of quality. We would argue that any attempt to create a baseline in Reception is subject to the same problems we discuss here, and potentially has the same negative effects (Bradbury and Roberts-Holmes 2017). Thus, there are lessons to be learnt and new possibilities to be considered, in the light of this cautionary tale.

New possibilities

In this book we have sought to ask critical questions about the use, accuracy and neutrality of data, and how they have an impact on people and practices. It makes sense then to use this final section to consider the alternative possibilities. Research on data and education has a responsibility to 'suggest appropriate responses that can minimise inequalities and potential abuses', as well as critique (Perrotta 2013). As Thompson and Cook argue, drawing on Deleuze:

> Of course, there are other possibilities, or lines of flight, that we may see teachers beginning to manifest (if we are not already) such as the teacher who becomes indifferent to the database, who neither tries to ignore the changing expectations of the teacher nor manipulate the data by saying: 'So, you've created some data-points. So what!'
>
> *(2014, 140)*

Around the world, many early childhood education scholars have sought to challenge the norms and discourses we discuss here, notably the idea of learning as measurable and linear (Cannella 1997; Dahlberg and Moss 2005; Fendler 2001; Hultqvist and Dahlberg 2001). Drawing on similar theoretical tools from Foucault and Deleuze used here, there are calls to question 'our need and desire ... to represent and recognize' (Dahlberg and Moss 2009, xiv discussing Olsson 2009), and 'unmask the uncritical truths about the child that govern [educators'] work' (MacNaughton 2005, 38). Similarly, critical policy studies scholars have discussed the alternative possibilities for a more democratic education system (Apple 2013), with examples of projects and systems that seek to disrupt the neoliberal market hegemony. With more specific reference to data, Selwyn has called on researchers to 'make visible the flow and circulation of data' (2015, 76), in order to reveal its power – something we hope to have achieved in part here – and perhaps use data to '*counter* rather than compound dominant cultures of accountability, auditing and performativity' (2016b, 66).

Alternatives in context

Our discussion here considers the possibilities for an alternative future for data and education, but we begin with a series of caveats. In a context where 'productivity is everything' (Ball 2017, 43), we must be cognizant of the context within which teachers currently operate. As has been apparent throughout our discussion, teachers are constrained by the neoliberal framework of education which values efficiency and 'quality' as numerically proven. Many of the teachers we interviewed felt disempowered as their locally produced, context-dependent and meaningful baseline systems were overlaid, duplicated and subverted by the power of national, commercially produced and DfE-endorsed assessment that the teachers felt was of little value. In our interviews, teachers were clear that Baseline Assessment was 'transforming what were complex, interpersonal processes of teaching, learning and research into a set of standardised and measurable products' (Ball 2007 cited in Fielding and Moss 2011, 24), but were not able to challenge this transformation. Any attempt to 'fold' or 'opt out of the data deluge' has costs (Souto-Otero and Beneito-Montagut 2016, 27). Where there is resistance, or rebellion perhaps, it is in attempts to challenge the principles of progress-based measures through 'gaming' or manipulating scores, engaging in a process of fabrication (Ball 2003), rather than through outright refusal.

We need to remember that in the current context teachers are subject to immense pressures in terms of workload; in a survey conducted by the Association of Teacher and Lecturers union in 2016, 87 per cent of respondents cited workload as the reason why they were considering leaving the profession (ATL 2016). In our own survey about Baseline, 84 per cent of respondents said the assessment had increased their workload outside the classroom. Data production is often an addition to teachers' workload, done after hours and on a variety of devices; it represents a 'reconfiguration of the *character* of teachers' work' (Selwyn, Nemorin and Johnson 2016, 12). As Selwyn, Nemorin and Johnson argue, online work particularly is a 'public presentation of self' within a system of surveillance, control and discipline (2016, 12); thus it represents a new development in existing struggles over power and control in schools. Data are controlling and occupying, and thus we must note how this reduces any teacher's time to think about alternatives or challenge existing 'regimes of truth' about how they are viewed.

Furthermore, we note that the teachers were professionally diligent in their attempts to make sense of these assessments, even though they struggled to find the value and purpose within them. For instance, teachers were anxious that the effects of the assessments with their focus upon literacy and mathematics might have the effect of further narrowing the EYFS towards such outcomes and away from the broader EYFS play-based learning. Others adapted the assessment to meet their own aims – for example, by focusing on social and emotional development – which is in itself a form of localised resistance. While recognising this agency, we also want to emphasise that any discussion of alternatives must be framed by the context in which teachers operate.

Towards a democratic accountability

Some of the teachers in our study demonstrated a passive compliance to the hyper-governing audit culture now embedded within their datafied schools. For them, Baseline was just another accountability hurdle to be negotiated like all the others; 'we just kind of had a group hug at the meeting, rolled our eyes, and thought here we go again' (Head, Alder). To a certain extent, it could be argued that these headteachers were ground down by the relentless performative machine and were resigned to becoming tightly governed subjects; as one said, they are 'so beaten and broken'. Despite being aware that there would be a different government with a different agenda in seven years, when Baseline could be assessed, they felt compelled to volunteer for the Baseline trial. Within the current punitive high-stakes regime, for these headteachers to do anything more than comply might have been perceived as irresponsible and hence a gamble not worth taking. Nevertheless, within this harsh context there were some 3000 primary school headteachers for whom there were 'other lines of flight' (Thompson and Cook 2014, 140), alternatives and possibilities, and so refused to participate in the 2015 voluntary trial (Ward 2015c).

For these headteachers, Baseline was yet another national standardised test and representative of the argument from the 'More Than a Score' campaigning organisation that 'the current system of testing every individual child in order to judge the effectiveness of teachers and schools is deeply flawed, and has had negative effects' (MTAS 2017). In line with academic work in this field, the coalition of organisations represented by More Than a Score note that within early years and primary education there has been a misplaced and damaging conflation of assessment with accountability, such as, for example, primary school Sats being used for both children's assessment and school accountability. Within the context of the highly successful Finnish system, Sahlberg (2014, 66) similarly argues that such 'frequent standardized student testing is *not* a necessary condition' for improvement. Within Finland, there are three categories of assessment; first, class-based formative and summative assessments, where teachers are solely responsible for their own class; second, a local school-based evaluation of children's progress after each term; and third, external national assessment tests from age 11, where only 10 per cent of the age cohort are sampled (Sahlberg 2014, 67). Sahlberg goes on to say that 'since there are no standardized high stakes tests in Finland prior to the end of upper-secondary education, the teacher can focus on teaching and learning without the disturbance of frequent tests to be passed' (2014, 67). The Finnish assessment and accountability system is a much more professionally trusting approach towards teachers and is much more respectful of children's learning than England's current system.

Headteacher Dame Alison Peacock, who was a member of the DfE's Commission for Assessment Without Levels and who advised the DfE on teacher training and professional development, was perhaps the best known headteacher who publicly stated 'We are not doing the baseline' (Ward 2015b). Peacock's outspoken democratic assertion of the complexity of young children's learning demonstrated that locally based and contextual possibilities and alternatives were preferable and possible to Baseline's reductionist approach:

> Understanding children's thinking and their developing ideas through building and sustaining dialogue is an expert form of teaching that enables high challenge within a richly supportive environment. This is the beauty and the art of early years teaching that cannot be reduced to scores on a page, or to boxes on a tracking screen … we need to put assessment back in its box; thereby refusing temptation to place labels on children or their teachers.
>
> *(Peacock 2016)*

Refusing the simplistic and reductionist labelling of Baseline Assessment, Peacock's actions demonstrated that an apparently dominant, totalising and monolithic accountability regime was in fact 'fragile and open to challenge' (Dahlberg, Moss and Pence 2007, 33). Although at the time Baseline was voluntary, Peacock's and other headteachers' ethical and political *refusal* of the dominant 'regime of truth' within a harshly punitive and disciplinary audit culture can be considered as an ethical and political act rather than a compliant *enactment* of policy. In Foucauldian terms, Peacock was 'caring for the self', for herself, the staff and the children as she embraced complexity, diversity and uncertainty as opposed to closure, universality and regulation.

Through embracing ongoing narrative formative assessment for learning (AfL) as a counter-discourse to a crude, numerical summative assessment for accountability, Peacock enabled a politics of hope, possibilities and alternatives. For Peacock, summative assessment data were simply used as 'a background metric' and did not dominant, dictate and steer pedagogy. Instead of Pupil Progress Review (PPR) meetings being focused on 'data sheets and prior attainment grids' (Peacock 2016, 52), professional pedagogical conversations occurred that 'built knowledge about how to inspire future learning' (2016, 105). Central to this dialogic approach to assessment was that children engaged in their own reflective learning. Here the transformation of PPR meetings away from an obsession on numerical data led the way to accountability systems based on 'trust, openness, generosity and professional courage' (Peacock 2016, 132). For Fielding and Moss (2011), such self-care through refusal is a demonstration of a 'democratic accountability' that 'is morally and politically situated, not merely technically and procedurally delivered'. Peacock and other headteachers took the ethical and political power to ensure a more democratic, locally based and ethically responsible version of early years and primary education assessment. Such democratic versions of assessment demand the political and ethical image of a 'rich' child, that is:

a child born with great potential that can be expressed in a hundred languages; an active learner, seeking the meaning of the world from birth, a
co-creator of knowledge, identity, culture and values; a child that can live,
learn, listen and communicate, but always in relation with others; the whole
child, the child with body, mind, emotions, creativity, history and social
identity; an individual, whose individuality and autonomy depend upon
interdependence ... and a citizen and a subject of rights.

(Moss 2014, 88)

This understanding of the rich, competent and socially connected child allows for
democratic and participatory forms of assessment and evaluation, such as pedagogical documentation. Selwyn asks, 'What would educationally nuanced and/or
"meaningful" data look like?' (2016a, 66). For Carr and Lee (2012, xi) pedagogical
documentation as an assessment process is necessary in the early years for the construction and enabling of positive learner identities. Respectfully listening to children's narrative-based learning stories allows for a democratic co-construction of
children's' learning identities, processes and possibilities of a learner self in process.

It is through narrative that we create and re-create selfhood, and self is a
product of our telling and re-telling. We are, from the start, expressions of
our culture. Culture is replete with alternative narratives about what self is or
might be.

(Bruner 2002, 86 cited in Carr and Lee 2012, 3)

Through storytelling and dialogue with early childhood teachers, children's learner
story narratives and 'possible learner selves' (Carr and Lee 2012, 3) are enabled. In
reciprocal relationships with adults, children learn to produce, generate and construct positive learning identities by focusing upon their dispositions and characteristics of learning. These learning stories are creatively produced through a range of
artefacts that make learning visible and hence open to multiple interpretations from
adults and children. These alternatives and possibilities of the self are located within
a child's socio-cultural milieu of the school and home. Learning stories and pedagogical documentation are located within the postmodern paradigm and can therefore
embrace diversity, uncertainty, contingency and unpredictable learner identity outcomes. Through an engagement with a 'discourse of meaning making' over a 'discourse of quality' we can reclaim the idea of judgement but as a 'discursive act
always made in relationship with others' (Dahlberg, Moss and Pence 2007, 86).

Unlike positivist norm-based assessment, which seeks to govern and control
through its simplistic categories, numbers and linear outcomes, pedagogical documentation focuses upon the learning process itself, such as 'participation, dialogue,
confidence-building, imagination and creativity' (Elfsrom, 2013, 15 cited in Moss
2014, 144). It embraces a democratic co-construction of knowledge between children and adults that is driven by children's questions and curiosity. The young
learner is ascribed with agency and enabled to take on an 'authoring role' in the

construction of themselves. Here educational outcomes become 'the appropriation of a repertoire of learner identities and possible selves' (Carr and Lee 2012, xv) and the role of formative assessment is to make such learning visible and open to interpretation. Although learner stories and Baseline Assessment were developed for different purposes, it is the effects upon young children that are the focus here. National summative assessment represents the antithesis of pedagogical documentation as it is in danger of producing a negative understanding of young children's learner identities. It tells a quasi-scientific, deficit-based story to a young child about what they are incapable of and cannot do, and closes down who and what they might become.

Concluding thoughts

Accountability-based assessments such as Baseline can be understood as 'new concentrations of power' (Crawford *et al.* 2014 cited in Selwyn 2016b, 64), We have analysed these 'concentrations of power' as being places of intense forms of digital comparison, dataveillance and governmentality, producing disciplined, competitive and individualised child and teacher subjectivities. We argue that data form an essential part of the 'considerable management' and hyper-governing required to produce the desired neoliberal subjectivities. If we view the subject as constituted through discourse, we can also see how the subject is constituted through data – a 'data double', or in our terms, a datafied subject. Data have discursive power to judge, group, define and demand action, whether this be the blue dots on a Baseline sheet that mean a child requires extra support, or a numerical value which places a child as 'below expected progress'. As well as recording educational 'attainment', data in schools increasingly record biopolitical information on character traits, behaviour and attendance (Williamson 2016a); an area which requires further research.

To think about a datafied subject means to recognise that educational data have an impact on agency, further constraining how we are recognised, interpellated and made intelligible. But this is not to say that responses to datafication are simple; as we have seen throughout, responses are varied and changing in terms of practice and pedagogy, affect and manipulation. There is always space for change, to think differently about how we use data, how they shape and define us, and therefore to challenge how we are subject to their power.

Note

1 For example, More Than A Score (https://morethanascore.co.uk/who-we-are/) was established after the 2016 Sats results were published in which 53 per cent of primary children were deemed not ready for secondary school.

REFERENCES

Adams, R. (2015) *Schools opt to replace 'test too far' for reception children*. Available online at: www.theguardian.com/teacher-network/2015/jun/09/schools-replace-test-too-far-recpetion-class (accessed 6 March 2017).

Alexander, R. (2009) *Children, their world, their education: Final report and recommendations of the Cambridge Primary Review* (London, Routledge).

Alexander, R. J. (2010) 'World class schools' – noble aspiration or globalised hokum? *Compare: A Journal of Comparative and International Education*, 40(6), 801–817.

Allen, G. (2011) *Early intervention: Smart investment, massive savings*. Report for HM Government (London, Cabinet Office).

Andrews, R. (2009) *Review of research in English as an additional language (EAL)*. Report for Institute of Education, for the Training and Development Agency (London, Institute of Education).

Apple, M. W. (2006) *Educating the 'right' way: Markets, standards, god, and inequality* (2nd edition) (London, Routledge).

Apple, M. W. (2009) *Global crises, education and social justice* (London, Routledge).

Apple, M. W. (2010) The measure of success: education, markets, and an audit culture, in: T. Monahan and R. Torres (Eds) *Schools under surveillance: Cultures of control in public education* (New Jersey: Rutgers University Press).

Apple, M. W. (2013) *Can education change society?* (London, Routledge).

Apple, M. W., Kenway, J. and Singh, M. (2005) *Globalizing education: Policies, pedagogies, and politics* (New York; Oxford, Peter Lang).

ATL (2016) *Workload drives teacher recruitment and retention crisis*. Available online at: www.atl.org.uk/latest/press-release/workload-drives-teacher-recruitment-and-retention-crisis-new-survey-finds (accessed 23 March 2017).

Au, W. (2011) Teaching under the new Taylorism: High stakes testing and the standardization of the 21st century curriculum. *Journal of Curriculum Studies*, 43(1), 25–45.

Ball, S. (1990) *Politics and policymaking in education* (London, Routledge).

Ball, S. (2003) The teacher's soul and the terrors of performativity. *Journal of Education Policy*, 18(2), 215–228.

Ball, S. (2013a) *The education debate* (2nd edition) (Bristol, Policy Press).

Ball, S. (2013b) *Foucault, power and education* (London, Routledge).

Ball, S., Junemann, C. and Santori, D. (2017) *Edu.Net: Globalisation and education policy mobility* (London, Routledge).

Ball, S., Maguire, M. and Braun, A. (2012) *How schools do policy: Policy enactments in secondary schools* (London, Routledge).

Ball, S. J. (2000) Performativities and fabrications in the education economy: Towards the performative society? *The Australian Educational Researcher*, 27(2), 1–23.

Ball, S. J. (2012a) *Global education inc: New policy networks and the neo-liberal imaginary* (London, Routledge).

Ball, S. J. (2012b) The reluctant state and the beginning of the end of state education. *Journal of Educational Administration and History*, 44(2), 89–103.

Ball, S. J. (2015) Education, governance and the tyranny of numbers. *Journal of Education Policy*, 30(3), 299–301.

Ball, S. J. (2016) Subjectivity as a site of struggle: Refusing neoliberalism? *British Journal of Sociology of Education*, 37(8), 1129–1146.

Ball, S. J. (2017) *Foucault as educator* (Switzerland, Springer).

Ball, S. J. and Junemann, C. (2012) *Networks, new governance and education* (Bristol: Policy Press).

Ball, S. J. and Olmedo, A. (2013) Care of the self, resistance and subjectivity under neoliberal governmentalities. *Critical Studies in Education*, 54(1), 85–96.

Ball, S. J., Maguire, M., Braun, A. and Hoskins, K. (2011a) Policy actors: Doing policy work in schools. *Discourse: Studies in the Cultural Politics of Education*, 32(4), 625–639.

Ball, S. J., Maguire, M., Braun, A. and Hoskins, K. (2011b) Policy subjects and policy actors in schools: Some necessary but insufficient analyses. *Discourse: Studies in the Cultural Politics of Education*, 32(4), 611–624.

Bassok, D., Latham, S. and Rorem, A. (2016) Is kindergarten the new first grade? *AERA Open*, 2(1), http://dx.doi.org/10.1177%2F2332858415616358.

Bauman, Z. (2000) *Liquid modernity* (Cambridge, Polity).

Bauman, Z. and Lyon, D. (2013) *Liquid surveillance: A conversation* (Cambridge; Malden, MA, Polity Press).

Beer, D. (2013) *Popular culture and new media: The politics of circulation* (Basingstoke: Palgrave Macmillan).

Beer, D. (2015) Productive measures: Culture and measurement in the context of everyday neoliberalism. *Big Data & Society*, 2(1), http://dx.doi.org/10.1177%2F2053951715578951.

BERA (2011) *Ethical guidelines for educational research*. Available online at: www.bera.ac.uk/wp-content/uploads/2014/02/BERA-Ethical-Guidelines-2011.pdf (accessed 5 April 2017).

Biesta, G. (2009) Good education in an age of measurement: On the need to reconnect with the question of purpose in education. *Educational Assessment, Evaluation and Accountability (formerly: Journal of Personnel Evaluation in Education)*, 21(1), 33–46.

Biesta, G. (2017) Education, measurement and the professions: Reclaiming a space for democratic professionality in education. *Educational Philosophy and Theory*, 49(4), 315–330.

Bodrova, E. and Leong, D. (2007) *Tools of the mind: The Vygotskian approach to early childhood education* (Upper Saddle River, NJ: Pearson/Merrill Prentice Hall).

Booher-Jennings, J. (2005) Below the bubble: 'Educational triage' and the Texas accountability system. *American Educational Research Journal*, 42(2), 231–268.

Bourne, R. and Shackleton, L. (2017) *Getting the state out of pre-school and childcare* (London, Institute of Economic Affairs).

Bowker, G. (2005) *Memory practices in the sciences* (Cambridge, MA, MIT Press).

Bowker, G. C. and Star, S. L. (1999) *Sorting things out: Classification and its consequences* (Cambridge, MA, MIT Press).

Bradbury, A. (2011a) Equity, ethnicity and the hidden dangers of 'contextual' measures of school success. *Race, Ethnicity and Education*, 14(3), 277–291.

Bradbury, A. (2011b) Rethinking assessment and inequality: The production of disparities in attainment in early years education. *Journal of Education Policy*, 26(5), 655–676.

Bradbury, A. (2012) 'I feel absolutely incompetent': Professionalism, policy and early childhood teachers. *Contemporary Issues in Early Childhood Education*, 13(3), 175–186.

Bradbury, A. (2013a) Education policy and the 'ideal learner': Producing recognisable learner-subjects through early years assessment. *British Journal of Sociology of Education*, 34(1), 1–19.

Bradbury, A. (2013b) 'Slimmed down' assessment? Policy contradictions related to 'burdensome bureaucracy' in early years and KS1, paper presented at the 'We need to talk about teaching' symposium, London, February 2013.

Bradbury, A. (2013c) *Understanding early years inequality: Policy, assessment and young children's identities* (London, Routledge).

Bradbury, A. (2014) Learning, assessment and equality in early childhood education (ECE) settings in England. *European Early Childhood Education Research Journal*, 22(3), 347–354.

Bradbury, A. and Roberts-Holmes, G. (2016a) Creating an Ofsted story: The role of early years assessment data in schools' narratives of progress. *British Journal of Sociology of Education*, 1–10, http://dx.doi.org/10.1080/01425692.2016.1202748.

Bradbury, A. and Roberts-Holmes, G. (2016b) *'They are children, not robots': The introduction of baseline assessment.* Report for ATL/NUT (London, UCL Institute of Education).

Bradbury, A. and Roberts-Holmes, G. (2017) *The proposed baseline assessment is just the return to a failed policy and we must fight it.* Available online at: www.tes.com/news/school-news/breaking-views/proposed-baseline-assessment-just-return-a-failed-policy-and-we-must (accessed 5 April 2017).

Braun, A., Maguire, M. and Ball, S. (2010) Policy enactments in the UK secondary school: Examining policy, practice and school positioning. *Journal of Education Policy*, 25(4), 547–560.

Brighenti, A. (2007) Visibility: A category for the social sciences. *Current Sociology*, 55(3), 323–342.

Broadhead, P. (2006) Developing an understanding of young children's learning through play: The place of observation, interaction and reflection. *British Educational Research Journal*, 32(2), 191–207.

Broadhead, P. and Burt, A. (2012) *Understanding young children's learning through play: Building playful pedagogies* (London, Routledge).

Bryce, T., Nellis, M., Corrigan, A. J., Gallagher, H., Lee, P. and Sercombe, H. (2010) Biometric surveillance in schools: Cause for concern or case for curriculum? *Scottish Educational Review*, 42(1), 3–22.

Butler, J. (2010) *Frames of war: When is life grievable?* (New York, Verso).

BWB (2015) *Why is it better without baseline assessment: 4 core reasons.* Available online at: www.newman.ac.uk/files/w3/24feb/pdf/Better%20without%20Baseline_Some%20concerns%20-%20Nancy%20Stewart.pdf?q=122 (accessed 22 June 2017).

Cambridge Primary Review Trust (2013) *Consultation response form: Primary assessment and accountability under the new national curriculum.* Available online at: http://cprtrust.org.uk/wp-content/uploads/2014/12/CPRTs-response-to-consultation-on-Performance-Descriptors.pdf (accessed 5 November 2016).

Camden, B. (2015) *Baseline assessment provider Early Excellence admits data 'anomalies'.* Available online at: http://schoolsweek.co.uk/baseline-assessment-provider-early-excellence-admits-data-anomalies/#comments (accessed 26 October 2016).

Camden, B. (2016) *Baseline test sign-up plummets.* Available online at: http://schoolsweek. co.uk/baseline-test-sign-up-plummets/ (accessed 6 March 2017).

Camden, B. (2017) *Baseline provider 'surprised' at DfE preference for formal reception test.* Available online at: http://schoolsweek.co.uk/baseline-provider-surprised-at-dfe-preference-for-formal-reception-test/ (accessed 7 April 2017).

Cannella, G. S. (1997) *Deconstructing early childhood education: Social justice and revolution* (New York, Peter Lang).

Carr, M. and Lee, W. (2012) *Learning stories: Constructing learner identities in early education* (London, SAGE).

Carr, M., Mitchell, L. and Rameka, L. (2016) Some thoughts about the value of an OECD international assessment framework for early childhood services in Aotearoa, New Zealand. *Contemporary Issues in Early Childhood*, 17(4), 450–454.

CEM (2017) *About us.* Available online at: www.cem.org/about-us (accessed 14 March 2017).

Cheney-Lippold, J. (2011) A new algorithmic identity: Soft biopolitics and the modulation of control. *Theory, Culture & Society*, 28(6), 164–181.

Dahlberg, G. and Moss, P. (2005) *Ethics and politics in early childhood education* (London, RoutledgeFalmer).

Dahlberg, G. and Moss, P. (2009) Foreword, in: L. M. Olsson (Ed.) *Movement and experimentation in young children's learning: Deleuze and Guattari in early childhood education* (London, Routledge).

Dahlberg, G., Moss, P. and Pence, A. (2007) *Beyond quality in early childhood education and care: Languages of evaluation* (2nd edition) (London, Routledge).

Davids, N. (2017) On the un-becoming of measurement in education. *Educational Philosophy and Theory*, 49(4), 422–433.

Davies, W. (2014) *The limits of neoliberalism: Authority, sovereignty and the logic of competition* (London, SAGE).

DCSF (2008) *Early years foundation stage: Themes and principles* (London, Department of Children, Schools and Families).

de Wolf, I. F. and Janssens, F. J. G. (2007) Effects and side effects of inspections and accountability in education: An overview of empirical studies. *Oxford Review of Education*, 33(3), 379–396.

Deleuze, G. (1995a) *Negotiations: 1972–1990* (New York, Columbia University Press).

Deleuze, G. (1995b) Postscript on societies of control, in: G. Deleuze and M. Joughin (Eds) *Negotiations 1972–1990* (New York, Columbia University Press).

DfE (2010) *The importance of teaching: Schools white paper 2010.* Available online at: www.education.gov.uk/publications/eOrderingDownload/CM-7980.pdf (accessed 8 August 2012).

DfE (2012) *Statutory framework for the early years foundation stage* (London, Department for Education).

DfE (2013a) *More great childcare: Raising quality and giving parents more choice* (London, Department for Education).

DfE (2013b) *New advice to help schools set performance-related pay.* Available online at: www.gov.uk/government/news/new-advice-to-help-schools-set-performance-related-pay (accessed 7 March 2017).

DfE (2013c) *Primary assessment and accountability under the new national curriculum.* Available online at: www.gov.uk/government/consultations/new-national-curriculum-primary-assessment-and-accountability (accessed 17 October 2016).

DfE (2014a) *EAL pupils by LEA, 2004–2013* (London, Department for Education).

DfE (2014b) *Raising the achievement of disadvantaged children.* Available online at: www.gov.

uk/government/policies/raising-the-achievement-of-disadvantaged-children (accessed 28 April 2015).

DfE (2014c) *Reforming assessment and accountability for primary schools*. Available online at: www.gov.uk/government/uploads/system/uploads/attachment_data/file/297595/Primary_Accountability_and_Assessment_Consultation_Response.pdf (accessed 15 November 2016).

DfE (2015a) *Policy paper: 2010 to 2015 government policy: School and college funding and accountability* (London, Department for Education).

DfE (2015b) *Reception baseline research: Views of teachers, school leaders, parents and carers*. Available online at: www.gov.uk/government/publications/reception-baseline-research (accessed 15 November 2016).

DfE (2016a) *Early years foundation stage profile results in England, 2015/16: Sfr 50/2016*. Available online at: www.gov.uk/government/statistics/early-years-foundation-stage-profile-results-2015-to-2016 (accessed 19 January 2017).

DfE (2016b) *Reception baseline assessment: Guide to signing up your school (updated 16 April 2016)*. Available online at: www.gov.uk/guidance/reception-baseline-assessment-guide-to-signing-up-your-school (accessed 6 March 2017).

DfE (2017a) *Expressions of interest for a national centre to administer the Organisation for Economic Co-operation and Development's (OECD) International Early Learning Study (IELS)*. Available online at: www.tenderlake.com/home/tender/9dbc8b1f-a9dd-4ef8-9230-4b8c8ca5a466/international-early-learning-study-iels-for-child-well-being-national-centre-for-england (accessed 26 June 2017).

DfE (2017b) *National pupil database: Third-party data requests*. Available online at: www.gov.uk/government/publications/national-pupil-database-requests-received (accessed 20 March 2017).

DfE (2017c) *Primary assessment in England consultation*. Available online at: https://consult.education.gov.uk/assessment-policy-and-development/primary-assessment/consultation/intro/ (accessed 6 April 2017).

Dunphy, E. (2008) *Supporting early learning and development through formative assessment: A research paper* (Dublin, National Council for Curriculum and Assessment).

Early Excellence (2016) *EExBA baseline assessment*. Available online at: http://earlyexcellence.com/eexba2016 (accessed 14 March 2017).

Ehren, M. C. M., Jones, K. and Perryman, J. (2016) Side effects of school inspection; motivations and contexts for strategic responses, in: M. C. M. Ehren (Ed.) *Methods and modalities of effective school inspections*. (Cham, Springer International Publishing).

Eynon, R. (2013) The rise of big data: What does it mean for education, technology, and media research? *Learning, Media and Technology*, 38(3), 237–240.

Fendler, L. (2001) Educating flexible souls: The construction of subjectivity through developmentality and interaction, in: K. Hultqvist and G. Dahlberg (Eds) *The child in a changing world: Refiguring early childhood education*. (London, Routledge).

Fenwick, T. J., Mangez, E. and Ozga, J. (2014) *Governing knowledge: Comparison, knowledge-based technologies and expertise in the regulation of education*. (London, Routledge).

Fielding, M. and Moss, P. (2011) *Radical democratic education and the common school* (London, Routledge).

Finn, M. (2016) Atmospheres of progress in a data-based school. *Cultural Geographies*, 23(1), 29–49.

Fischer Family Trust (2017) *Target-setting*. Available online at: www.fft.org.uk/fft-aspire/target-setting.aspx (accessed 20 April 2017).

Fleer, M. (2010) *Early learning and development: Cultural-historical concepts in play* (Cambridge, Cambridge University Press).

Fleer, M. (2013) *Play in the early years* (Cambridge, Cambridge University Press).

Fleer, M. and Richardson, C. (2009) Mapping the transformation of understanding, in: A. Anning, J. Cunning and M. Fleer (Eds) *Early childhood education: Society and culture* (2nd edition) (London, SAGE).

Foucault, M. (1977) *Discipline and punish: The birth of the prison* (London, Allen Lane).

Foucault, M. (1980) *Power-knowledge: Selected interviews and other writings, 1972–1977* (Brighton, Harvester Press).

Francis, B., Archer, L., Hodgen, J., Pepper, D., Taylor, B. and Travers, M.-C. (2015) Exploring the relative lack of impact of research on 'ability grouping' in England: A discourse analytic account. *Cambridge Journal of Education*, 47(1), 1–17.

Gaunt, C. (2013) *Ofsted chief calls for review of early years assessment*. Available online at: www.nurseryworld.co.uk/article/1187290/ofsted-chief-calls-review-early-years-assessment (accessed 19 July 2013).

Gee, J. P. (2007) Reflections on assessment from a sociocultural situated perspective. *Yearbook of the National Society for the Study of Education*, 106, 362–375.

Gillborn, D. (2008) *Racism and education: Coincidence or conspiracy?* (London, Routledge).

Gillborn, D. and Youdell, D. (2000) *Rationing education: Policy, practice, reform and equity* (Buckingham, Open University Press).

Gilliom, J. (2010) Lying, cheating and teaching to the test: The politics of surveillance under no child left behind, in: T. Monahan and R. Torres (Eds) *Schools under surveillance: Cultures of control in public education* (New Jersey, Rutgers University Press).

Goldstein, H. and Moss, G. (2014) Knowledge and numbers in education. *Comparative Education*, 50(3), 259–265.

Gorur, R. (2014) Towards a sociology of measurement in education policy. *European Educational Research Journal*, 13(1), 58–72.

Graue, E. (2008) Teaching and learning in a post-DAP world. *Early Education and Development*, 19(3), 441–447.

Grek, S. (2009) Governing by numbers: The PISA 'effect' in Europe. *Journal of Education Policy*, 24(1), 23–37.

Grek, S. (2013) Expert moves: International comparative testing and the rise of expertocracy. *Journal of Education Policy*, 28(5), 695–709.

Grek, S. and Lindgren, J. (2014) *Governing by inspection* (London, Routledge).

Grek, S., Lindgren, J. and Clarke, J. (2015) Inspection and emotion: The role of affective governing, in: S. Grek and J. Lindgren (Eds) *Governing by inspection*. (London, Routledge).

Haggerty, K. D. and Ericson, R. V. (2000) The surveillant assemblage. *The British Journal of Sociology*, 51(4), 605–622.

Hardy, I. (2014) A logic of appropriation: Enacting national testing (NAPLAN) in Australia. *Journal of Education Policy*, 29(1), 1–18.

Hardy, I. (2015) 'I'm just a numbers person': The complexity, nature and effects of the quantification of education. *International Studies in Sociology of Education*, 25(1), 20–37.

Hardy, I. and Boyle, C. (2011) My school? Critiquing the abstraction and quantification of education. *Asia-Pacific Journal of Teacher Education*, 39(3), 211–222.

Harvey, D. (2007) *A brief history of neoliberalism* (New York, Oxford University Press).

Heavey, A. (2016) *Counting the costs of baseline*. Available online at: www.atl.org.uk/latest/blog/counting-other-costs-baseline-assessment (accessed 8 November 2016).

Higham, R. (2014) 'Who owns our schools?' An analysis of the governance of free schools in England. *Educational Management Administration and Leadership*, 42(3), 404–422.

Hogan, A., Sellar, S. and Lingard, B. (2016) Commercialising comparison: Pearson puts the TLC in soft capitalism. *Journal of Education Policy*, 31(3), 243–258.

Hope, A. (2016) Biopower and school surveillance technologies 2.0. *British Journal of Sociology of Education*, 37(7), 885–904.

Hultqvist, K. and Dahlberg, G. (2001) *Governing the child in the new millennium* (London, RoutledgeFalmer).

Hursh, D. (2013) Raising the stakes: High-stakes testing and the attack on public education in New York. *Journal of Education Policy*, 28(5), 574–588.

Hutchings, M. (2015) *Exam factories? The impact of accountability measures on children and young people* (London, National Union of Teachers).

Jennings, J. and Pallas, A. (2016) How does value-added data affect teachers? *Educational Leadership*, 73(8), www.ascd.org/publications/educational_leadership/may16/vol73/num08/How_Does_Value-Added_Data_Affect_Teachers%C2%A2.aspx (accessed 10 August 2017).

Judd, A. (2012) *School test cheating thrives while investigations languish*. Available online at: www.ajc.com/news/education/school-test-cheating-thrives-while-investigations-languish/XAPhfpyjT6Zc0RCLOl9J4K/ (accessed 5 April 2017).

Junemann, C. and Ball, S. J. (2013) Ark and the revolution of state education in England. *Education Inquiry*, 4(3), http://dx.doi.org/10.3402/edui.v4i3.22611.

Kelly, A. and Downey, C. (2011) *Using effectiveness data for school improvement: Developing and utilising metrics* (London, Routledge).

Kelly, A., Downey, C. and Rietdijk, W. (2010) *Data dictatorship and data democracy: Understanding professional attitudes to the use of pupil performance data in schools* (Borough of Reading, CfBT Education Trust).

Kilderry, A. (2015) The intensification of performativity in early childhood education. *Journal of Curriculum Studies*, 47(5), 633–652.

Kitchin, R. (2014) *The data revolution: Big data, open data, data infrastructures and their consequences* (London, SAGE).

Koyama, J. and Menken, K. (2013) Emergent bilinguals: Framing students as statistical data? *Bilingual Research Journal*, 36(1), 82–99.

Laevers, F., Declercq, B. and Thomas, F. (2010) *Implementation of the process-oriented approach in early years settings in Milton Keynes*. Final report. (Leuven, Belgium: CEGO Leuven University).

Lawn, M. (2013) *The rise of data in education systems: Collection, visualisation and uses* (Didcot, Symposium).

Lazzarato, M. (2009) Neoliberalism in action inequality, insecurity and the reconstitution of the social. *Theory, Culture & Society*, 26(6), 109–133.

Leckie, G. and Goldstein, H. (2017) The evolution of school league tables in England 1992–2016: 'Contextual value-added', 'expected progress' and 'progress 8'. *British Educational Research Journal*, 43(2), 193–212.

Legg, S. (2005) Foucault's population geographies: Classifications, biopolitics and governmental spaces. *Population, Space and Place*, 11(3), 137–156.

Leonardo, Z. (2007) The war on schools: NCLB, nation creation and the educational construction of whiteness. *Race, Ethnicity and Education*, 10(3), 262–278.

Lewis, S. and Hardy, I. (2015) Funding, reputation and targets: The discursive logics of high-stakes testing. *Cambridge Journal of Education*, 45(2), 245–264.

Lingard, B. (2009) Testing times: The need for new intelligent accountabilities for schooling. *QTU Professional Magazine*, 24(November), 13–19.

Lingard, B. and Sellar, S. (2013) 'Catalyst data': Perverse systemic effects of audit and accountability in Australian schooling. *Journal of Education Policy*, 28(5), 634–656.

Lingard, B., Martino, W. and Rezai-Rashti, G. (2013) Testing regimes, accountabilities and education policy: Commensurate global and national developments. *Journal of Education Policy*, 28(5), 539–556.

Lingard, B., Sellar, S. and Savage, G. C. (2014) Re-articulating social justice as equity in schooling policy: The effects of testing and data infrastructures. *British Journal of Sociology of Education*, 35(5), 710–730.

Lipman, P. (2013) Economic crisis, accountability, and the state's coercive assault on public education in the USA. *Journal of Education Policy*, 28(5), 557–573.

Lupton, D. (2016) *The quantified self* (Cambridge, Polity Press).

Lupton, D. and Williamson, B. (2017) The datafied child: The dataveillance of children and implications for their rights. *New Media & Society*, 19(5), 780–794.

Lynch, T. L. (2015) *Hidden role of software in educational research: Policy to practice* (London, Routledge).

Lyon, D. (2001) *Surveillance society: Monitoring everyday life* (Maidenhead, McGraw-Hill Education UK).

Lyon, D. (2014) Surveillance, Snowden, and big data: Capacities, consequences, critique. *Big Data & Society*, 1(2), http://dx.doi.org/10.1177%2F2053951714541861.

Mackey, G., Hill, D. and Vocht, L. D. (2016) Response to the colloquium 'The Organisation for Economic Co-operation and Development's International Early Learning Study: Opening for debate and contestation'. *Contemporary Issues in Early Childhood*, 17(4), 447–449.

MacNaughton, G. (2005) *Doing Foucault in early childhood studies: Applying poststructural ideas* (London, Routledge).

Malaguzzi, L., Edwards, C., Gandini, L. and Foreman, G. (1996) The hundred languages of children: The Reggio Emilia approach to early childhood education (New Jersey, Ablex Publishing Corporation).

Manovich, L. (2012) Trending: The promises and challenges of big social data, in: M. Gold (Ed.) *Debates in the digital humanities*. (Minnesota, University of Minnesota Press).

Manovich, L. (2013) *Software takes command: Extending the language of new media* (London, Bloomsbury).

Mansell, W. (2007) *Education by numbers: The damaging treadmill of school tests* (London, Politico's).

Marks, R. (2016) *Ability-grouping in primary schools: Case studies and critical debates* (St Albans, Critical Publishing).

McGimpsey, I. (2017) Late neoliberalism: Delineating a policy regime. *Critical Social Policy*, 37(1), 64–84.

McGimpsey, I., Bradbury, A. and Santori, D. (2016) Revisions to rationality: The translation of 'new knowledges' into policy under the coalition government. *British Journal of Sociology of Education*, 1–14, http://dx.doi.org/10.1080/01425692.2016.1202747.

McHoul, A. W. and Grace, W. (1998) *A Foucault primer: Discourse, power, and the subject* (London, UCL Press).

Meckes, L. and Carrasco, R. (2010) Two decades of SIMCE: An overview of the national assessment system in Chile. *Assessment in Education: Principles, Policy & Practice*, 17(2), 233–248.

Mercer, N., Dawes, L. and Staarman, J. K. (2009) Dialogic teaching in the primary science classroom. *Language and Education*, 23(4), 353–369.

Metro (2017) *Teachers 'worn out by demand for data'* (Metro, 4 April).

Meyer, H. and Zahedi, K. (2014) Open letter to Andreas Schleicher, OECD, Paris. *Global Policy Journal*, 5 May. Available online at: www.globalpolicyjournal.com/blog/05/05/2014/open-letter-andreas-schleicher-oecd-paris (accessed 22 June 2017).

Monahan, T., and Torres, R. (eds) (2010) *Schools under surveillance: Cultures of control in public education* (New Jersey, Rutgers University Press).

Moss, P. (Ed.) (2013) *Early childhood and compulsory education: Reconceptualising the relationship* (London, Routledge).

Moss, P. (2014) *Transformative change and real utopias in early childhood education: A story of democracy, experimentation and potentiality* (London, Routledge).

Moss, P. (2015) There are alternatives! Contestation and hope in early childhood education. *Global Studies of Childhood*, 5(3), 226–238.

Moss, P. (2016) *Is a preschool PISA what we want for our young children?* Available online at: https://ioelondonblog.wordpress.com/2016/08/08/is-a-preschool-pisa-what-we-want-for-our-young-children/ (accessed 28 February 2017).

Moss, P., Dahlberg, G., Grieshaber, S., Mantovani, S., May, H., Pence, A., Rayna, S., Swadener, B. B. and Vandenbroeck, M. (2016) The Organisation for Economic Co-operation and Development's International Early Learning Study: Opening for debate and contestation. *Contemporary Issues in Early Childhood*, 17(3), 343–351.

Moss, P., Dahlberg, G., Olssen, L. M. and Vandenbroeck, M. (2016) *Why contest early childhood?* (London, Routledge).

MTAS (2017) *More Than a Score*. Available online at: https://morethanascore.co.uk/ (accessed 23 March 2017).

Neaum, S. (2016) School readiness and pedagogies of competence and performance: Theorising the troubled relationship between early years and early years policy. *International Journal of Early Years Education*, 24(3), 239–253.

NFER (2016) *Summer-born pupils: What's the evidence?* Available online at: www.nfer.ac.uk/pdf/summer-born.pdf (accessed 28 June 2017).

O'Neil, C. (2016) *Weapons of math destruction: How big data increases inequality and threatens democracy* (New York, Crown Publishing Group).

OECD (2015) *Call for tenders: International Early Learning Study* (Paris, Organisation for Economic Co-operation and Development).

Ofsted (2014) *Inspecting schools: Handbook for inspectors*. Available online at: www.gov.uk/government/publications/school-inspection-handbook (accessed 11 June 2015).

Olmedo, A. (2014) From England with love … ark, heterarchies and global 'philanthropic governance'. *Journal of Education Policy*, 29(5), 575–597.

Olsson, L. M. (2009) *Movement and experimentation in young children's learning: Deleuze and Guattari in early childhood education* (London, Routledge).

Osgood, J. (2006) Deconstructing professionalism in early childhood education: Resisting the regulatory gaze. *Contemporary Issues in Early Childhood*, 7(1), 5–14.

Ozga, J. (2009) Governing education through data in England: From regulation to self-evaluation. *Journal of Education Policy*, 24(2), 149–162.

Ozga, J. (2016) Trust in numbers? Digital education governance and the inspection process. *European Educational Research Journal*, 15(1), 69–81.

Ozga, J. and Segerholm, C. (2015) Neo-liberal agenda(s) in education, in: S. Grek and J. Lindgren (Eds) *Governing by inspection* (London, Routledge).

Ozga, J., Dahler-Larsen, P., Segerholm, C. and Simola, H. (Eds.) (2011) *Fabricating quality in education: Data and governance in Europe* (London, Routledge).

Ozga, J., Segerholm, C. and Simola, H. (2011) The governance turn, in: J. Ozga, P. Dahler-Larsen, C. Segerholm and H. Simola (Eds) *Fabricating quality in education: Data and governance in Europe* (London, Routledge).

Peacock, A. (2016) *Baseline u-turn: 'Superhead' Alison Peacock describes her relief*. Available online at: www.tes.com/news/school-news/breaking-views/baseline-u-turn-superhead-alison-peacock-describes-her-relief (accessed 23 March 2017).

Perrotta, C. (2013) Assessment, technology and democratic education in the age of data. *Learning, Media and Technology*, 38(1), 116–122.

Perry, T. (2016) English value-added measures: Examining the limitations of school performance measurement. *British Educational Research Journal*, 42(6), 1056–1080.

Perryman, J. (2009) Inspection and the fabrication of professional and performative processes. *Journal of Education Policy*, 24(5), 611–631.

Piattoeva, N. (2015) Elastic numbers: National examinations data as a technology of government. *Journal of Education Policy*, 30(3), 316–334.

Piattoeva, N. (2016) The imperative to protect data and the rise of surveillance cameras in administering national testing in Russia. *European Educational Research Journal*, 15(1), 82–98.

Power, M. P. (2013) *The audit society: Rituals of verification* (Oxford, OUP).

Pratt, N. (2016) Neoliberalism and the (internal) marketisation of primary school assessment in England. *British Educational Research Journal*, 42(5), 890–905.

Rabinow, P. and Rose, N. (2006) Biopower today. *BioSocieties*, 1(2), 195–217.

Report Bee (2017) Homepage. Available online at: www.reportbee.com/#home (accessed 14 February 2017).

Richards, C. (2016) Our data-obsessed school system is way too complicated, *TES*, 1 November 2016.

Roberts-Holmes, G. (2012) 'It's the bread and butter of our practice': Experiencing the early years foundation stage. *International Journal of Early Years Education*, 20(1), 30–42.

Roberts-Holmes, G. (2013) 'If the teaching is good, the data should be good and if there's bad teaching there is bad data': Understanding early years teachers' responses to the revised Early Years Foundation Stage Profile, paper presented at the BERA Conference, University of Sussex, Brighton.

Roberts-Holmes, G. (2015) The 'datafication' of early years pedagogy: 'If the teaching is good, the data should be good and if there's bad teaching, there is bad data'. *Journal of Education Policy*, 30(3), 302–315.

Roberts-Holmes, G. and Bradbury, A. (2016) Governance, accountability and the datafication of early years education in England *British Education Research Journal*, 42(4), 600–613.

Roberts-Holmes, G. and Bradbury, A. (2017) Primary schools and network governance: A policy analysis of reception baseline assessment. *British Education Research Journal*, http://onlinelibrary.wiley.com/doi/10.1002/berj.3285/epdf.

Rose, N. (1999) *Powers of freedom: Reframing political thought* (Cambridge, Cambridge University Press).

Rustin, S. (2016) *New test for 'growth mindset': The theory that anyone who tries can succeed.* Available online at: www.theguardian.com/education/2016/may/10/growth-mindset-research-uk-schools-sats (accessed 24 March 2017).

Sahlberg, P. (2014) *Finnish lessons 2.0: What can the world learn from educational change in Finland?* (New York, Teachers College Press).

Saltman, K. J. (2015) *Capitalizing on disaster: Taking and breaking public schools* (London, Routledge).

Samuelsson, I. P. and Fleer, M. (2009) *Play and learning in early childhood settings: International perspectives* (New York, Springer).

Sellar, S. (2015) A feel for numbers: Affect, data and education policy. *Critical Studies in Education*, 56(1), 131–146.

Sellar, S. and Lingard, B. (2013) The OECD and global governance in education. *Journal of Education Policy*, 28(5), 710–725.

Sellar, S. and Lingard, B. (2014) The OECD and the expansion of PISA: New global modes of governance in education. *British Educational Research Journal*, 40(6), 917–936.

Selwyn, N. (2010) *Schools and schooling in the digital age: A critical analysis* (London, Routledge).

Selwyn, N. (2015) Data entry: Towards the critical study of digital data and education. *Learning, Media and Technology*, 40(1), 64–82.

Selwyn, N. (2016a) *Is technology good for education?* (Cambridge, Polity Press).

Selwyn, N. (2016b) 'There's so much data': Exploring the realities of data-based school governance. *European Educational Research Journal*, 15(1), 54–68.

Selwyn, N., Henderson, M. and Chao, S. H. (2015) Exploring the role of digital data in contemporary schools and schooling – '200,000 lines in an Excel spreadsheet'. *British Education Research Journal*, 41(5), 767–781.

Selwyn, N., Nemorin, S. and Johnson, N. (2016) High-tech, hard work: An investigation of teachers' work in the digital age. *Learning, Media and Technology*, 1–16, http://dx.doi.org/10.1080/17439884.2016.1252770.

Shore, C. and Wright, S. (2015) Governing by numbers: Audit culture, rankings and the new world order. *Social Anthropology*, 23(1), 22–28.

Sig+ (2017) *The school data company*. Available online at: www.sigplus.co.uk (accessed 14 March 2017).

Silliman, M. (2015) The use of data in the governance of education systems (Conference Paper). Available online at: www.researchgate.net/publication/303703115_The_Use_of_Data_in_the_Governance_of_Education_Systems (accessed 28 November 2016).

Simmons, L. (2010) 'The docile body in school space', in: T. Monahan and R. Torres (Eds) *Schools under surveillance: Cultures of control in public education* (New Jersey: Rutgers University Press).

Simon, B. (2005) The return of panopticism: Supervision, subjection and the new surveillance. *Surveillance & Society*, 3(1), https://ojs.library.queensu.ca/index.php/surveillance-and-society/article/view/3317.

Simons, M. (2014) Governing through feedback, in: T. E. Fenwick Mangez and J. Ozga (Eds) *Governing knowledge, comparison, knowledge-based technologies and expertise in the regulation of education (world yearbook of education 2014)* (London, Routledge).

Siraj-Blatchford, I. (2010) A focus on pedagogy, in : K. Sylva, E. Melhuish, P. Sammons, I. Siraj-Blatchford and B. Taggart (Eds) *Early childhood matters – Evidence from the effective pre-school and primary education project* (London, Routledge).

Siraj, I., Kingston, D. and Melhuish, E. C. (2015) *Assessing quality in early childhood education and care: Sustained shared thinking and emotional well-being (SSTEW) scale for 2–5-year-olds provision* (London, Institute of Education Press).

Slee, R. (2011) *Irregular schooling: Special education, regular education and inclusive education* (London, Routledge).

Smith, S. (2016) *Against race- and class-based pedagogy in early childhood education* (New York, Palgrave Macmillan).

Souto-Otero, M. and Beneito-Montagut, R. (2016) From governing through data to governmentality through data: Artefacts, strategies and the digital turn. *European Educational Research Journal*, 15(1), 14–33.

St. Pierre, E. A. (2012) Another postmodern report on knowledge: Positivism and its others. *International Journal of Leadership in Education*, 15(4), 483–503.

STA (2014) *Reception baseline: Criteria for potential assessments* (Coventry, Standards and Testing Agency).

STA (2016) *Reception baseline comparability study*. Available online at: www.gov.uk/government/publications/reception-baseline-comparability-study (accessed 6 April 2017).

Stobart, G. (2008) *Testing times: The uses and abuses of assessment* (London, Routledge).

Strand, S. (2016) *Educational outcomes among children with English as an additional language (EAL)* (Oxford, Migration Observatory, University of Oxford).

Sylva, K. and Taggart, B. (2010) *ECERS-E: The four curricular subscales extension to the Early Childhood Environment Rating Scale (ECERS-R)* (New York, Teachers College Press).

Taylor, E. (2013) *Surveillance schools: Security, discipline and control in contemporary education* (Basingstoke, Palgrave Macmillan).

Thompson, G. and Cook, I. (2014) Manipulating the data: Teaching and NAPLAN in the control society. *Discourse: Studies in the Cultural Politics of Education*, 35(1), 129–142.

Thompson, G. and Cook, I. (2017) The politics of teaching time in disciplinary and control societies. *British Journal of Sociology of Education*, 38(1), 26–37.

Thrift, N. (2005) *Knowing capitalism* (London, SAGE).

Tsapkou, D. (2015) From surveillance to dataveillance: Disappearing bodies and the end of optics. *Birkbeck Law Review*, 3(1), www.bbklr.org/3-1-6.html.

Unicef (2011) *Children's wellbeing the UK, Sweden and Spain: The role of inequality and materialism* (London, Unicef).

Urban, M. (2015) From 'closing the gap' to an ethics of affirmation: Reconceptualising the role of early childhood services in times of uncertainty. *European Journal of Education*, 50(3), 293–306.

Urban, M. and Swadener, B. B. (2016) Democratic accountability and contextualised systemic evaluation. A comment on the OECD initiative to launch an International Early Learning Study (IELS). *International Critical Childhood Policy Studies Journal*, 5(1), 6–18.

Valenzuela, J. P., Bellei, C. and Ríos, D. D. L. (2014) Socioeconomic school segregation in a market-oriented educational system. The case of Chile. *Journal of Education Policy*, 29(2), 217–241.

Vince, S. (2016) *Data-based accountability in the Early Years Foundation Stage*, unpublished MA dissertation (London, UCL Institute of Education).

Ward, H. (2015a) *Ofsted fears baseline assessments for four-year-olds will hurt the most disadvantaged*. Available online at: www.tes.com/news/school-news/breaking-news/ofsted-fears-baseline-assessments-four-year-olds-will-hurt-most (accessed 6 March 2017).

Ward, H. (2015b) *Superhead Dame Alison Peacock snubs baseline tests for four-year-olds*. Available online at: www.tes.com/news/school-news/breaking-news/superhead-dame-alison-peacock-snubs-baseline-tests-four-year-olds (accessed 23 March 2017).

Ward, H. (2015c) *Test-heavy baseline assessments rejected by schools*. Available online at: www.tes.com/news/school-news/breaking-news/test-heavy-baseline-assessments-rejected-schools (accessed 6 March 2017).

Ward, H. (2016) *Baseline assessments dropped as accountability measures in major DfE u-turn*. Available online at: www.tes.com/news/school-news/breaking-news/baseline-assessments-dropped-accountability-measures-major-dfe-u-turn (accessed 6 March 2017).

Weale, S. (2016) *Are children born in the summer really at a big disadvantage?* Available online at: www.theguardian.com/world/2016/oct/14/what-happened-to-allowing-children-born-in-summer-to-start-school-later (accessed 28 June 2017).

Wertsch, J. V. and Del Rio, P. (1995) *Sociocultural studies of mind* (Cambridge, Cambridge University Press).

West, A. and Bailey, E. (2013) The development of the academies programme: 'Privatising' school-based education in England, 1986–2013. *British Journal of Educational Studies*, 61(2), 137–159.

Whitebread, D. and Bingham, S. (2012) School readiness: A critical review of perspectives and evidence, *TACTYC Occasional Paper no. 2*.

Whitebread, D. and Coltman, P. (2015) *Teaching and learning in the early years* (London, Routledge).

Wilkins, C. (2011) Professionalism and the post performative teacher: New teachers reflect on autonomy and accountability in the English school system. *Professional Development in Education*, 37(3), 389–409.

Williamson, B. (2014) Reassembling children as data doppelgangers: How databases are making education machine-readable, paper presented at the Powerful Knowledge Conference, University of Bristol, 16 May.

Williamson, B. (2015a) Digital education governance: Data visualization, predictive analytics, and 'real-time' policy instruments. *Journal of Education Policy*, 31(2), 123–141.

Williamson, B. (2015b) Governing methods: Policy innovation labs, design and data science in the digital governance of education. *Journal of Educational Administration and History*, 47(3), 251–271.

Williamson, B. (2016a) Coding the biodigital child: The biopolitics and pedagogic strategies of educational data science. *Pedagogy, Culture & Society*, 24(3), 401–416.

Williamson, B. (2016b) Digital education governance: An introduction. *European Educational Research Journal*, 15(1), 3–13.

Williamson, B. (2016c) Digital methodologies of education governance: Pearson plc and the remediation of methods. *European Educational Research Journal*, 15(1), 34–53.

Williamson, B. (2016d) Silicon startup schools: Technocracy, algorithmic imaginaries and venture philanthropy in corporate education reform. *Critical Studies in Education*, 1–19, http://dx.doi.org/10.1080/17508487.2016.1186710.

Williamson, B. (2017) Decoding ClassDojo: Psycho-policy, social-emotional learning and persuasive educational technologies. *Learning, Media and Technology*, 1–14, http://dx.doi.org/10.1080/17439884.2017.1278020.

Wrigley, T. (2015) *Predicting children's potential: Baseline tests.* Available online at: https://reclaimingschools.org/2015/06/11/predicting-childrens-potential-baseline-tests/ (accessed 20 April 2017).

Wrigley, T. and Wormwell, L. (2016) Infantile accountability: When big data meet small children. *Improving Schools*, 19(2), 105–118.

Wyse, D. and Ferrari, A. (2015) Creativity and education: Comparing the national curricula of the states of the European Union and the United Kingdom. *British Educational Research Journal*, 41(1), 30–47.

Wyse, D. and Torrance, H. (2009) The development and consequences of national curriculum assessment for primary education in England. *Educational Research*, 51(2), 213–228.

Youdell, D. (2006a) *Impossible bodies, impossible selves: Exclusions and student subjectivities* (Dordrecht, Springer).

Youdell, D. C. (2006b) Subjectivation and performative politics – Butler thinking Althusser and Foucault: Intelligibility, agency and the raced-nationed-religioned subjects of education. *British Journal of Sociology of Education*, 27(4), 511–528.

INDEX

Page numbers in *italics* denote tables, those in **bold** denote figures.